Whispered Secrets

By

Toni Auberry

ISBN: 1-4107-6665-9 (e-book)
ISBN: 1-4107-6663-2 (Paperback)
ISBN: 1-4107-6664-0 (Dust Jacket)

Library of Congress Control Number: 2003094304

This book is printed on acid-free paper.

Printed in the United States of America
Bloomington, IN

1stBooks - rev. 01/31/04

Acknowledgements

I wish to thank my family and friends who have supported and encouraged me during the lengthy time it took for me to finally complete this novel. Without their support and guidance I would have given up and put the manuscript upon a shelf where it never would have seen the light of day.

Chapter 1

April 5, 1990
8:00 AM

Sterling Funeral Home, the final destination after death for the majority of Scottsdale's affluent citizens, had been architecturally designed to resemble the surrounding older Victorian homes. It stood serenely nestled between two majestic maples with thick trunks and reaching branches that boldly swept the sky on windy days. Towering hedges, strategically positioned along the side and back boundaries of the mortuary's flawlessly groomed lawn, offered a sense of privacy to visitors of the establishment and to neighboring residents. In the front courtyard a multitude of bright yellow tulips lined both sides of the forty-foot sidewalk that trailed from the street, between the maples, to the spacious porch where two white wicker chairs offered tired mourners a place to rest and gather their thoughts.

1

On this fine April morning while robins were waking up the world with songs of cheer, fifty-year-old Randy Tedrow lay with a peaceful look displayed upon his face in the finest satin-lined casket that Sterling had to offer. He had been tastefully dressed in his most expensive black suit and appeared as formidable in death as he had in life. The red silk tie he had always referred to as his power tie had been properly arranged by his wife so that he looked as though he was preparing to face the city council for one of his famous debates, just as he had done hundreds of times over the past twenty years. A distinguished city councilman, a dedicated church member, and president of Tower Enterprise, the fastest growing engineering company in Indiana, he had long been upheld as a brilliant energetic spokesman no matter what the circumstances in which he had to speak.

Intelligent...worldly...enterprising. Those were the words the town's newspaper editor had used to describe the man Randy Tedrow had been before death had staked its odious claim. Empty useless words really, since the dynamism that had flowed so easily from Randy no longer existed. The only thing left of him now was a cold, empty shell totally devoid of energy.

Mr. Randy Tedrow would never again stand in front of a crowd and mesmerize the masses with his persuasive mannerisms. In reality, he would never do anything again.

And his daughter felt an odd gladness deep in her heart because of that very fact.

+++++

Amy Tedrow, Randy's eighteen-year-old daughter, stood nervously clutching her hands into tight little fists at the front door of the mortuary. Her face looked ashen in the bright morning sunlight. The black mourning dress her mother had forced her to wear had somehow stolen most of the color from her cheeks.

She swayed unsteadily as a sudden wave of dizziness sent the porch moving on its own. The wavering feeling launched an attack of nausea that threatened to hurl the contents of her stomach right out at her feet. She reached for one of the wicker chairs for support and waited for the queasiness clutching at her belly to slowly subside. Her heart hammered wildly in her chest, and she struggled with her self-control in a hopeless attempt to regain some sense of composure.

The very last thing I need to do this morning, she thought anxiously, *is to get sick and throw up on the front porch of the funeral home. That would send Mom over the edge for sure. She'd probably start screaming I'd done it on purpose just to embarrass her, and I don't think I could handle that right now.*

Amy shuddered as a sudden gust of wind wrapped itself tightly around her body. Yet she didn't appear to notice how it molded the dress to her slender frame, showing the world a dramatic glimpse of sensual, graceful curves. Nor was she aware of how the brisk, spring breeze made her beautiful, waist-length, raven hair dance in wild ripples across her back.

In fact, the only thing she was really paying attention to was the strange uneasiness that was lurking furtively somewhere far back in her mind.

I've got to go into the funeral home whether I want to or not, she thought as her insides twisted into a hundred tight knots. *It's really foolish to be so scared. After all, there's nothing to be afraid of any longer; Dad's dead and he can't hurt me now. What's he going to do—reach out and grab me from his casket? Of course not! Things like that only happen at the movies, not in real life.*

Tentatively she reached out to open the door. A subtle tremor shook her hand as it encircled the doorknob. *I can't do this. I just can't do it.* She froze with her fingers clutched so tightly they blanched at the knuckles. She wanted to turn and run as fast as her feet could carry her from the fear that was cascading down and drowning her under its heavy weight.

From somewhere in her unconscious mind came the terrifying image of what waited for her inside the mortuary. For some reason she kept seeing the frightening vision of her father's enormous hands reaching out to touch her face as blood steadily dripped from each finger.

"Please God, can't I just go home? I don't want to be here," Amy pleaded in a small whisper of a voice. Her troubled hazel eyes frantically searched for an escape that did not exist because even as she desperately dreamed of leaving, she knew she couldn't. Her mother had demanded this morning that she attend the funeral service, and she didn't have the strength to refuse. Years of strict obedience to her parents had left her powerless to act on her own wishes.

Suddenly a flicker of movement caught Amy's attention, and she whirled toward it halfway expecting to see—what? A demon?

Or maybe the devil himself reaching up from his fiery pit to drag her down into the dark abyss where her father must surely be residing right at this moment?

In her heart the fears were real enough. Hadn't he sworn she'd never be free from him no matter what happened?

A small gasp of relief escaped her lips when all she saw was her own reflection in the window located directly behind the wicker chairs. Unfortunately this feeling of relief didn't last long. Disturbed by the dark circles under her eyes and the way her hair now lay in tangled disarray, the tension returned even stronger than before. She stared at her image and realized her father had been right about one thing—she should be ashamed of the way she looked.

She warily brushed away a stray wisp of hair from her face, and she remembered how much her father had despised its darkness. "That black hair of yours is a sure sign that the devil has marked you as one of his," he had shouted during one of his wild rampages as his belt had lashed upon her back for what had seemed the hundredth time. "Satan's accursed finger has touched you, and it is up to me to save your soul from eternal damnation."

Despair overwhelmed Amy as she stared at the awful reflection of her ugliness in the window. *Was Dad right? Have I been cursed for some terrible sin I can't remember? Something I did when I was only a young child or maybe before I was even born, something so abhorrent it was impossible for even my own father to love me?*

"You little bitch!" Her father's enraged voice suddenly shrieked in her ears. "You did this to me. This is all your fault."

Shocked by the force of the words from the man she thought was dead, Amy stumbled backward a couple of steps and almost collapsed. *No...No, you can't be here, you're dead!* A flaming wildfire of panic raced through her terrified mind and torched her soul with a terror that became absolute when a man's heavy hand unexpectedly appeared on her shoulder.

"Dad!" Amy cried out, her heart pounding wildly within her chest. She spun around, expecting to see her father standing behind her with his cold gray eyes piercing deep into her soul, and she raised her hands in front of her face as if to ward off the devil himself.

"Amy, it's only me," Edward, her brother, spoke softly as he looked upon his sister's face. He had mistaken the fear burning in Amy's eyes as grief, and he desperately wanted to wrap his arms around her to try to protect her from the pain he knew was ripping apart her heart.

The moment Amy gazed up into Edward's gentle brown eyes she felt relief flow over her. The concern on his face touched her deeply and immediately eased the overwhelming panic that had only seconds before almost sent her running wildly down the sidewalk. Edward, four years her elder, had always been her best and actually her only friend. Compassionate and gentle-hearted, he had been the one person in her family who had ever really cared about her. Tall and handsome with strong broad shoulders and wavy chestnut hair that threatened to curl if allowed to grow too long, Edward was almost an exact physical copy of their father. Fortunately their similarities ended there. Her brother's eyes were always filled with warmth. Not like *his*...cold and hard with the power to pierce your heart with their sharp daggers. And Edward really cared about people. He didn't use them to suit his own means, or try and control them through quiet manipulation. Edward was special, cut from the same mold as their father, yet so different, so very, very different.

"Are you all right?" Edward asked, worried over the shocked look on his sister's face. "Maybe you should come inside with Mom and me and sit down for a few minutes."

"No! I...I'm fine. Really I am. It's just—," Amy paused for a second, "for a moment I thought I heard Dad's voice and it startled me."

"I know what you mean," Edward replied. "When I woke up this morning I swore I heard him calling me down for breakfast. It was a terrible shock when I realized it couldn't possibly be true."

Amy felt a small ache of bitterness worming its way into her heart as Edward gently gathered her up into the comfort of his arms. *There's no way you can possibly know what I mean,* she thought. *Dad loved you.*

"We're all hurting right now, but somehow, the three of us will get through this together," Edward replied tenderly in a voice that was meant to console Amy. "In a way we're lucky. You and me and Mom, we still have each other."

Amy didn't say a word. Anything she would have said would have only upset him more. Feeling trapped within the confines of her

7

brother's arms, she stepped back and broke the physical contact between them.

"Oh Amy, don't pull away from me," Edward said, saddened by the misery he saw in her troubled eyes. "I really do need you right now. How can I possibly get through today without your support? And think how much Mom needs you. She—"

"I doubt very much it's me Mom needs," Amy said, wanting to stop Edward before he said anymore. "She hasn't needed me for years."

"Now, Sis, that's not true. I know you two have had differences, but all teenage girls have problems with their mothers. It's natural for you not to see eye-to-eye on a lot of things."

Amy fought back tears as Edward's words tore holes in her heart. She and her mother hadn't seen eye-to-eye on anything for a very long time. In fact, she wasn't even sure she really had a mother. The woman who was supposed to be her mother acted as though she was something that should be despised instead of someone who should be loved.

Edward cupped Amy's hands in his. Anguish cast a heavy shadow across his face, and his voice was deep from the sorrow weighting it down.

"Without the two of you I'd be falling apart right now. Dad's death is almost more than I can handle. I mean…it was so damn unexpected. Last week he was talking about running for mayor, and now he's gone. I just don't understand what happened. He never said one word about having any kind of chest pains, not even to Mom."

Grief overwhelmed Edward sending silent tears rolling down his cheeks.

Amy couldn't speak. Edward's pain cut deeply into her soul, but she couldn't find a single word within herself that might bring him comfort.

"How could he have a heart attack without ever having any symptoms?" he asked.

"I…I…don't know," Amy stammered, her face suddenly growing even paler than it had been a few seconds earlier.

Edward instantly became alarmed by Amy's appearance. "I think you'd better come inside and sit down. You don't look very well."

"No, I want to stay out here a little longer." Amy rubbed her temples as the tiny threads of a headache started weaving their way through her brain.

Edward watched her hands and instinctively knew what was happening.

"Are you getting another migraine?" he asked.

"Only a small one. If you don't care, I'd like to sit out here on the steps for a while. Maybe the fresh air will keep the pain from getting worse. You go on in with Mom, and I'll join you later."

"Are you sure? I could wait out here with you if you want me to."

"No, I'll be all right. It's probably the flowers in the viewing room that are causing the headache anyway. You know my head starts pounding unmercifully the moment I get around roses and the viewing room is literally packed with them."

"Well, if you're positive that you want to stay out here by yourself, I'm not going to try to force you to change your mind," Edward said, his thoughts already directed elsewhere. From inside the mortuary, he could hear the sounds of his mother's desperate sobbing floating across the air. Without thinking another thought about Amy, he hurried though Sterling's front door leaving his sister alone with her now throbbing migraine.

Chapter 2

Amy sat quietly on the front steps of the mortuary trying to ignore the migraine's increasingly painful intrusion. Closing her eyes, she focused on the pleasant touch of the morning sun stroking her face with its warmth. Slowly the migraine began to ease as she forced her thoughts to travel to places where her father's memory couldn't intrude. Years ago she had learned the only escape she had from reality was to pretend the horrors she faced every day weren't real. This illusion of happiness had been the key to her survival in a world where the truth of her existence had been too painful to bear.

Suddenly the joyful sound of laughing children floated across on the spring breeze flowing gently around her. Her eyes sprang open, and her gaze shifted toward the direction of the laughter. At the house across the street, she could see a group of children playing tag. The oldest boy, who looked to be about eight, purposefully slowed down so that a younger blond-headed girl could catch him. The girl's gleeful cry of joy echoed down the street.

Amy's heart suddenly seemed heavier, and the weight made her feel as though it had turned to solid stone right in the center of her chest.

As she watched the children playing it reminded her of when she and Edward had played tag, and he had purposely allowed her to win. She remembered how he had run from her and then pretended to fall so she could catch him. "You're it!" she had screamed in delight each time she had tagged him.

A single tear slowly inched its way down Amy's cheek. Edward was the only one she had ever laughed with. No one else had even cared if she was alive.

Through tear brimmed eyes Amy noticed the blond-headed girl eagerly beckoning to the boy. Her small hand was waving fervently for him to hurry to her side. "Chris, come here," she shouted across the yard. "I have a secret to tell you." When Chris approached, Amy watched him stoop on bended knee so he could hear the girl's whispered words more clearly. Because she was too short to reach the boy's ear without standing on tiptoes, the blond-haired girl held tightly to his arm for balance as she stretched upward. "Come closer," the girl said. "It's a secret that I don't want anyone else to hear."

Without warning Amy found herself tumbling down into a black bottomless pit that had unexpectedly opened directly under her feet.

Secrets—a word she knew far too well. How many secrets had she wanted to tell her brother but could never find the words?

How many tears had she cried in the loneliness of her despair because there had been no one she could whisper her terrible secrets too?

More than she could ever count. More than she dare remember.

+++++

Sixteen-year-old Ricky Kells felt a wave of excitement swell through his entire body as he pulled away from Montana's Flower Boutique in the shop's old, beat-up delivery van. Today was his first day on the job, and he was on his way to make his very first delivery. He felt very important and sat as tall and straight in the driver's seat as his thin, five-foot, six-inch frame would allow. A broad smile crossed his face as the wondrous call of freedom eagerly beckoned him to head down the road and straight out of town.

With each shift of the gears, Ricky felt the vibration of the van's unbalanced wheels as it sped down Main Street, and he realized that he was actually happy for the first time in years.

This van might be old, but it's going to be my ticket out of town, he thought remembering how his friend Shane had laughed when he'd heard about the job. "That old junker of Montana's won't even make it across town," Shane had teased. "You'll get stuck riding your thumb for sure." *But what did Shane know? He didn't even have his driver's license yet. So how could he possibly understand?*

Ricky gripped the steering wheel tightly, thrilled by the feeling of power surging through him. Soon he would be free of Scottsdale and his stepfather Jack. All he had to do was earn enough money to buy a bus ticket, and he'd be gone before Jack had the opportunity to smack him around like a punching bag again.

As he carefully threaded his way through the sparse morning traffic, Ricky glanced into the rearview mirror. He couldn't help noticing the proof of the confrontation he had last night with Jack. A fresh two-inch bruise below his right eye had colored his cheekbone a dark blue. He had tried to use a little of his mother's makeup to hide it, but he hadn't been too successful.

Ricky frowned as he surveyed his damaged face. He was surprised Montana hadn't said something this morning when he showed up for work. But then again, this wasn't the first time his new boss had seen one of his black eyes.

One Saturday night about a month ago, Montana had discovered him hiding from Jack in the alley behind the flower shop. His right eye, swollen shut from a direct hit with Jack's fist, had told Montana everything. "Your Dad?" Montana had asked. "Yes," he had replied, and then nothing more had been said. Montana had opened the backdoor to the flower shop, pulled him in, fixed him an ice bag, lugged out an old cot from behind a work bench, and then prepared to leave. "I've got to get on home, but you're welcome to stay the night," Montana had said without a second thought. "Just be sure the door is locked when you decide to go."

Ricky had been surprised that Montana had trusted him enough to leave him alone in his shop all night, but he had been thankful for the chance to sleep somewhere other than the alley. He had felt safe in Montana's workroom full of half-finished silk flower arrangements. There had been something peaceful and non-threatening in the colorful surroundings, and he had lingered until late Sunday morning before he had decided it would be safe to go back home.

It was three weeks later that Montana had offered him the job. "You need something to keep you out of trouble," Montana had said, "and I've got plenty of work that needs done around here. You could come right after school and stay as late as you like. I don't care if you bring your homework and study when things get a little slow. You could even set up that cot there in the back room if you had to spend the night sometime."

Without blinking an eye, he'd jumped at the offer.

Even Jack had shown some enthusiasm when he'd heard about the job. Ricky figured that was because his stepfather had plans for confiscating his paycheck to buy that gut-wrenching booze he swigged down every night. But there was no way in hell he was going to let that happen. As soon as he got his hands on that first paycheck, he would be history. He would head as far West as he could possibly get, maybe even to California, and his mother and Jack would never hear from him again.

Thoughts of sunny beaches and tiny bikinis supported by firm tanned breasts kept Ricky's mind occupied as he headed toward Sterling's Funeral Home. Sitting precariously on the passenger seat right beside him was an enormous bouquet of two dozen red roses addressed to the family of Randy Tedrow.

15

When he turned a corner too fast, Ricky almost smashed into the back of a brand-new silver pickup that had unexpectedly pulled out directly in front of him. The moment he hit the brakes the bouquet of roses toppled forward. He frantically attempted to keep them from pitching off the front seat while trying not to ram into the back of the truck. With one hand on the steering wheel and one on the flowers, he managed to prevent both accidents from occurring.

A cold sweat broke out across Ricky's forehead as he imagined what Jack's reaction would have been if he had somehow managed to wreak Montana's van the first day on the job. Jack would more than likely drag out his special belt for that...the one with the metal studs that left tiny bruises and cuts wherever they landed.

Ricky knew by heart what that belt felt like.

Worried about the roses, Ricky pulled off to the side of the street so he could check for damage. He immediately noticed that two of the roses were dangling from broken stems.

No one will know if there are two less roses, he thought as he painstakingly removed the two ruined flowers from the vase. *I could probably even take one for Jenny and no one would even guess.*

He hurriedly removed one more of the blood-red roses. *I'll stop by her house on the way back to the shop and surprise her. Maybe I'll get that kiss she's been promising me.*

Visions of Jenny's shining green eyes dancing excitedly as she thanked him for the flower kept Ricky occupied the rest of the way to the funeral home. However, all thoughts of his girlfriend vanished the moment he spied Amy Tedrow sitting on the front steps of the mortuary staring with sad eyes across the street at a couple of kids whispering to each other.

A sudden surge of primal heat swept through Ricky as his eyes traveled over Amy's slender frame draped in the long black dress that accented the sensual curves of her body. *Amy has got to be the most beautiful girl in town,* he thought longingly as he tried to imagine what it would be like to kiss her. He felt his heart start to pound wildly as he looked in awe at the sunlight dancing across her raven hair making it shine like pure black silk.

Amy's hair had always fascinated him. His fingers ached to touch it, to feel it slip softly across his palm. He wanted to bury his face in it to simply breathe in the smell. Once he had deliberately crowded right behind her when they were boarding the school bus just for the chance to touch it. He had no difficulty remembering what her hair had felt like...satiny, unbelievably sexy.

He also distinctly remembered the disturbing expression that had instantly darkened her face the moment she had realized someone's hands were touching her. The fear that had arisen from her had been so absolute, so distinct, he had felt as though she had breathed it out in a breath of frozen air.

At that moment he had known something about her no one else knew. *Someone had hurt Amy! Hurt her real bad.*

He had seen the same frightened look staring back at him from his own bedroom mirror late one night right after Jack had beaten him with a cane. Bruised and bleeding, his face had reflected the same look of endless despair he had seen on Amy's that day.

17

+++++

Ricky stepped away from Montana's delivery van carrying the immense bouquet designated for Amy and her family. The elaborate flower arrangement was so huge it partially blocked his view as he headed up the sidewalk toward the front steps of the mortuary where Amy sat with her eyes focused somewhere off into the distance.

She looks so lonely, Ricky thought as he caught subtle glimpses of her through the roses' thick green foliage. *Like she doesn't have a friend in the world.*

Ricky was instinctively aware of the aura of sadness…or maybe it was pain…that completely surrounded Amy. She appeared to be encased in a dark heavy cloud that somehow kept people from getting too close to her.

Maybe Amy would go with me when I leave town, Ricky hopefully thought, his heart filling with empathy for the girl who appeared to be as alone as he was. *I could find a way to take care of her. I know I could.*

Thrust into a daydream where he was the hero, Ricky stood on the sidewalk a few feet in front of Amy hoping she would turn and glance his way. A full minute passed before an unexpected burst of wind swirled around him sending the bouquet's abundance of greenery flapping wildly in his face.

Ricky, though, didn't even realize it was happening. That same wind was whipping Amy's skirt up around her legs allowing him a glimpse of soft, ivory skin.

Ricky felt a pink flush instantly spread unbidden across his face. The flush quickly deepened to a crimson red when Amy's eyes shifted their gaze toward him. As Amy stared at him with a shocked look blanketing her entire face, a strange new emotion surprised Ricky. He suddenly felt the need to rescue Amy. He wanted to take her away from whatever pain lay hidden so deep in her soul.

"Amy, as soon as I get my first paycheck I'm getting out of this godforsaken town," Ricky said. "Do you want to go with me? You'd be safe with me; I'd never let anyone hurt you. I promise."

+++++

Rationally, Amy knew it no longer mattered if her secrets were never told to anyone. *Dad can't hurt me any longer,* she thought as the image of her father towering over her like a crazed giant fought its way from the very back of her mind. *Now that he's dead, I'm finally free of him.*

"You'll never be free of me," her father's voice hissed softly in her ear. "I'll always be right behind you, and if you ever tell anyone about us—"

No! Amy shouted desperately in her mind. *Leave me alone! Please just leave me alone!* Her eyes, widened by fright, futilely glanced around, and when she saw her father standing right in front of her carrying a bouquet of red roses she almost screamed.

For an instance, all the terror from all her nightmares combined to fill her soul with indescribable fear.

She felt herself slipping away, heading toward that safe place within herself where she had always taken refuge as a child, but she was instantly pulled back when a voice that was not her father's spoke. "Amy, as soon as I get my first paycheck I'm getting out of this godforsaken town. Do you want to go with me? You'd be safe with me; I'd never let anyone hurt you. I promise." And Amy realized it was Ricky Kells standing in front of her.

Her fears vanished as quickly as they had arisen. She had seen Ricky at school, and he'd always seemed shy and non-threatening, although lately he had been looking at her with a strange expression cloaking his face...an expression she hadn't been able to decipher. She kept getting an uneasy feeling he knew something about her, and that had made her very uncomfortable.

"I...I don't think I should," Amy finally stammered.

"Away from here we'd both be safe. They can't hurt us if they can't find us." Ricky's eyes filled with hope because she hadn't answered no right away. "I have a friend in Seattle who would let us crash with him until we could find work."

"Who couldn't hurt us?" Amy asked, a small tremor in her voice underscoring her words. She suddenly became worried that Ricky knew something about her father and their dark secrets.

"Well, for me it's Jack, my stepfather. He's one mean son of a bitch, and I'm sick and tired of him knocking me around all the time. As soon as I get the chance I'm going to go so far away he'll never be able to get his hands on me again."

"What has that got to do with me?" Amy nervously replied, her eyes locking on the bruise below Ricky's right eye.

"Jack's got nothing to do with you, but I think somebody else has been at you. I've seen it in your face. Your eyes can't hide what they've seen. At least not from someone who has seen the same thing."

"I don't know what you're talking about," Amy anxiously licked her dry lips, "and I think you'd better leave right now!" She was afraid her father might hear Ricky and decide to do something to them. Ricky knew way too much.

"You do know what I'm talking about! You don't have to—"

"Please, just go before something terrible happens," Amy turned her eyes away from Ricky's insistent stare. Ricky didn't have any idea what could take place. If he really knew, he'd realize her father could kill them both. Even if he was dead!

"Amy, listen to me. Don't say no right now. Just think about it for a few days."

Ricky sensed Amy had started to mentally isolate herself from him, so he quickly pressed on. "I'll check back with you next week after you have had some time to think about it. I'd planned to leave Friday afternoon right after I cashed my paycheck, but I could wait a few more days if you needed some time to get your things together."

"I'm sorry, but I can't go with you," Amy responded in a voice that was almost a whisper. "I can't go anywhere right now." Without waiting for Ricky to say another word, she turned and dashed through the front door of the mortuary leaving the young man standing alone on the steps staring after her with a questioning look upon his face.

21

Toni Auberry

Chapter 3

Amy ducked into one of Sterling's unoccupied viewing rooms in an attempt to seek some kind of refuge from the strange overwhelming panic that had driven her to flee so quickly from Ricky. Within the darkened shadows of the room she managed to regain her composure, and she waited and listened behind closed doors until she heard Ricky deliver the roses and then drive away. Only when she felt positive she wouldn't have to face the young man again did she cautiously open the door and reenter the hallway.

Moving silently—years of hiding had taught her that trick—Amy walked through the funeral home's dimly lit foyer toward the main viewing room were she knew her mother and brother would be waiting for the first of the visitors to arrive. As she walked, her eyes anxiously darted from one end of the hallway to the other. The area before her appeared dark and dangerous. She felt trapped, constrained unwillingly by the four walls surrounding her, and she began to have difficulty breathing as a tight band of dread wrapped

23

itself around her chest. The sound of her shallow breathing echoed in the room. A cold sweat broke out across her forehead, and her heart began to pound furiously. She wanted to run, to somehow escape the memories of the man who had held her captive for so many years…but she couldn't. It was impossible to escape the memories when they had been beaten into her with iron fists that broke her bones and shattered her spirit. The best she could hope for would be to find the strength to push them back into her mind where she would never have to think of them again.

She shook her head as though to clear her mind of the obsessive thoughts that were tormenting her, and then she headed toward the room where the mayor, city councilmen, physicians, lawyers, and the rest of Scottsdale's high and mighty townspeople would soon be gathering to pay their last respects to her father. Before long, mourners would be lined up all the way out to the street waiting for the opportunity to say how sorry they were over the sudden, unexpected death of her father from a heart attack.

As Amy slowly moved toward the viewing room, her presence remained undetected. The hall's thick burgundy carpet cloaked whatever slight sounds her footsteps made. When she reached the entrance to the room where her father rested in his death sleep, she stopped.

Neither her mother nor Edward noticed her standing motionless at the doorway.

Not wanting to draw her mother's attention, Amy silently waited. As the seconds slipped past and she remained unnoticed, her mind worked on piecing together the jumble of emotions that were swirling around inside her head and in her heart.

Anger...relief...guilt...hate. She couldn't truly decide how she felt, and to make matters worse, a deep sense of shame overlay all of the other emotions.

I'm not supposed to be relieved that my father is dead, she thought, *but I am. What's wrong with me?*

The shame filling her heart deepened as she glanced over at her brother standing in front of their father's casket. His sorrow showed in each subtle movement of his body, and Amy knew she should be feeling the same way...but she didn't. She also knew God would some day punish her for hating her father so much. *Surely I'm going to go to hell for feeling this way. Children are supposed to honor their fathers, not hate them or be thankful when they die.*

Yet as much as she tried, Amy couldn't put out the tiny spark of gratification that glowed deep within her soul.

She remembered a time when she was fourteen that she had actually wished for this very thing to happen. Lying in bed, curled tightly around a pillow, seeking comfort in the darkness of her bedroom, she had wished for it with every bit of strength she had left. In fact, she had even prayed for it, begging God to end her torment.

For years she had known death would be the only way she would ever be able to escape the pain of her father's angry fists. However, she had always believed it would ultimately be her death, not his, that would finally put an end to her suffering.

And she had suffered year after year.

The sad part was no one ever noticed. The angry, biting words her father had spat at her, the slaps across the face, the twisted arms, the kicks, the shoves... all had been done when they were alone behind the closed doors of their home. The only witness to her private nightmare had been her mother, who had turned and walked away, pretending none of it had happened.

Amy wiped away the solitary tear that had moistened her cheek, and she suddenly felt overpowered by a feeling of great loss. But the feeling of loss wasn't over what had been. It was over what would never be. Now she would never get the chance to hear her father say he was sorry for hurting her, nor would she ever find out why he had hated her so much. That chance had disappeared the moment his heart had stopped beating.

Chapter 4

Connie Tedrow stared forlornly down into her husband's casket. The desolate look in her eyes spoke silent words of misery to anyone looking upon her face. Her dull, gray-streaked, brown hair framed her gaunt face in a wretched mask of despair. Her thin frame sagged like that of an old woman and a strange listlessness hung around her like a cloak. Even the simple movement of brushing a loose strand of hair from her face appeared too difficult to perform

Edward watched his mother carefully, and his concern for her was growing with each passing minute. He thought that the tiny lines on her face looked deeper, more etched into her skin, and her eyes, puffy and red from crying, seemed to have aged her at least ten years. He truly believed that she was precariously close to having a nervous breakdown, and he had doubts that she would be able to make it through the funeral.

Gently, he placed a hand upon his mother's shoulder. "It's going to be all right Mom. I know things will be hard for awhile, but you'll make it through this. And I promise you that Amy and I will help all we can."

"Amy!" Connie lashed out angrily and abruptly pushed her son's hand away. "This is all her fault. I don't want her helping me with anything."

"What in the world are you talking about?" Edward asked. "How could Dad's death possibly be Amy's fault? She didn't do anything to him. He died from a heart attack."

"But she caused it! If she hadn't been arguing with him, it would never have happened." Connie turned toward her son and let the bitterness she felt toward Amy roll off her tongue. "Randy is dead, and your sister killed him, as sure as if she had placed a gun to his head and pulled the trigger. She killed him! Can't you understand that? This is all her fault."

"How can you even think such a terrible thing?" Edward was dumbfounded. He couldn't believe the anger-driven words he had just heard flowing from his mother's mouth. "You know the doctor warned Dad about taking better care of himself. He refused to take his blood pressure medicine. He wouldn't eat right or exercise. He thought he was indestructible. He—"

"He died because Amy broke his heart. She drove his blood pressure up by arguing with him all the time. That's what killed him. His heart couldn't take the strain of all that constant bickering. If she'd been a better daughter, it wouldn't have happened."

"What do you mean if Amy had been a better daughter? Amy is one of the finest girls I know. Any man would be proud to have her in his family."

"You don't know what you're talking about," Connie retorted sharply. "There are things...evil things...about your sister that you know nothing about."

"Mom, you're talking crazy. There's nothing evil about Amy."

"I am not crazy!" Connie cried out, her voice shrill and teetering on the edge of hysteria. "If you could've seen the wicked things that she did to your father you wouldn't—" Connie suddenly stopped her verbal rampage in mid-sentence when a sharp gasp echoed loudly across the room. Then before she had the chance to say another word she heard the sound of running footsteps fleeing down the hall.

"Amy! Oh, my God! She must have heard you." Edward said, and without even looking at his mother, he turned and sprinted after his sister, leaving his mother standing alone by the casket

"Wait, Sis! Mom didn't mean it," Edward shouted. "She's just confused. That's all. Please don't go."

But Amy didn't respond to Edward's frantic plea not to leave. By the time the words had left his mouth, she had already made it out the front door of the mortuary.

Edward charged quickly after her and literally ran into the first group of visitors who were arriving to pay their respects to his father.

"Excuse me." Edward apologized as he hurriedly pushed his way between Earl Gibson, the county treasurer, and his wife, Amanda. "I've got to talk to Amy."

"I think you're going to have to move a lot faster than that," Mr. Gibson sharply retorted. "The way she shot out of that door she's probably halfway across town by now."

Edward ignored the remark and raced down the front steps, taking them two at a time. When he reached the street, he stopped. Amy wasn't anywhere in sight, and he didn't know which direction to take. *Would she have headed home?* He turned toward his car parked a few feet away and began to frantically search through his pockets for keys, but before he found them, he heard his name being called.

"Edward, wait." Mrs. Gibson said anxiously as she placed a trembling hand on his shoulder. "I think you need to come inside. Your mother just fainted."

Torn between his desire to find Amy and his need to help his mother, Edward didn't know what to do. He hesitated, looking first down the street and then up at the mortuary.

"Please," Mrs. Gibson pleaded. "My husband is with her, but he's not a doctor, and I think she may be hurt. She hit her head when she fell"

Edward's concern for Amy immediately vanished, and he turned toward the funeral home and dashed up the steps without a second thought for his sister.

Chapter 5

Amy stood motionless at the entrance to the viewing room. Her hazel eyes were fixed upon her mother and Edward as they talked. She had no difficulty hearing the anger and loathing in Connie's voice at the very mention of her name.

My fault? Mom thinks I did this to Dad? The words stabbed deeply into Amy's soul, and her heart ached from the anguish and grief her mother's words had inflicted. *I could never hurt anyone. Doesn't she know that? Oh God, Oh God—*

Caught up in a whirlwind of confusion, Amy allowed instinct to take control, and it sent her running straight out of the funeral home and down the sidewalk toward the street. She didn't hear Edward calling her name and begging her to stop. The only thing she heard was her mother's awful accusation echoing loudly in her mind. *"She killed him. Can't you understand that? This is all her fault."*

Running blindly down the middle of the street with no destination in mind, Amy obeyed only the driving need to escape her mother's hurtful words. *The evil things I did to Dad?* Her mind shouted in a deafening roar that only she could hear. *What about the horrible things Dad did to me? What about me?*

As she ran, one shoe fell off unnoticed, and then the other one disappeared. But Amy took no heed. Bare feet steadily hit the pavement sending her further and further away from the anguish converging all around her. The roughness of the road shredded her hosiery, and a small sliver of glass sliced deep into her heel. The wound's urgent message of pain went ignored by her brain as she ran with blood oozing steadily from the cut. A bright red trail followed in her wake as the injured foot repeatedly slapped the road.

Unconsciously she headed toward home. At the corner of Fifth and Vine, a car almost hit her, but she didn't notice. Nor did she pay any attention to the small black dog that chased after her when she invaded his territory. The animal snapped angrily at her heels, but that didn't stop her. Onward she ran, leaving the animal's incessant barking behind her in only a few seconds. Five minutes later, she moved from the road to the sidewalk and continued her journey homeward.

+++++

Nellie Patrick, a long-time neighbor of the Tedrow family, watched in surprise from her front window as Amy raced wildly past her house. "George," she said, turning to face her elderly husband, "what do you suppose that crazy Tedrow girl is up to this time. I just saw her running barefoot down the sidewalk in her funeral clothes."

George Patrick shook his head in disgust and didn't even look up from his newspaper. "You know she's a little touched in the head. Nothing about that girl should surprise you. You've heard some of those stories Randy has told me about her."

"Well, do you think we should do something? After all her father is being buried today, and she did look as though she had been crying."

"No! Tedrows' business is for the Tedrows. Just keep your nose out of it. I'm sure her family can handle that girl without any help from us."

"But she seemed so upset."

"I told you to mind your own business. I learned a long time ago not to interfere with other people's family matters. Especially the Tedrows. You go messing with that group and you're just asking for trouble, so get back to your knitting, old woman, and leave well enough alone."

+++++

Suddenly, without realizing how she got there, Amy found herself on the front porch of her home. The sturdy oak door that had opened to her for eighteen years stood unlocked and patiently waiting for the touch of her hand. She reached up with both arms and shoved the door open. Her feet automatically carried her into the house, and without thinking she dashed up the winding staircase to the second floor. A deep penetrating hurt now clouded her mind with a dense fog, and she moved upward through the house totally unaware of her destination. She didn't even stop at her bedroom door. Instead, instinct continued to guide her steps further down the second-floor hallway and then up the back stairwell to the attic.

+++++

In the attic, back in the darkest corner of the room, located next to a bookcase stacked high with discarded novels and musty old magazines stood the antique writing desk that had belonged to her grandfather. When she was little, she frequently used it as a place of refuge. She would crawl into the desk's leg space and tuck herself far back into its deepest shadows to escape the terrors that had been waiting for her downstairs.

And under the desk, just as there had been years ago, lay a tattered, old, teddy bear with only one arm. Amy used to crawl into this secret hiding place and embrace the bear tightly to her chest. The bear had been a gift from Edward on her eighth birthday, and its presence had always provided her with some sense of comfort.

Now years later, burdened by a hurt she could not control, Amy sought her old refuge. Quickly she crossed the attic floor, expertly dodging piles of scattered junk as thick cobwebs parted readily before her. Her eyes frantically searched for the desk and for the dust-covered bear that lay beneath it waiting silently for her return.

When she finally reached her destination, she dropped to her knees and crawled like a wounded animal beneath the desk. In the process, she scraped her knees on the floor's rough wooden planks, but she paid no heed to the throbbing ache it produced.

Somehow she managed to squeeze herself into a fetal position under the desk. She clutched the teddy bear tightly in her arms and sobbed pitifully as the agonizing grief in her heart flowed like a river from her eyes. The bear's dusty exterior quickly became streaked from the great outpouring of tears washing down upon it.

Minutes later, Amy sent herself away to a place within herself where her wounded spirit would be safe, a place where the pain ripping though her heart no longer existed, a place where she never cried.

+++++

Four hours later, Edward discovered Amy still huddled under the desk, curled in the fetal position with her arms wrapped tightly around the one-arm bear. He had found her by following a trail of bloody footprints that lead through the house and up the stairs.

"Amy, I'm sorry about what happened. Mom didn't really mean what she said. She knows it isn't your fault that Dad died."

But Amy didn't say a word. She remained curled up under the desk like a speechless baby with her eyes vacant and staring off toward some faraway realm that he couldn't see.

Edward reached out and took her hands in his. "Please, Sis, don't let this happen again. You might not come back to us this time."

Tears began streaming down his face when she didn't respond.

"Oh, Amy, what have we done to you?" he cried, pulling her into his arms and then gently picking her up.

As he carried her downstairs, Edward prayed with all his heart and soul that she would be all right.

Chapter 6

March 28, 1998
8 years later

Amy was abruptly awakened in the middle of the night by a strange noise that had originated from somewhere in her house, and without even thinking about what she was doing, she swiftly threw off her covers and jumped out of bed. She knew if someone had managed to break into the house she definitely didn't want to be found hiding under the blankets.

The moment her feet hit the floor she froze, and all of her senses went on alert, just like a marine who had suddenly been jarred awake in his foxhole by the sound of a single shot echoing in the jungle. The hairs on her arms stood up as though they were electrically charged. She was so attuned to the changes going on that she actually felt a cool draft of air as it subtly brushed against her skin, and the smell of her own fear seemed strong as she quietly took in a carefully drawn breath.

Somehow a prowler must have gotten past the security system, she thought, as the distinct sounds of softly treading footsteps reached her ears.

Without warning, panic struck like a searing bolt of lightning. It sent her heart racing wildly as adrenaline pumped instantaneously throughout her body, and when she heard the footsteps begin to move stealthily down the hall toward her bedroom the cold sweat of fear swiftly drenched her from head to toe. When she realized that the intruder would soon be at her bedroom door, her legs began to tremble violently, and she was afraid they were going to collapse beneath her.

She suddenly felt as though she had been hopelessly abandoned to stand alone at the brink of hell's fiery inferno.

The door...I need to lock the door, she realized, as the noise from the hallway grew even closer. *If I'm really lucky I should be able to snap the lock in place before he can open it. And maybe that would give me enough time to reach my gun.*

But time turned against her. Before she could take one step forward the soft click of a turning knob resounded through the room, and when the creaking of an opening door quickly followed, her terror escalated almost beyond control.

Oh no! Please, God, not again.

An immense shadow suddenly filled the doorway, and she saw two glistening, gray eyes piercing the darkness with a cruel, hungry look. Unyielding, the eyes found Amy's, and they wordlessly demanded she give up her soul.

She opened her mouth to scream, but no sounds were given voice. A band of fear had wound itself so tightly around her chest that it was squeezing all the air from her lungs. She had to struggle to draw in even one small breath.

The dark shadow moved forward, and she stumbled backward in an attempt to avoid being grabbed by muscular hands with strong, thick fingers that looked as though they could rip her heart out with one quick swoop. And as the hands reached out, she saw enormous arms covered with coarse, dark hairs, and she knew the thing before her was not a man, but a monstrosity formed in the bowels of hell...a devil-beast sent to destroy her body and her soul.

The beast's fingers tightly wrapped themselves around her wrist. She tried to pull away but lost her balance and fell backward upon the bed. The hands grabbed-touched-probed. She struggled to escape as hurtful fingers sought out places that shouldn't be sought.

Somehow, though she didn't know how, her nightgown twisted itself up around her waist. She could feel the heat of the beast's hands upon her thighs pushing and pulling, trying to tear her legs off. Then she felt a terrible pain rip through the softness of her belly, like a knife was being plunged again and again deep inside of her. She screamed and screamed, but the sounds disappeared into the darkness without being heard by anyone.

A strange odor of stale sweat saturated the air. The stench filled her nostrils with a burning, nauseating sensation. She tried to scream again, but this time there wasn't enough air in her lungs. Her breaths came in short quick gasps, and she knew she was dying because her whole body was incased in a raging fire of pain. Over the sound of her own ragged breathing she heard a low growl close to her ear. Deep and coarse it grated across every nerve in her body.

"Whore." The beast's growl became a deep guttural voice. "Jezebel. Slut."

Shocked, she could only lie unmoving in her bed bound tightly by overwhelming terror and pain.

"You'll pay for doing this to me," the beast threatened viciously as its cold, gray eyes stared madly into hers. "This is all your fault."

+++++

Amy awoke from her horrible nightmare in a crazed panic. The images running through her mind were so real that at first she didn't realize she had only been dreaming. Uncontrolled terror continued to surge through her body consuming all rational thought. The moment she opened her eyes she bolted upright in bed and violently kicked off her covers to escape their heavy restraining weight. Then she leaped from the bed in a frenzied attempt to flee from the beast that had come for her in the middle of the night.

She sprinted out of her bedroom and raced down the hallway into the living room, where the outdoor security lights were shining through the windows and she could see that no hideous, snarling beast was chasing after her. She groaned from the pain of the mental anguish she had just gone through and quickly ran her fingers through her sweat-soaked hair as she wondered if her nightmares were ever going to stop.

+++++

After Amy's fears had diminished enough for her to consider sleep, she crawled back into bed, but before she pulled the covers around her she reached over to the bedside dresser and switched on the lamp. She needed the light, because the very last thing she wanted to do was to return to the darkness of that nightmare.

Snuggled safe and warm beneath her grandmother's wedding ring quilt, she lay listening to the howling winds of an unusually late winter storm and wondered if the wailing of the wind could have made her dream of that vile, depraved beast again.

+++++

An hour later, as the intensity of the storm outside of her bedroom window increased, she could hear gusts of shrieking winds wrapping themselves around the trees. The sound reminded her of a werewolf's howl, and from within her mind came the vivid vision of hairy, malformed hands that touched and hurt as they invaded secret places.

She closed her eyes and tried to clear her thoughts of the awful images. She needed to rest, but relaxing seemed to be an impossible feat. No matter how hard she tried, she couldn't escape the tension holding her captive, even when she realized it wasn't the stormy weather that was feeding her restlessness. Bad weather had never bothered her. She had learned early there were worse storms in life that had to be endured than the ones caused by Mother Nature.

Actually, she derived pleasure from almost any type of weather. The kiss of a gentle spring breeze, the warming heat of the summer sun, an invigorating autumn frost, and the cool softness of winter snow were all wondrous things to behold. There was goodness and purity in what was natural.

It was the unnatural that frightened her, and she didn't mean events such as tornadoes, blizzards, or floods. Even though such destructive forces could come into play and cause great havoc there was no intended evil thrust upon the world from those earthly elements. Real evil disguised itself in other forms—not dressed up as wind, snow, or rain.

Tired, but deeply troubled, Amy unconsciously resisted sleep because of the chance she might start dreaming again. Dreaming had become very unpleasant. Entering the world of dreams meant entering a place where unspeakable horror waited around every corner. Lately she hated even going to bed. Staying up past midnight had become a very annoying habit. It was no wonder she felt tired all the time. She had mistakenly thought if she stayed up until exhaustion took over she might not dream, but that theory had proved to be wrong...very wrong. Instead, the dreams were coming more frequently, each one progressively more realistic, and this last one was no exception.

Shivering, Amy pulled the quilt more tightly around her. *Why do I keep dreaming about werewolves? Maybe I should go buy a box of silver bullets for my gun. Or is that crucifixes and wooden stakes that are supposed to kill werewolves? A vial of holy water probably wouldn't hurt either,* she thought as she lay tossing and turning restlessly in bed.

After an hour she finally drifted off to sleep. Fortunately, this time there were no further nightmares waiting for her in the dark.

Chapter 7

Early the next morning Amy hurriedly threw on a gray sweatshirt and burgundy sweatpants. It didn't matter if her outfit wasn't a perfect match as long as it was comfortable. She didn't have time to waste worrying about such trivial matters as clothes. The important thing was to study for the strategic marketing exam she had to take on Monday. She had to have an A in the class to keep up her grade-point average.

Until this year she had only been taking classes part-time at the university to keep current with all the changes constantly going on at work, but now everything was different. A couple of months ago she had made a major decision that made it imperative she maintain a high academic standing. It was a decision she hadn't told anyone yet.

Amy smiled when she thought of her new plans and let her mind drift from her studies.

This is one secret I don't mind keeping, she thought happily. *At least for now. When I find out if my dream can turn into reality, then I'll tell someone. There will be plenty of time for talk later if things go the way I hope, and if they don't, then no one will know I failed.*

"But maybe I won't fail," she said, speaking out loud to give herself confidence. "Maybe it will all turn out the way I'm praying it will."

For the past three years she had worked for Comtec, a highly competitive computer company. While the work had proven to be very challenging, the job no longer fit her needs. She wanted to-*no, she needed to*-do more with her life than tap in words on a keyboard. She had a great desire to help other people…especially kids, and she had finally found a way to do it.

Hardly anyone ever bothered to stand up and speak for the battered and abused children who couldn't speak for themselves. Unfortunately, a lot of parents appeared to be worrying only about themselves instead of their children, and the government agencies that were supposed to protect those children were too overwhelmed to work efficiently. Like wispy ethereal ghosts, many unseen and unheard children were being cast upon the wind to land wherever they might be blown by the strong winds of injustice.

I have to do something to help, she thought, feeling a strong burst of courage filling her heart with its warm radiating touch. *I can't spend my life sitting behind a desk shuffling paperwork knowing all those voiceless, young faces need someone to speak for them until they are old enough to speak for themselves. I know from personal experience how important it is that someone cares enough to say what needs to be said, and I can be that someone if I can only get the chance. That's why I have to go to law school. I'll be a lawyer, and make sure those children's voices are heard. All those speechless ghosts out there drifting on the wind will be able to find a way to talk...by using me. No one heard my silent screams for help, and I never want that to happen to another child. To need help and not be able to find the words to ask for it is one of the worst nightmares that could happen to anyone.*

Amy wishfully picked up the brochures from Indiana University that were lying on top of the bedroom dresser and reread them for the hundredth time. She had an appointment to talk to an admissions officer in two weeks, and as each day passed her determination grew stronger. Given the chance, she would quit her job and start law classes immediately.

She breathed in a hopeful breath. *It could really happen. There is always that possibility; some dreams do come true.* Going back to school full-time would be rough, but others had done it. And she was just as strong-willed as the next person, maybe even more so. After all, she had survived her father.

Laden with a stack of books, notes, and paper she headed for the kitchen. "Maybe," she said, placing the heavy load down on the table, "just maybe, if I work really hard I'll make a very good lawyer, and I will make a difference in this world."

+++++

Amy stared at the pile of books she had just laid down on the kitchen table. She sighed, sat down and then started reading.

After an hour she became restless. It was hard to concentrate with the clock on the wall steadily ticking off the minutes. The noise grated at her nerves making her jittery and tense.

If I don't finish reviewing this test material this morning, I won't have another chance before the exam on Wednesday, she thought, glancing over her shoulder at the calendar posted on the refrigerator. *I'm going to be covered up the rest of the weekend, and there is no way I'll be able to get back to this if I don't do it right now.*

She paused from her studies and frowned. Unfortunately, the rest of her weekend plans revolved around the fact that today was her twenty-sixth birthday, and that was something she really didn't care to think about.

She forced herself to resume studying but found it very difficult to focus. She had to keep rereading the same paragraphs over and over. Nothing seemed to be making any sense. Her mind kept pulling her away with intruding thoughts about her birthday. Annoyed, she admonished herself.

The last thing I should be doing right now is thinking about my birthday. I definitely don't understand why people always want to make such a big fuss over birthdays anyway. Personally I rank them right up there with catching the flu or breaking a leg, and it's not because I'm afraid of getting old. A few gray hairs and extra wrinkles are the least of my worries. Wrinkles only show that a person has character, not that she's getting old. Women should stop worrying so much about how they look and concentrate on improving their minds. They'd feel better if they did. A woman can't stop time from leaving its mark upon on her face, but she can sure avoid letting stupidity show up there.

Birthdays aren't something I want to celebrate, she thought bitterly, *and I dearly wish Edward wouldn't insist every year that I have a party. I mean, it's not that I don't like parties. The problem is Edward always invites Mom. He has this strange idea it's good for us to spend time together. Well, spending a whole evening stuck in the same room with Mom isn't my idea of a good time. That woman never has a kind word to say. She's always criticizing me no matter what I do, and it seems like every time we get together the static in the air increases ten-fold. Edward really ought to think about anchoring a lightening rod in the middle of his living room to draw out some of the charge if he wants us to be together for longer than an hour. Of course that isn't the way I want it to be, but there are some things no one can change, and unfortunately, one of them is Mom's attitude toward me. That will never alter, at least not as long as she continues to blame me for Dad's death.*

Conceivably, I could be partially responsible for Dad's heart attack. After all, if he hadn't gotten so upset with me it might not have happened. But then again, if Mom hadn't been inclined to hysteria, the heart attack might not have been fatal. That afternoon when Dad stumbled out on the front porch and collapsed red-faced at Mom's feet, she could have started CPR on him. But instead, she stood screaming for help when she knew there'd be no one to hear the cries. By the time she had regained her senses and finally called for the paramedics, he'd stopped breathing and had started turning blue.

+++++

Amy laid down her textbook. She didn't want to think about the day her father had died, but the images kept filling her mind anyway.

She had never argued with her father. She had been too smart for that. Arguing with him only made life tougher. He always had his way in the end, so it had been much simpler to give in at the very first. Giving in had saved her a lot of heartache and a lot of pain. It had been safer for her to do exactly whatever he had demanded than to question his authority.

The old biblical adage about the meek inheriting the earth was absurd. Being meek didn't get you anywhere, and it sure didn't protect you from those stronger than you. She had learned early that the people who had power were the ones who had control. If you were small and defenseless there wasn't anything you could do if someone bigger and stronger wanted things done differently than you, especially if there wasn't anyone to stick up for you. And in her family it had been her father who had all the power and control. There hadn't been anyone to protect her from him. Her mother had never tried to help, and her father had made sure that Edward hadn't been around when his anger had gotten out of hand. Her brother never knew about the well-kept family secret.

Amy thought about that last day with her father. The fight she had with him just before he died had been the first time she had ever stood up to him. Without his consent she had applied for a scholarship at the University of Southern Indiana. It had been an important scholarship and she had been shocked and then very excited when she found out she had been awarded it. She had thought her father would be thrilled, but she had been wrong.

She grimaced as the textbook in front of her eyes blurred then vanished. Even though she didn't want to go, her mind took her back to the afternoon her father died. Unable to resist the pulling force of her memories, she followed them back to a day she wished she could forget.

Chapter 8

April 2, 1990
4:00 PM

Amy raced breathless up the front steps of her house and barged though the door without even pausing long enough to shut it behind her. Without thinking, she headed toward the library where she knew her father would be working on his new building project for the city council.

I can't believe it! Amy grinned, her thoughts ablaze with the astounding news she had just received. Of all the students who had applied for the University of Southern Indiana's Presidential Scholarship, the selection committee had chosen her. Her father would be ecstatic when he heard.

As she dashed down the hallway, she caught a glimpse of herself in the mirror by the stairs. Her cheeks were flushed, and her eyes actually seemed to be sparkling. She laughed at her own

53

appearance. It was a buoyant, spirited laugh that matched her light-heartedness, and she beamed with delight. The scholarship was proof she was as smart as Edward...maybe even smarter. When her brother had graduated from high school his grades hadn't been good enough for a scholarship.

She knew the news would be a big surprise. Her father didn't even know she had applied for admission to the university let alone for a scholarship. It had been a secret between her and the guidance counselor. She had decided not to tell anyone until she knew for a fact she'd been accepted.

Now she wouldn't have to keep it a secret any longer. She was really going to go to college. All those heartfelt hopes and dreams she had been wishing the past four years were actually going to come true. What better news could an eighteen-year-old girl have!

She burst through the library door like a whirlwind without even bothering to knock. Her eyes quickly scanned the room and stopped when they rested upon her father working diligently at his desk.

"Dad! Dad! They picked me! They picked me!" Her voice, high pitched and loud from excitement, echoed off the walls.

Without even glancing up from his work, he asked emotionlessly, "Who picked you, and what did they pick you for?"

"U.S.I. The University of Southern Indiana. They picked me for one of their Presidential Scholarships. I can't believe it! The scholarship will cover not only my tuition, but also my books and housing for all four years if I maintain my grades. Isn't this the best news ever!"

Amy expected a return show of enthusiasm when she revealed the exciting news and had not expected the violent reaction that her father exhibited the moment the announcement passed her lips. His fist slammed down angrily upon his desk, and the force of the blow was so strong that the desk shook upon its sturdy legs sending Edward's picture toppling to the floor.

Stunned, Amy didn't even flinch as she watched the glass from the picture frame shatter into a hundred tiny pieces at her feet. She realized right then that she should run, but shock had riveted her feet to the floor. Only her pounding heart moved as she looked hopelessly at her father's enraged face.

The news should have made Dad happy. What had gone wrong?

Her father glared at her through hostile stormy eyes and bellowed, "Who in hell gave you permission to apply to that university? It sure wasn't me. No one came to me asking about going to any damn college. I would have told you right off to stop thinking about such foolishness."

The sparkle that had been dancing in Amy's eyes only moments earlier died a quick death. From the tone of her father's voice she knew instantly he was more than a little upset, but she didn't need to hear him to recognize that fact. When he got mad he clutched his teeth so tightly his jaw muscles would start making little jerking movements. Now, even from several feet away, she could see those muscles twitching like mad.

It was a very bad sign, a dangerous one she knew all too well.

Dazed, she stood staring wide-eyed at her father. This was to have been her moment of victory, the day he finally acknowledged she was special, just like Edward. She couldn't believe his reaction. He was supposed to be happy…not angry.

"You stupid cow! I'm talking to you. Don't stand there staring at me all bug-eyed with your mouth hanging wide open like some kind of moron."

"Dad, I—"

"Shut your mouth, right now. You know better than to interrupt me."

For a moment only silence covered the distance between them. She did know better than to interrupt him.

"You're not going to waste your time or my money starting something you won't be able to finish. You at college? Where did you get a preposterous idea like that?"

"From you. You're always talking about how important college is."

"Yes, for people smart enough to handle it. Which of course, you're not. You're nothing but an idiot. I'd be the laughing stock of this town when you failed. And you would fail. I know that for a fact, and I will not allow myself to be the brunt of everyone's jokes because you're too stupid to finish what you started. I repeat—I will not allow that to happen."

"I won't fail! I promise." She looked at him and pleaded, "Why would you even think I couldn't do it? I had to work very hard these last four years to keep my grades up just to get this scholarship. I didn't fail at that. I can do this. I know I can. I promise I won't embarrass you."

"You only got that scholarship because you're my daughter. There is no way you could have earned it by yourself. You're just too damn dumb."

"You're wrong, Dad! I did earn it. The scholarship has absolutely nothing to do with being your daughter."

"Everything you have is because you are my daughter. Without me you are nothing…just another stupid girl, who thinks she's smart enough to make it on her own."

"Dad, I'm not stupid. My grades prove that. I'm even valedictorian this year. If I was dumb I wouldn't have been able to achieve that."

"Maybe you can fool them down at the school, but I know better. I'm telling you right now you can't go to U.S.I. or any other college. All you're good for is cleaning house, and you're not even very good at that. Hell, you can't even cook a decent meal."

"I'm just as smart as Edward. Maybe even smarter. Why can't you see that?" She could tell his anger was growing, but she couldn't stop from trying to make him listen.

He scowled at the mention of Edward's name and the rage in his voice grew stronger. "The only thing I see is that you're stepping way over your boundaries. I'm the boss in this house, not you. I've

57

only allowed you to stay here because I couldn't send you any place else. No man would have wanted a little slut like you in his home. So pay close attention. I want you to stop all this nonsense about college. You're not going anywhere, and I won't discuss it anymore."

Amy unconsciously stepped back a couple of steps to put a little distance between them. Her skin had started tingling from a nervous itch as tiny goosebumps shot from the base of her neck straight down her spine. Arguing with her father would only make him angrier and that was a very risky thing to do.

"Dad...listen...I...I don't understand why you're acting like this."

"You don't have to understand. You're my daughter, and therefore you will do exactly as you're told. Which means you are going to stay right here in this house where you belong."

"I can't stay here forever. I'm eighteen now. What are you trying to do to me?"

"The only thing I am trying to do is protect you. You couldn't make it out in the real world, not without me."

"Protect me! You've never protected me from anything in your life. Why start now?" Amy bit her lip and tried hard to keep tears from forming in her eyes. She didn't want to cry. This was far too important. The moment she started crying he would know he had won, and then she would be trapped there forever in the house with him, and that would be a fate worse than death itself.

"Watch your mouth, young lady, or you will regret it...I promise you," he threatened.

"The only thing I've ever needed protection from was you!" Amy cried out unexpectedly. "You're a cruel, hateful man. I wish you weren't my father. I wish you were dead!"

Shocked at her own words, Amy knew she should start running before he got the chance to get out of his chair. If she moved fast enough he might not be able to catch her.

"You little bitch, who do you think you're talking to?" he demanded to know, standing up looking as menacing as a striking cobra. "You're not ever going to leave this house as long as I'm alive. You belong here, not anywhere else. I want you right where I can keep an eye on you at all times. I'm not going to give you the chance to mess up someone else's life the way you have messed up mine. Do you understand?"

"I understand more than you think I do," she barely whispered, the cold hostility from his eyes freezing her with fear. From his stance she could tell he was getting ready to come after her. She wanted to flee from the room, but her feet wouldn't move.

There was no question in her mind what would happen next. Her father's rage showed plainly on his face. His hands were clinched tightly into huge fists, and she knew what that meant. Those hands were terrible weapons when fueled by the madness that sometimes took control, a madness that would only be calmed by her pain.

Cautiously she started backing out of the room carefully placing one foot behind the other. Her eyes sought his, and she thought he looked like a cougar stalking its kill. She instinctively knew that once she took to flight he would be right on top of her.

Everything seemed to happen in slow motion. As she cautiously inched backward, her eyes followed his advance. Malice emanated from him like a deadly, black aura. The piercing glare from his stone-cold granite eyes sent sharp daggers deep into her heart. She knew this time would be different...this time he would kill her. She could feel the powerful force of his anger driving him and realized he wouldn't be able to stop once he started.

As he reached to grab her arm to pull her toward another journey into hell, an unanticipated burst of wild fury coursed through her whole body, a fury so intense it broke through the terror that had held her in bondage for so long. From somewhere deep inside, courage...or maybe desperation...took charge.

I've worked too hard for this chance to escape, and he isn't going to take it away from me! Not now...not ever, she thought, as the rapidly growing fire inside her began to blaze furiously, Instead of fleeing, she abruptly dodged his groping hands and darted to the other side of the room. She stood so his desk was placed between them like a shield and then turned to face her father. Only this time the fear that had been her constant companion for so many years had vanished and had been replaced by a powerful determination to be free.

"I think you'd better stop right there. Don't you dare come one step closer," she lashed out in a controlled voice full of anger and hate. "You have hit me for the last time. I'm not a defenseless child anymore, and if you even touch me again this whole town will find out exactly what you are—a monster—a terrible, awful monster who brutally abused his own daughter. What do you think the members of the Town Council would say about that? And what about your precious Church Board? Would they still worship you if they knew?"

Her father was shocked by her insolence and for the longest time he didn't move or even speak. But as he stood silently in front of her, the rage on his face started to ebb and was quickly replaced by arrogance. "It doesn't matter what you tell anyone," he said. "No one will believe you. You have absolutely no proof I've done a single thing wrong. Anyway, they all know you're crazy. After some of the stories they've heard about you in town I'm surprised that someone hasn't suggested I have you committed."

"Stories you made up to protect yourself," Amy replied bitterly.

"Prove it. Even the doctor thinks you're a very disturbed young lady. I could have you locked up in that mental hospital across town for years with no problem at all. So you'd better think twice before you say one word to anybody."

"Edward would believe me. I would make him believe me."

"How would you like to spend the next ten years in the loony bin strapped in a straight-jacket? It could be arranged very easily," he said, reaching for the phone. "I only have to call, and they would come and get you, no questions asked."

"You'd better listen and listen carefully, you bastard!" she shouted, her heart racing as fast as her thoughts. "You're dead wrong about there being no proof. I don't think you'd want to put your precious reputation on the line right now. If your friends ever discover what has really happened behind the closed doors of this house, you'd be run out of town. And what about Edward? What would he do? Do you think he would still see you as some kind of god when the truth becomes known?"

"I haven't done anything to you that you haven't deserved. You have always been an insolent little brat." Her father pulled back his hand without touching the phone. Then he slowly started moving around the desk toward her. "Besides, what kind of proof is a bruise? That's all anyone has seen…a few little bruises. I don't think I will be labeled a monster over that."

Artfully, Amy quickly sidestepped him again. The unabated fury flowing through her body gave her the strength to continue. "Do you remember that camera you lost about five years ago? You know, the one with the timer that lets you take self-photos. Well, guess what? The camera wasn't lost. It's only been hidden away in a very safe place."

"So, who gives a damn about that stupid camera," he said, glaring at her with a penetrating gaze of animosity.

"You had better, that's who. You want proof. I have lots of proof. I took pictures of every single bruise you gave me over the last five years. Somewhere, safely hidden away, is a very explicit photographic testimony of your love for me."

"You really are crazy," he said, clenching his hands into tight fists. "I should've had you put away years ago."

"Crazy enough to take pictures of the hell you put me through. How many rolls of film do think there might be after five years? Two, three, maybe four at the most? Wrong! The last time I counted there were seven rolls. Seven rolls of film documenting my wonderful life here in this house. Remember that time a couple of years ago when you slammed me up against the stove because supper wasn't ready? I think you broke a couple of ribs that day. It took weeks for the bruising on my chest to finally fade. The coloring in that photo should be real interesting."

"You stupid little whore! All this time you've been setting me up. I should just—"

"You should just shut up and listen! Unless you want those pictures posted all over town, this is what you're going to do. Number one-you will stay as far away from me as possible at all times. Number two-you will never hit me again. Don't even raise your hand in the attempt. I know you can do that. Not once have you ever attempted to hit me when anyone else except Mom was around, so we both know you have the self-control to do this."

"You can't tell me what to do!" Enraged by Amy's impudence he started shouting. "I'm your father, and I give the orders around here, not you."

"Not this time," Amy said, watching his face turn beet-red. She almost faltered when she noticed how the veins on his neck were bulging like little blue snakes attempting to break free from underneath the surface of his skin. She thought he looked as though he could explode at any moment.

But she knew she couldn't back down. If she stopped now, she might as well go shoot herself. If she didn't stand up to him today, the chance would never come again, and she would be his prisoner for life.

"Number three," she said with more courage than she actually felt at that moment. "You will not try to prevent me from attending college. I worked hard for that scholarship and deserve it. So, just sign any papers you have to sign and don't hassle me over it. And finally, don't go spreading any more lies about me. Just don't mention my name to anyone, because if you do I'll make sure those photographs I took are made public. And believe me, if that happens, all those stories you told about me will look like fairy tales compared to the ones everyone in town will start telling about you."

Then without waiting for a reply, Amy turned and with great dignity walked away. At the library door she couldn't resist looking back to be sure he wasn't coming after her. He wasn't. He was standing at the desk with one hand clutched tightly to his chest and the other one on the edge of the desk supporting his weight. She could see little beads of sweat forming across his brow, and his color had turned ashen. For a second she waited for his eyes to find hers, but he didn't even look in her direction. He was staring off into the air at nothing at all.

Wild thoughts raced through her mind as she forced herself to calmly walk out of the house. For right now she would be safe. His precious reputation was his most prized possession, and he would do anything to protect it. She was fairly certain he wouldn't try to get even…at least not for a while.

As it turned out, she didn't have to worry about her father's reprisal. The very next time she saw him was at the mortuary lying stone-cold in a fancy wooden box, and she knew he couldn't hit her from there.

Toni Auberry

Chapter 9

March 29, 1998

Amy lay down her textbook and sat back in the kitchen chair. After she had wasted her precious time reliving those dreadful last few minutes with her father, she had forced herself to think of nothing but the textbook positioned in front of her face. For over two hours now she had been concentrating exclusively on her homework, and her mind was overflowing with information.

Studying isn't much fun, but it's sure easier than thinking about Dad, she thought, as she stretched to ease the dull ache in her lower back. *I just don't understand why I can't get him out of my head. He's been dead for eight years now, yet somehow he still manages to intimidate me. He has a horrid way of sneaking into my mind when I least expect it and messing me over. He's like a hungry tiger waiting to pounce on its next meal, and like that tiger's meal I'm never prepared for the moment of attack.*

Amy glanced at the clock and was surprised to find it was almost noon. She marked her place in the textbook and closed it. *I've got to take a break. If I sit here one minute more, I'll go stark raving mad. Besides, if I don't get some caffeine into me soon, I'm going to have a raging migraine.* Giving in to the caffeine craving that was gnawing greedily at her nerves, Amy filled a kettle with water and then placed it on the stove to heat. A few minutes later just as she started pouring the boiling water into her teacup, the front doorbell unexpectedly chimed, and her arm jerked back with a nervous twitch. Steaming hot water splashed onto the table and threatened to saturate the homework she had so diligently worked on all morning. She grabbed a nearby dishtowel and hurriedly mopped up the mess. As the last drop of water was wiped away, the doorbell sounded again with four short repeated rings.

Someone's awfully impatient this morning, she thought. Annoyed, she tossed the wet towel into the sink. When the bell chimed for the sixth time, she felt more than a twinge of apprehension take control of her thoughts. *Who in the world could that be?* she wondered warily.

She nervously peered through the window of the front door trying to get a glimpse of her unknown caller. But the late winter storm that had howled so wildly through the night had painted a multitude of frosty images on the pane making it impossible for her to see who was standing on the other side. Her hand lingered on the deadbolt. She just couldn't bring herself to release it until she was sure who her surprise visitor was.

"Come on, Amy, open up," Edward shouted. His boisterous voice boomed through the door as though it wasn't even there. "And hurry, it's damn cold out here."

Amy was instantly relieved at the sound of Edward's voice and threw the door open allowing an uninvited blast of freezing air to force itself into the house. It briskly gusted down the hall and into the kitchen where it swept her pile of neatly stacked notes off the table and scattered them across the white tile floor.

The moment Edward stepped into the house the wind blew in a light dusting of snowflakes that danced around him before falling quietly to the floor. He stamped his boots on the doormat to loosen the snow clinging to them, and then he quickly shut the door to keep the storm outside where it belonged. As the door closed, the wind started howling louder as if it were angry over being shut out.

"Who would have expected it to be so cold on your birthday?" Edward asked as he took off his gloves." I can't remember the weather ever being this bad in March. We should be thinking about wearing our shorts instead of these heavy winter coats."

The sight of her brother all bundled up like a small child in his heavy winter parka made Amy smile. "Thanks a lot for making a mess of the house," she teased. "You've managed to get snow all over the floor, which by the way, I just cleaned last night, and to make it worse you have made a complete disaster of my homework. I'll never be able to place all those notes back in order. I'm not so sure now that it was a good idea to let you in."

"If you hadn't, you wouldn't have gotten this." Edward hoisted up the large package he had set inside the door upon entering the house.

Amy eyed the package with delight. Of course it had to be a birthday present and it would be something spectacular! Edward had always gone out of his way to pick out an extra-special birthday gift. Every year he surprised her with the perfect present. Sometimes she felt that he knew her tastes better than she did.

The package was immense. At least three feet tall and nearly as long, it was wrapped in plain brown shipping paper that gave absolutely no clue to what could possibly be inside. She eagerly took the gift from Edward hands, and in her excitement she almost dropped it.

"Careful now," Edward laughed. "Don't break your present before you even get the chance to enjoy it."

Amy carefully carried the gift to the living room and sat down on the couch. She cautiously began loosening the package's heavily taped edges. She had learned from experience not to hastily open any of Edward's presents. A person could never really be sure what she might find inside a gift bearing her brother's name. Edward's sense of humor was well known, and his gifts sometimes literally jumped out of their packages. Last year he had rigged her present so that colorful confetti exploded into the air the moment she had opened it. She had been so surprised she had dropped the package and almost broke the delicate music box inside.

Amy's eyes flashed with excitement as the last of the paper fell away. This year no unwelcome surprises were hidden inside. Instead, a lovely oil painting of a young girl lay hidden within the many layers of brown wrapping paper. The child, dressed in an old-fashioned, blue nightgown, sat nestled in an antique, four-poster bed with her arms wrapped around a magnificent collie. She was a tiny thing with an air of frailty about her. She looked to be about seven or eight and had huge, hazel eyes. Her dark brown hair, tied back at the base of her neck by a wide, navy ribbon, hung in large ringlets down to her waist. It was easy to tell from the painting she had been from a well-to-do family. The background suggested luxurious surroundings, and the collie had the majestic look of a purebred.

"Oh Edward, this painting is fabulous! I really do love it. You know, the only thing I like about my birthdays are the presents I get from you." Amy stood up from the couch, went over to Edward and wrapped her arms around him giving him a loving hug. "But it really isn't the presents that are so important. It's the fact you always go out of your way to find something you know I will adore. That alone makes whatever it is you give me extra special. You have always had a way of making me feel cherished."

"Well, you deserve to be pampered once in awhile. Whether you realize it or not, you really are a wonderful person. You just never give yourself credit for anything. You always seem to be putting yourself down, and I just don't understand why."

"Let's not get into that discussion again." Amy frowned and backed away from Edward. Her eyes no long sparked with excitement. Instead, they flashed a warning that Edward was starting to tread on dangerous ground and should back off. "I really don't want to talk about that particular subject right now," she said with a slight touch of resentment in her voice.

"All right, I won't say any more for now, but only because it's your birthday." Edward bent down and placed a small brotherly kiss on Amy's forehead. "You have the right not to get a lecture today, but next week we really need to sit down and have a serious discussion about your self-esteem. I think you need to see a professional to help you get over feeling so negatively about yourself all the time."

Amy sat quietly for a moment without saying a word; then she expertly directed the conversation away from herself. "I was just about to fix some hot tea when you showed up. Would you like some? It wouldn't be a bother to fix an extra cup."

"No thanks, Sis, I can only stay for a few minutes. But I do want you to know I had an ulterior motive for coming over here today."

"And what's that?" Amy saw the suspicious twinkle in her brother's eyes and realized immediately that he was up to something.

"I know how much you hate coming to the house when Mom is there, and I figured you might try to use this bad weather as an excuse not to show up this evening for your birthday party. So I'm here to offer up an enticement to get you there."

"I think you messed up on that one," Amy teased. "You already gave me my present. Now what other reason would I have for coming over?"

"Well, that was only one of your presents. The best is yet to come, but you're going to have to show up in person to get it. So I expect you to be at my house at precisely seven o'clock this evening. And please try to come with a positive attitude. I know you and Mom don't get along very well, but try for my sake. I do love both of you, and it really upsets me when the two of you argue all the time."

"I promise to show up, but I can't promise anything else. It all depends on how Mom acts. I refuse to just sit around and let her rip me to pieces with that sharp tongue of hers. I know you think I overreact, but you really have no idea how vicious she can be. She is so subtle with those cutting words of hers that no one recognizes she is actually trying to open old wounds just to watch me bleed."

"I'll talk to her before you get there. I really do want this party to be an enjoyable time for everyone concerned. I don't want my wife upset because you and Mom aren't willing to be nice to each other for one evening. The pregnancy has Ellen going through enough mood swings the way it is without the two of you making it worse."

"For Ellen's sake I promise to be on my best behavior." Amy sighed in resignation and then made a tiny cross over her heart. "Now, tell me how you managed to find the painting. It's so unusual, and it is really the most perfect present."

"Well, you know me, the perfect brother," Edward laughingly commented. "I did have to rummage through several antique shops to find it. I'd begun to think you would have to settle for another music box this year. Then there it was…hanging on the back wall of a small antique shop. The moment I saw it I immediately thought of you. The girl in the painting looks just the way I remember you as a child. She has the same misty, faraway look in her eyes that you always had. Back when we were kids it seemed to me that you lived in a different world than the rest of us. Sometimes you would just sit for hours and stare off into space, looking at some unknown place we couldn't see. And that dog in the painting reminds me of Thomas, the pup you got when you were seven. I remember how you used to worship that mutt like it was the only friend you had in the world. You would whisper secrets in his ears that you wouldn't even tell me. I can still vividly recall a couple of times when I came upon you sitting on the front porch steps with tears steaming down your face, and you would be talking to Thomas so quietly no one else could hear what you were saying. When I would ask you what was wrong, you'd just look at me with those big, sad eyes of yours and silently shake your head. If I tried to force you to tell me what was wrong, you'd run away and hide. I used to get so frustrated because you wouldn't talk to me."

In a small almost inaudible voice Amy whispered, "Maybe someday I'll tell you my secrets…but not now…not today."

Edward didn't know how to respond. He knew there were things about their childhood Amy needed to talk about. He just didn't know how to get her to open up. Every time he tried, she would only withdraw more.

Finally, Amy broke the tense silence. "You really shouldn't spend so much money on me. With Ellen expecting, you need to start thinking more about saving for the baby. Raising a child is going to put a bigger demand on your budget. I suspect you spent way too much on me this year."

Edward shook his head and smiled. "There you go again, worrying about things you shouldn't be worrying about. If I couldn't afford something I simply wouldn't buy it. Usually I don't tell people the price of their gifts, but if it will ease your mind I will tell you I didn't spend a lot of money on the painting. In fact, you would be amazed how much it really cost. I actually got it so cheap it feels like I stole it!"

Amy grinned, allowing the lost sparkle to return to her eyes. "Here I am believing you spent a small fortune on me, and you're telling me how cheap you really are. I should have realized you haven't changed. I still remember the time you actually did steal one of my birthday presents. In the middle of the night you slipped over to Old Lady Grime's flower garden and picked all her spring tulips. When I found them on the bedside dresser the next morning, you lied, saying you had bought them as a special surprise just for me."

"Well, they were a special surprise for you, and you have to admit those tulips did make a beautiful bouquet."

"Yes, but you really got into big trouble over it. That old woman was hopping mad. She had been bragging all week how those tulips were the first ones up in the neighborhood that spring, and when she discovered they were gone she called the police. If Dad hadn't sweet-talked her out of it, I think you would have ended up spending the night in jail."

"I didn't get off the hook easily, you know. Dad forced me to work for her for a whole month. I swear she must have made me plant a hundred different flowers. Working for her was terrible! She was worse than an army drill sergeant. 'Weed this…trim that…dig those.' By the time that month was over I was actually starting to think I was in the army!"

"You have to admit she did have the best-looking flower garden in the neighborhood that year. Guess your hard work was worth something."

"It was worth more than a bunch of old tulips." Edward's eyes drifted over to the painting, and he thought about Amy's dog, Thomas. "You know, I might not have had to work so hard if that crazy pup of yours hadn't kept digging up everything I planted. It seemed like every time I planted a flower Thomas would dig it up. There were a couple of times I actually thought about killing that mutt for making me work so hard."

"Killing Thomas!" Amy grabbed Edward's arm and stared at him through eyes wide with alarm. "Why would you have even thought of such a horrible thing?"

"Oh Amy, that was only an expression. You know I wouldn't have hurt Thomas."

"I know, but—" Her fingers dug deep into Edward's arm, and she held on as though he would disappear if she were to let go. She closed her eyes to try to avoid seeing the terrible picture that had started to form in her thoughts, but she was unsuccessful. From somewhere far back in the dark recesses of her mind came the horrible image of Thomas lying dead with bright crimson blood pouring from a ragged wound in his neck. The sight was so hideous she had to struggle to keep from screaming out in alarm.

"Sis, you can let go of my arm now." Edward said gently. "You're going to leave bruises if you don't."

"Sorry." Amy released her hold and stood back, her face flushing from embarrassment.

"What was that all about? You honestly weren't thinking I would've hurt Thomas?"

"No, that's not it. It's just…well, when you mentioned killing Thomas…oh I don't know how to explain it." Frustrated, Amy turned away, avoiding the questioning look on Edward's face. Unconsciously she rubbed her temples as a dull aching pain started throbbing above her eyes.

"Another migraine?" Edward asked, his concern for Amy showing in his voice. "That's the third one this week, isn't it?"

"It's only a little one. Nothing for you to worry about, and besides it's more a feeling of pressure than pain anyway."

"Well, lately your little headaches have all ended up as big ones. What brought this one on?"

"Maybe because I started thinking about Thomas. It still upsets me that we never did find out what happened to him when he disappeared. We both know he wouldn't have run away. Every time I think about him I get this strange sensation in my head that feels like tiny little bugs are crawling around in my skull."

"Amy! That doesn't sound good. If you don't make an appointment to see the doctor soon, I'm going to drag you there myself."

"Well, right now you just need to drag yourself home. I'm not in the mood to discuss doctors." Amy handed Edward his coat and walked with him to the door. "I don't want you to think I'm chasing you out, but if I'm going to attend your party tonight I have to rest. Once a migraine takes root it's hard to kill."

"Listen, Sis, you seem to be having headaches almost every day now. I'm serious about you going to see your doctor. I'm really concerned you might have something gravely wrong."

"Over the last eight years I've seen plenty of doctors, and they just keep shoving more pain medicines at me. The last one had me so doped up I couldn't think straight for weeks, so it's really safer for me to try to sleep the pain away."

"You've been having headaches since you were a kid. I don't understand why someone can't find out the cause. I know Dad wouldn't take you to a doctor because he didn't have any faith in them, but that is no reason for you to feel that way."

"Dad thought I was just trying to avoid school," Amy replied bitingly. "Maybe if he had taken me to a doctor I wouldn't be having so much difficulty now."

"I don't want to start an argument over what Dad should have done. I'm simply concerned about you. That's all. Your headaches are getting worse, and you are showing signs of depression again. The last time you were depressed, you talked about taking a high dive off of the State Bank building. I don't want you to end up as some piece of bloody art work on the sidewalk."

"That was over nine years ago, and I have matured a little since then. I admit I was a little confused back in high school. After all, Dad did try his best to make my life hell. You were the lucky one. He never cared what you did, but with me it was different. I couldn't even leave the house without giving a full report of my every movement. If I showed up late even by one minute, he would come out screaming before my feet hit the front porch steps."

"Now, Amy, I know Dad was harder on you than on me, but after all you were his little girl. He didn't want you to end up in trouble like some of the other girls in town. In his own way he was only looking after you. I really don't believe it was as terrible as you think it was."

"That's easy for you to say. You weren't the one he dragged into the house after being caught on the front porch getting a good night kiss. I can still see him storming out the door yelling and hollering, calling me a slut. He scared my date so badly the boy never did ask me out again. After word got around school about how Dad

79

was such a raving manic, I never got asked out again by anyone. Which might not have mattered since most of the time, I wasn't even allowed to leave the house. Why wouldn't I have been depressed?"

"Amy it wasn't that bad."

"Yes, for me it was. But how would you know? You were gone most of the time. Dad didn't keep you locked up in the house like some kind of prisoner."

"You weren't locked up."

"The same as. Every move I made he monitored. He treated me like I was a whore who wanted sex with every guy I met. He was totally obsessed with the idea that some boy might touch me."

"He was just being a good father. He knew what guys wanted when they went out on dates."

"Good fathers don't call their daughters sluts because of good night kisses. Good fathers don't imprison their daughters because of their own fears. Good fathers—"

"Amy, chill out! This isn't going to make your headache any better." Edward placed a hand on each of Amy's shoulders and stared right into her eyes. "Just try to relax."

"I know I shouldn't get so uptight, but it makes me so angry when I start thinking about how Dad treated me." Amy brushed Edward's hands away with a push and continued bitterly, "You just don't understand at all. Dad let you go out all the time. The more dates you had, the better he liked it. He was always pushing you to have sex with every girl you dated. It almost seemed as though he were keeping score. Like he was going to present you with some big trophy when you reached a certain total. I can still hear him bragging to those old fools he called friends about what a great stud you were."

"Amy, I said chill out. This particular discussion is not an option for today. Remember it's your birthday, and you are supposed to be happy. So, let's not drag out old family issues. We can talk about this next week. Today you have a party to attend, and you still have another extra special present waiting for you at my house."

"You're right." Amy suddenly felt too tired to continue arguing. "I'm sorry."

"Apology accepted. Now, I need to get home. There are things that have to be done before the party tonight, and you need to head into your bedroom and lie down for a few minutes. I don't want you using that headache as an excuse not to come."

After Edward left, Amy went back into the kitchen to fix the hot tea she had been craving earlier. While the water heated she began gently massaging her temples in small circular motions. The pain in her head had started to throb again, and she had to fight hard to keep tears of frustration from flowing.

Chapter 10

Why are my headaches getting worse? Amy worried, while her fingers carefully kneaded the knotted pressure points at her brow that were sending sharp bolts of pain across her forehead and behind her eyes. *Maybe I should get a checkup, but I can't see what good that would really do? Doctors never pay attention to what their patients are trying to tell them. They don't want to know the truth if it is something different than what they want to believe. They only see what they want to see. Just like Dr. Stevenson. If he hadn't been so busy trying to impress Dad, he might have noticed something very wrong was going on at my house. If he had bothered to look at me, even once, as a real person, maybe I wouldn't have had to suffer so much all those years. One of these days I'm going to visit him and describe in detail the price I had to pay because of his negligence. Of course, it might not matter to him. There are some men you can never reach. Still, it would certainly make me feel better. Maybe that sounds vindictive, but he deserves to know the part he played in the hell I had to live through as I was growing up under his care.*

Amy felt a fiery anger igniting deep within her heart as she thought about how much suffering she had endured as a direct result of Dr. Stevenson's lack of concern. As the anger flared higher and higher, the pain in her head also grew stronger. She cringed as it pounded with the power of a sledgehammer slamming forcefully again and again on a concrete block.

Hopeful that the caffeine from the freshly brewed tea would somehow help ease her misery, Amy sipped at the hot brew while she painstakingly gathered the papers that the wind had scattered earlier across the kitchen floor. A few minutes later, she sat at the table staring unhappily at the stack of unfinished homework that seemed to be staring back at her demanding her immediate attention. Unable to face the task of studying while her head was exploding with pain, she piled all her notes and textbooks on one of the kitchen chairs and then shoved it under the table so she wouldn't have to look at it. *Out of sight, out of mind,* she hoped.

She tried to think herself into a state of relaxation, but the headache had filled her thoughts with its presence, and she couldn't focus well enough to meditate successfully. Staring into her teacup like a psychic trying to read a customer's fortune from tea leaves, she tried to remember when she had first started have the migraines.

There was one distinct episode deeply imprinted in her memory...the school's Christmas play when she was ten...her head had hurt so severely during the performance that she'd almost passed out on the stage from the pain.

My angel costume was so beautiful that night, she remembered sadly. *The snow-white gown had been covered with silver threads and twinkling sequins that had shimmered and sparkled even under the dimmest of lights. And attached to the back of the gown there had even been delicate white-feathered wings, which actually fluttered gracefully as I danced.*

Tears filled Amy's eyes as she remembered how excited she had been to be given the part of the angel in the play. Her heart had been brimming with a spirited joy as she had dressed for the performance. The costume had fit her perfectly, and the moment she had it on she had danced with delight across her bedroom floor, spinning in a circle, sending the gown's full skirt twirling and glittering like a night full of stars. Her soft satin shoes had appeared to move almost on their own as they lifted her gracefully up on her toes.

For one short moment, she had actually felt like a real angel, one that could truly fly. She remembered thinking that she could go anywhere she wanted to, even past the clouds, the moon, and as far as the Milky Way. Up among the stars-flying, soaring, gliding-she would be free from all the pain and heartache she had to face every day at home with her father.

Spinning and twirling, laughing and giggling, she had danced, and her heart had been filled with a magical joy.

That is...until she saw herself in the mirror.

She seriously doubted that she would ever forget the way she had felt at that awful, terrible moment.

For one small minute of time she had actually thought she really did look like an angel, beautiful and pure, one of God's most favorite things. Then an excruciating pain had cut through her temples, stopping her feet in mid-step, bringing her down to her knees. She remembered believing the pain was a punishment sent by God for daring to think she could be one of his heavenly spirits.

As the pain in her head had increased, so had the realization that the image in the mirror was deceptive. She had known deep in her heart there couldn't be anything beautiful about her. No matter how pretty and angelic the costume looked outside, it couldn't hide the ugliness inside. The mirror had lied. There could be no beauty in her reflection.

+++++

Amy set down the teacup and cradled her head in her hands. She wanted to make the memory of that night vanish, disappear into the blackness of her mind like so many of her other memories. She didn't want to think about it anymore. But the images wouldn't recede. Instead they came in sharper, clearer, as though she were living it all again.

She vividly recalled walking up to the mirror, touching her reflection, and slowly running her fingers across the glass as she followed the lines of her face. Despair, hopelessness, desperation had seemed to live in the eyes of the pitiful creature staring back at her.

What if? She had thought. *What if I go on stage and the audience sees through the beauty of the costume into the ugliness inside of me? What if they want to send me away? Where would I go? How would I survive? Dad says no one will ever want me because I'm so wicked, so evil.*

As she had stood peering into her own eyes, the fears about getting on stage had grown with each passing second, as had the headache pounding unmercifully in her skull. Finally the pain had become so intense her head had felt as though it would explode. She had wanted to lie down in her bed and bury herself as far as possible under the covers to hide from the shame consuming her soul. But she had known that she couldn't hide or disappear into the shadows of the night. Not with her father waiting for her. He had already called upstairs once for her to hurry, and experience had taught her that it wasn't wise to make him call twice. She had wanted to cry as she had forced her feet to carry her from the safety of the bedroom, down the hallway, and then to the stairs leading to the last place she want to go to.

+++++

As the memory of that terrible trek down the stairs filled Amy's mind with forms and images she didn't really want to see, her stomach twisted and turned a thousand times. She found it difficult to draw in a full breath of air as a strange tension wrapped itself around her chest. She suddenly became light-headed and had difficulty focusing…just as she had the night of the play.

That night, as she had descended the stairs that took her to her father, she had been so dizzy the steps under her feet had actually seemed to move on their own accord. She remembered how her hands had clutched the banister so tightly that her fingers had ached for days afterward. She also remembered how she had desperately pleaded to be allowed to remain home.

But it hadn't mattered to her father that her head hurt so severely she thought she might die. He didn't offer up one word of compassion or understanding; he had only told her she had no choice, it was her duty to go. Then he had refused to attend the play, saying he didn't want to go and be embarrassed when she messed up her part.

Her mother had gone though, and in a rare motherly moment had held her hand, kissed her on the cheek, and promised everything would turn out just fine.

But it hadn't turned out fine.

With a throbbing headache and a dominating fear of failure, she had forced herself to go on stage, and it was there that she had proved her father right—she did fail.

The constant aching in her head didn't go away, even though she had prayed with all of her heart for it to stop hurting. Instead, it remained with her through the whole play. The pain messed with her mind, and she couldn't remember her lines. She had stood in front of the whole school assembly with her mouth open wide and couldn't force a single word to come out. She could still picture the three little girls that had sat on the front row of the audience talking and pointing their fingers at her. They had actually giggled loudly enough for the whole auditorium to hear. Those three little girls don't know how lucky they really were that night. She could still remember being so nauseated she almost threw up on them.

Afterwards during the trip home, there had been no acts of solace or words of encouragement from her mother. Only looks of disdain were given as the silence in the car had mounted with each passing mile.

She had managed to embarrass and disgrace the whole family, just as her father had said she would.

As soon as they had arrived home, her mother had wasted no time in reciting the whole terrible ordeal. After the story had been told, her father had grabbed her arm and yanked her up the stairs behind him so quickly she had stumbled several times as she tried to keep in step. The next morning she had huge bruises on both of her knees from where she had fallen.

All the way up the stairs her father had bellowed like a wild bull how ashamed he was of her and how lucky she was that he didn't throw her out of the house for shaming the whole family. When they finally reached her room he yanked open the door, jerked her inside, and threw her down on the floor.

She remembered how vividly he had looked like a murderous giant as she had lain at his feet shaking in fear, watching him pull his belt from around his waist.

If Thomas hadn't been hiding under her bed, she couldn't begin to guess what might have happened. Thomas, her savior, had sprung from under the darkness of the bed, his pointed fangs gleaming like silver daggers, and his eyes glowing with the rage of a wild beast. He had growled at her father, low and threatening, like a wolf ready to attack.

For a few moments Thomas and her father had locked eyes like mortal enemies about to do battle. Then her father had slowly backed out of the room without touching her. The sound of the door locking behind him as he left the room had been heaven sent. He might have thought he was locking her in, but in reality he had locked himself out. She had known that as long as the door stayed locked she would be safe and secure within her prison.

Afterwards, in the darkened confines of the bedroom, she had whispered to Thomas that she was sure everyone at school had realized what a terrible person she was. They had to have been able to recognize the badness, the wickedness, which existed within her.

As she had told Thomas about the three little girls who had laughed at her, he had simply looked at her with adoring eyes that spoke only of unconditional understanding. Then she had buried her face in his soft fur and cried a river of tears while Thomas had stood patiently waiting until she finished. Then he had gently licked away the remaining tears. The rest of the night he had stayed at the foot of her bed as if stationing himself as a shield between her and the world.

Later that same night as she lay curled under the protection of the soft blankets wrapped tightly around her small body, there had been a wonderful dream of a beautiful angel, who flew down from heaven and carried her away to a safe place. The angel's wings were as soft as downy feathers and a golden halo had glowed over the top of her head. Her touch had felt kind and gentle, and her smile had promised sweet peace.

Upon awakening from the dream, there had been the sad realization she was still at home in her own bed. The angel had seemed so genuine, so real.

To this day she still regrets that the dream hadn't been a reality. If the angel had taken her away, she wouldn't have had to endure all those long years of her father's hateful abuse.

Toni Auberry

Chapter 11

Amy's thoughts of that terrible night of the school play only intensified the agonizing throbbing of her migraine. She finally gave up trying to control the pain and went to seek the quiet refuge of her bedroom. She reluctantly took two pain pills and then crawled into bed with all of her clothes still on. After several restless minutes her headache started to ease, and the lure of sleep's darkened depths beckoned with promises of peaceful relief. As she entered that short period between wakefulness and sleep, the faint cries of a small child echoed through her mind.

"Please help me," the child's pleading voice whispered urgently. *"It hurts so badly and he won't stop."*

Who won't stop? Amy wondered for one brief moment before the darkness of deep sleep carried her far away from the pain in her head.

+++++

After a two-hour nap, Amy awoke with only a dull throbbing in her head. She was able to face the prospect of the annual family get-together with a little more enthusiasm. While thoughts of spending the evening in the company of her mother weren't pleasant, the bad feeling was offset by the knowledge that Edward and his wife, Ellen, would be there to act as buffers. Edward and Ellen were more than just family; they were her best and dearest friends. It would be worth the price she would have to pay for being around her mother just to be in their company.

I suppose, Amy thoughtfully considered, *if people knew what really happened to me they might find it strange that I love Edward.*

She had realized early, however, that it wouldn't be right to blame her brother for their father's actions. Edward had been carefully sheltered from the evil side of their father. He really had no idea what had happened to her behind the closed doors of their home when only she and their father were there alone. Edward never saw or heard the blows that had been so unmercifully bestowed upon her. If he had, he would have tried to save her. She knew that in her heart, but she hadn't been able to tell him and he had never guessed.

+++++

Eager to take a closer look at the painting Edward had given her, Amy headed toward the living room. On the way out of the bedroom Amy caught a glimpse of her refection in the dresser mirror. Shocked by her appearance, she stopped to stare. Her clothes were a mess, wrinkled and disheveled from being slept in. Her hair stuck out in different directions like an old bag lady's, and her mascara had smeared, blackening both of her eyes.

What a fuss Mom would make if she saw me right now, she thought running her fingers through her hair. Even observing one hair out of place was enough to send her mother into a fit. Unfortunately for both of them, her mother had always put too much emphasis on appearances.

For a moment Amy thought about taking a picture of her new look and sending it to her mother in a thank-you card, maybe writing something in it like: *Dear Mom, Thank you for giving birth to me on this glorious day. I'm sending you this picture of me to remind you of all the wonderful moments we spent together as I was growing up. It was your love that made me what I am today. Aren't you proud of your accomplishment? Your loving daughter, Amy.*

But she couldn't do that. She really wasn't that kind of person. Besides, she didn't own a camera. She hadn't touched one since her father had died. She had already taken enough pictures to last her a lifetime.

She critically assessed her appearance in the mirror and wondered if she looked older than she really was. Some days she felt more like sixty than twenty-six. Hopefully it didn't show on her face, though she guessed it really didn't matter. There wasn't anyone she hoped to impress, and even if there were she wouldn't go out of her way to be something that she wasn't. A man would have to take her as she was, whether that included gray hairs, wrinkles, or whatever.

As she adjusted her clothes she suddenly remembered the child's pitiful cry for help she had heard earlier just before she had drifted off to sleep. Surely it had been only a dream? None of her neighbors had any children and neither the TV nor the radio had been on.

The poor child's voice had sounded so pathetic and desolate, Amy mindfully reflected. *What could I have possibly been dreaming about?*

+++++

Amy's troubled thoughts over the disturbing dream didn't stay with her long. They were quickly chased away by the desire to look at Edward's painting again. After quickly tugging a comb through her tangled hair and washing the smeared mascara from her eyes, she hurried into the living room to take another look at the marvelous present her brother had delivered earlier in the day.

She carried the painting over into the sunlight that was filtering in from the huge picture window near the couch, and she reflected on Edward's statements about it. After studying the picture more closely, she understood what he had meant when he had described the little girl's eyes as having a misty faraway look. The girl's eyes did appear to be focused on some distant shore, as though she was daydreaming about some mystical place that only she could see. It gave the painting a mysterious haunting quality.

Amy looked closely at the girl's facial expression and felt there was more than a hint of sorrow etched in the young face…like the child had already endured much unhappiness in her youthful life.

There appeared to be small lines of sadness drawn under the child's eyes. The faint markings made Amy wonder if the child had cried so many tears that the unhappiness had permanently left its wretched mark.

An old sixties song by Smoky Robinson, "Tracks of My Tears" started playing through Amy's mind as one of her fingers gingerly traced a path around the girl's eyes.

When she scrutinized the painting even further, she observed that the girl appeared to be clutching the collie very tightly against her body, as if afraid of letting go, and that the dog actually seemed to be guarding the child. His ears were perked up as if listening for some hidden danger, and his stance appeared alert and proud like a soldier standing watch from his outpost.

Perhaps the collie had reason to be on guard, Amy thought somberly. *Maybe the girl had whispered her secrets to him. Secrets so terrible they couldn't be told to anyone except her friend, who stood so diligently on guard within the circle of her arms.*

Suddenly Amy felt hot and flushed from the sunlight that was warmly caressing her shoulders. She quickly moved from the couch, carrying the painting with her, and sat in the recliner in the furthest, darkest corner of the room. There in the shadows the little girl's eyes no longer appeared so sad, and she felt foolish for attributing such negative feelings to an innocent looking portrait.

Upon examining the painting again, Amy discovered it no longer evoked images of sorrow, sadness, and whispered secrets, and she chided herself for having such gloomy notions.

Amy carefully contemplated where to hang her newly acquired work of art. After carefully studying the colors used by the artist, she thought of several places in the house where it would fit with the decor. Finally she decided that the subtle blue color of the child's nightgown would match perfectly with the blue in the heirloom wedding ring quilt in her bedroom. Pleased with the decision, she went into the bedroom, removed the old landscape picture that had hung for three years above the headboard, and with a ceremonious gesture, replaced it with the new painting.

"Well, little girl, I hope you like your new home," she announced as if speaking to a real person. "Sorry I can't stay and keep you company, but I have another important engagement to attend. You see, my brother is expecting me at his house this evening because today is my birthday, and he's giving me a party"

+++++

Amy dressed for the party in a simple black wool suit…thinking black was a good color to be wearing when meeting with her mother. Then she went on a search for her black heels. She finally located them under her bed, and in the process of retrieving them she accidentally smacked her head on the bed frame.

I can't believe it! Amy thought, rubbing her forehead. *Mom can cause me problems even when she isn't around. Why didn't I listen to my own mind and simply wear the jeans and tennis shoes I really wanted to wear. After all, that's what I would be most comfortable in. It's so foolish of me to keep trying to please Mom when she can't be pleased.*

Amy glanced up at the painting. "I hope your mother wasn't as hard to get along with as mine is. You probably got to wear whatever you wanted to, and I bet you didn't get yelled at all the time for being clumsy."

Feeling a small painful bump on her forehead, Amy looked closely in the mirror for any noticeable bruising. Luckily no discoloration showed, only a small dime sized knot had appeared near the hairline. With her hair combed just right it wouldn't be seen, and that was a good thing because then her mother couldn't make asinine comments to everyone at the party about how clumsy her daughter was. She had heard enough of those kinds of remarks growing up and didn't want to hear anymore. In fact, it wouldn't bother her much if she didn't have to hear her mother's voice for a very long time. The harsh tone always set every nerve in her body on edge. If she never heard another "Oh, Amy" pass from her mother's lips, she would be quite happy.

+++++

After washing her face and putting on fresh makeup, Amy stood in front of the full-length mirror attached to the bathroom door to take one final glance at her appearance before she left the house. She pivoted on her heels, looking in the mirror and carefully checking for anything that her mother might find wrong with the outfit. She wanted to be sure everything was perfect. She realized that worrying about her mother's opinion was one of the dumbest things she could ever do, but she still couldn't help it. It was a habit that had been ingrained into her subconscious since childhood. She was probably going to be doomed to be forever trying to seek approval, even while knowing she would never achieve it.

Amy frowned, partly from dissatisfaction with the way that she looked, and partly because she realized there would be no escaping her mother's influence. *Mom will probably hate this dress simply because I'm wearing it,* she thought as she carefully brushed a small bit of lint off the front collar.

Dressed in black, feeling as though she was preparing to attend a funeral instead of a birthday party, Amy stepped back from the mirror and headed into the bedroom to find her purse. When she entered the room, she felt compelled to stop and shift her gaze upward at the painting hanging above her bed. She was surprised to find that the little girl's eyes seemed to be focused right on her. Then she thought she saw two tiny tears start to trail down the girl's pale cheeks. But when she blinked her eyes, all traces of the tears vanished, and Amy realized her imagination had only been playing games with her mind.

"What do you think?" she asked the girl as she spun in a circle in front of the painting to show off her outfit. "Do you think this will pass my mother's approval?"

Amy paused as if waiting for an answer, and then she shivered when a strange chill passed through her body. For a moment, she had halfway expected to hear a reply.

Feeling foolish, Amy turned to go, but she couldn't resist the urge to look back. "You know," she said to the girl, "no matter what I wear, Mom will find something wrong with it. I don't understand why I even worry about what she thinks. You're lucky you don't have to be troubled about such things."

Amy gathered her coat and gloves and reluctantly prepared to leave. *Edward was right about one thing,* she thought, *I would have called the party off tonight if he hadn't insisted on having it. The weather really is too cold and I would rather just sit home where it is nice and warm and read a good book. Which I think would be much more fun than celebrating my birthday with my mother.*

Toni Auberry

Chapter 12

When Amy stepped away from her car she couldn't help noticing how cozy Edward's house looked from the outside. The bright lights shining from the windows seemed to light the entire front yard. Like a lighthouse sending out a beacon to lost sailors, the beams radiating from her brother's house beckoned her to seek refuge within its walls.

Instantly, Amy was glad she had decided to attend the party. As she headed up the sidewalk toward the front door, she definitely felt more enthusiasm than she had a few minutes earlier. And this enthusiasm spiked even higher when her sister-in-law Ellen zealously threw open the door before she even had the chance to ring the doorbell.

"Oh, I'm so glad you made it." Ellen said, eagerly embracing Amy in an affectionate hug, her bright blue eyes sparking with excitement. "After all, it is your party, and it would be a little strange if the guest of honor didn't show up."

"I wouldn't have passed up a chance to see my favorite people and to check up on how you and the little one are doing," Amy proclaimed good-naturedly, pleased with Ellen's gracious reception. She smiled warmly at her sister-in-law, thinking Ellen looked beautiful in a rose-colored maternity dress that did little to hide the fact the baby was due in a few weeks.

"I guess we're doing all right, but I still can't wait until this is all over with." Ellen grimaced and patted her tummy gently. "Thank God, I only have a couple more weeks to go. I'm beginning to feel like a fat waddling duck these days."

Ellen took Amy's coat and hung it in the hall closet. Then she ushered the way into the living room where Edward was waiting for them.

"Well, in my opinion, you look wonderful." Amy said. "A glow is positively radiating from your face. And I really like the new hairstyle; that pageboy cut frames your face perfectly."

"Amy's right." Edward lovingly kissed his wife on the cheek. "You do look fantastic. But then, I've always thought that, even at five o'clock in the morning when that blond hair of yours is—"

"Are you still planning to go back to work after the baby's born?" Amy asked quickly, not wanting to give Edward the chance to tease Ellen.

"After six weeks," Ellen said. "I can't leave my job unattended much longer than that."

"She thinks the hospital can't run without her," Edward said.

"Well, Dear," Ellen looked at Edward, "that's what they pay me to do, run the hospital. If St. Joseph could manage without its director, I wouldn't have a job."

"How about you, Edward," Amy asked, "are you taking any leave to spend time with the baby?"

"A couple of weeks at least and more if it can be arranged. Though I'm not sure if that will be possible. Tower Enterprise is right in the middle of a new project and there isn't anyone else that can do my job. Lately I've been able to understand why Dad wasn't able to spend more time with me. It seems no matter how much you do for that company, there always seems to be more that has to be done."

Ellen whispered to Amy. "Your Mom wants to baby-sit when I go back to work. What do you think of that idea? Do you think she could handle it?"

"No!" Amy almost screamed the word out. "She's not capable of handling a baby." Amy felt her nerves twisting into taut aching bundles. *Surely Ellen wasn't seriously considering the offer.*

"That's my opinion too," Ellen said. "But Edward doesn't want to hurt your mother's feelings. So we haven't really discussed it with her yet. I'm not sure how she'll take it when I say no."

"I wouldn't worry about it." Amy let her eyes glance over at Edward. "Your baby's welfare is more important than Mom's feelings. She'll get over it."

"Now Amy," Edward hastily replied, "just because you don't get along with Mom doesn't mean she couldn't handle caring for the baby. After all she did raise the two of us. And I think we turned out pretty well, don't you?"

"But you don't understand—" Amy said with a tremor of fear echoing in her words.

"Edward doesn't understand what?" Connie asked, interrupting Amy as she entered the living room.

"Oh, hello, Mother," Amy responded, forcing a tight smile.

"I guess I should wish you a happy birthday," Connie said with little enthusiasm behind her words as she disdainfully scanned Amy's attire. "You really shouldn't wear black. It simply isn't a good color for you. It makes you look so pale. Besides with all that black on, one would think you were going to a funeral instead of a birthday party. I would think you'd have sense enough to dress more appropriately."

Amy looked at her mother with a smoldering anger glowing in her eyes, but she didn't say a word.

"Don't listen to her," Ellen spoke up quickly. "Black is quite suitable for this occasion. That outfit gives you a very sophisticated look."

Amy smiled at Ellen, her eyes thanking her sister-in-law for the compliment.

Connie frowned at Ellen's defense of Amy. "I was only trying to give her some advice. But she never listens to me anyway, so I guess it doesn't really matter what I say." Connie shrugged, then moved toward the dining room and motioned for Amy to follow her.

"I have a wonderful surprise for you. I put your birthday present on the table so all of us could enjoy it during dinner."

Oh no, what has she got in store for me now? Amy wondered as she reluctantly followed her mother. At the entrance to the dinning room she stopped to stare at her Mother's present. In the center of Edward's elegant mahogany table set a beautiful bouquet of a dozen deep-red roses.

Roses...I can't believe she's doing this to me. Amy was astonished at her mother's insidious actions. *Dad always gave me red roses for my birthday, and I hated them. And Mom knows that.* As she stared with disgust at the bouquet on the table, Amy suddenly saw the frightening image of crimson roses covered in fresh blood. The blood had completely saturated the roses and was steadily dripping off the red petals and falling upon a pile of newly turned dirt. The terrible picture flashed unbidden through her thoughts before she had the chance to control it

Amy immediately closed her eyes to try to dispel the scene from her mind.

"Amy, what's wrong?" Ellen promptly asked when she noticed the strange look that had unexpectedly appeared on Amy's face.

"Oh nothing. Nothing at all," Amy guardedly replied. She didn't want to sound crazy, so she couldn't tell anyone about the blood-covered roses. Anyway, as quickly as the flashing images had materialized, they had now vanished, and it seemed foolish to say anything.

"Are you sure?" Edward looked at her quizzically. "For a second, you looked awfully pale."

"Oh, for heaven's sake. I'm fine." Amy responded abruptly.

Oblivious to her daughter's strange reaction to the roses, Connie moved the vase of flowers to the edge of the table and began to carefully rearrange the bouquet. "I thought you would enjoy these," she said, lovingly holding one of the roses in her hands. "I remember how your father always gave you red roses on your birthday, and I believe it is important that you think of him tonight."

Amy glared at her mother, but didn't say a single word. *The absolute last thing I need tonight is to be reminded of Dad,* she thought angrily. *Now I'm going to have to think about him all evening if I have to look at those roses all through dinner. If I hadn't promised Edward that I'd be on my best behavior, I would stuff the whole arrangement down the garbage disposal right now!*

"Do you remember those rose bushes that your father planted as a surprise for your eleventh birthday?" Connie wistfully commented, as she thought about her husband. "The night before your birthday, when Edward and I got home from his basketball game, I found your father out in the garden planting those roses in the moonlight. I have always thought it was so admirable of him to go to all that trouble." Her voice took on a petulant tone. "Of course, I recall that you didn't appreciate it one bit. I don't think you even thanked him."

"Mom, I really don't want to discuss Dad right now." Amy looked at Edward for assistance hoping he would help before she completely lost control of her temper and started saying things she really didn't want to say. She did remember that particular birthday, and her memory wasn't a pleasant one. She had hated those rose bushes, and one day when her father wasn't around she poured a full box of salt over them and had taken great pleasure in watching them die.

Connie continued talking as if Amy hadn't said a word. "Speaking of your father, Edward, I was wondering earlier today how his memorial is coming along. The last time I went by the library the plaque was already in place. I think all that has to be done now is for it to warm up enough for the flowers to be planted around it."

"What memorial?" Amy asked, her voice filled with disbelief. "What are you talking about?"

"Why the one the city council is building down in front of the library," Connie answered curtly. "The city council decided last year to erect this fantastic memorial to honor all the work your father did for the community when he was alive. I can't believe that you didn't read about it in the newspaper."

Shocked, Amy grabbed Edward by the arm. "Why didn't you tell me?"

"Because I know how you feel about Dad, and I didn't want to upset you." Edward looked at Amy beseechingly. He felt it was important that she understand. "He did do a lot for the community, you know. Those drug programs he sponsored have really helped some of the kids stay out of trouble."

"He did a lot for all of us," Connie quickly spoke up. "He always did what he thought was best for this family…including you, Amy."

Dumbfounded, Amy felt a bitter fury surging through her veins. Speechless, she choked on the words she wanted to say. *What my father did to me shouldn't have been done to anyone, let alone his own daughter. The town should be tearing down his headstone, not building a memorial. Why couldn't anyone see that?*

Chapter 13

The unpleasant silence that followed Connie's reference to her husband's memorial abruptly ended with the ringing of the front doorbell and the arrival of the other party guests. Three of Amy's friends, two of Edward's, and Ellen's mother arrived all at the same time and the house quickly filled with joyous birthday greetings, handshakes, and hugs.

The next two hours passed quickly, dinner was served, a little wine was consumed, the birthday cake was ceremoniously cut, and then the entire group returned to the living room to watch Amy open her birthday presents.

Amy smiled joyfully at everyone, including her mother. She was feeling happy and content for the first time in weeks. When she glanced at the presents piled upon the coffee table, she suddenly remembered the wonderful gift Edward had given her earlier. "You should see the delightful painting I received from Edward this morning. It's an antique oil of this precious little girl with her arms wrapped around the neck of a gorgeous collie."

"Edward thinks the girl looks like Amy when she was a child," Ellen said. "And Amy used to have a collie just like the one in the painting. Isn't that the neatest thing!"

"A collie...I know someone who breeds collies," one of Edward's friends spoke up. "He says that they are really loyal dogs and are supposed to make great pets."

"Well, the one Amy had was nothing but trouble," Connie replied. "He was a terrible nuisance, always digging up flower beds and dragging mud through my house."

"He was a good dog, Mom," Amy said quickly. "You shouldn't say anything bad about him. He was my best friend, and I cried for months after he disappeared."

"Disappeared?" Ellen's mother looked questioningly at Edward.

"It happened on Amy's eleventh birthday," Edward replied. "The dog simply vanished into thin air, and we never did find out what happened. Amy and I spent days looking for him, but we never found a trace of him anywhere."

Amy paled at the mention of Thomas' disappearance. *Thomas...could you possibly have known how much I missed you,* she thought sadly. *I cried forever when you left me.* The old wound in her heart started aching, and she began to feel odd, but she didn't know why. She couldn't explain the strange feeling that was crawling through her mind like a thrashing snake. But she didn't have time to decipher the bizarre sensation before a migraine swept like a vast tidal wave through her head. In less than a second, the room began spinning around her and dazzling flashes of light started bouncing off the walls.

Amy quickly excused herself from the party and carefully made her way down the hall by holding on to the walls. By the time she entered the bathroom her legs were shaking so severely she couldn't stand. She collapsed, sitting on the side of the bathtub and moaning as a series of sharp thrusting pains stabbed right between her eyes. She thought she would pass out from the tremendous pressure building within her head. Afraid that she might faint, she lowered her head down between her legs and took in several slow deep breaths. Moments later an insistent knocking on the bathroom door brought her back up.

"Are you all right?" Ellen asked from the other side of the door.

"I'll be fine. Just give me a couple of minutes." Amy didn't want to worry Ellen by telling her how bad she was feeling. "Guess I shouldn't have mixed the wine and cake. My stomach is a little upset, that's all."

"What's wrong with that girl now," Connie demanded to know as she appeared at Ellen's side.

"Nothing's wrong," Ellen answered.

"If Amy is sick, she shouldn't be here," Connie retorted angrily. "It could endanger you and the baby. I swear, she should have had more sense than to come here tonight. She never thinks about the consequences of what she's doing. All she ever thinks about is herself."

"Would you lay off your daughter for just one night," Ellen spat back at Connie. "She's a wonderful person and wouldn't do anything on purpose to hurt me or the baby. Just leave her alone for a few minutes, and I'm sure she'll join us as soon as she can."

Amy listened to her mother's rude remarks from the other side of the bathroom door and wondered if they would ever be able to spend time together without trying to rip each other's throat out?

+++++

After several tense minutes, the migraine's incessant throbbing finally began to ebb, and Amy decided to try to rejoin the party. When she paused at the sink to freshen up, she felt a strange coldness surrounding her. She shivered as little goosebumps traveled up her arms. She scanned the room looking for a source for the icy current of air that had wrapped itself around her, but she found nothing. The small bathroom window was tightly shut and locked, and there existed no clues to indicate where the chilly air had originated. Mystified over the sudden drop in room temperature, she wondered whether to report it to Edward. After all, cold drafts wouldn't be good for the baby. Maybe the furnace wasn't working right, and Edward might want to have it checked.

Amy turned on the faucets to wash her hands and her bewilderment grew stronger as the hot water turned icy cold. Then she gasped in surprise as the clear tap water started turning pink and then quickly became deep red. She jerked her hands from under the flowing water and stared at them in disbelief. Bright red blood coated both hands from wrists to fingers. Her eyes looked with disbelief at the sink. Blood was splattered everywhere...on the soap dish, the basin, the walls. She stepped back, holding her hands out in front of her so the blood wouldn't get on her clothes, and fought hard not to scream.

But she swore she could hear a little girl's voice doing the screaming for her.

Then an instant later, the water cleared, the blood disappeared, and the chill in the room vanished. Amy found herself standing quietly in frightened silence in front of a spotless, white sink with no possible clue to explain the mysterious happening. Her fears of the unexplained drove her from the bathroom. She quickly decided not to say a word to anyone about the strange chill that had came upon her in the room or about the bloody water that had poured from the faucet. She was sure no one would believe her anyway.

"Sorry, guys, I didn't mean to run out on you," Amy apologized when she returned to the living room. "Guess I had a little too much wine and it upset my stomach."

"Reminds me of the time—" one of Amy's friends started telling a funny wine story, which lead to an avalanche of other hilarious wine tales from the whole group. Soon everyone had forgotten Amy's sudden departure, and all were laughing and talking again. After awhile, Amy's headache eased to almost nothing. By the time she finally got around to opening her presents she had let the memory of the strange event bury itself with all the other secret and strange things she kept hidden somewhere in the back of her mind.

Laughing and joking with everyone as she opened her presents, she repeatedly thanked her friends for their wonderful gifts.

In the mist of the laughter, the sound of a car pulling up in the driveway caught Amy's attention. As she watched Edward move toward the front door, she wondered who could possibly be arriving that late. Curiosity got the best of her, and her eyes stayed upon Edward. When he opened the door and stood at the entrance engaged in earnest conversation with a tall, handsome, blond-haired man, her interest peaked even more.

"Hey Amy, who's that?" whispered Stacy, one of Amy's friends. "He's really cute."

"I don't know," Amy answered. "He must be a friend of Edward's."

"Look at his eyes," said Christi, another one of Amy's friends. "They're so blue."

"It's not his eyes I'm looking at," Stacy laughed with a girlish giggle. "What I wouldn't give to have those big arms of his wrapped around me."

"Or his fantastic legs," Christi sighed wishfully.

"Do you think Edward would introduce me to him?" Stacy asked hopefully.

"I don't know why not." Amy replied, glancing up at Edward. She was surprised to see him smiling at her with a mischievous twinkle sparkling in his eyes. At that moment, she instantly knew he was up to something.

"Remember this morning," Edward said, "when I promised you an even better present than the painting. Well, it has just arrived." He opened the door, and the blond-haired man came into the house leading the most gorgeous collie Amy had ever seen. It took her a few seconds to realize the magnificent creature was the present Edward had referred to.

"Sit," the man commanded, and obediently the dog sat back on its haunches.

The collie cocked his head to one side and began scanning the group of people in the room as if looking for someone special. Immediately the dog focused in on Amy, and he thumped his tail eagerly as he waited patiently for his trainer to give him permission to move.

Laughing, Edward said, "Well, it seems like our friend here has already picked out his new owner."

Astonishment, like a tremendous rush of adrenaline, flowed through Amy increasing her heart rate, flushing her face, and making her eyes glow with radiant wonderment.

Ted Bay, the collie's owner, couldn't believe what he was seeing. Right in front of him, almost in arms' reach, stood the most stunning woman he could ever imagine. As he watched Amy dash over and throw her arms around the collie, laughing and crying all at the same time, he was unprepared to deal with the sudden influx of emotions overtaking him. He had no time to put up the wall he always used when women were around. Before he realized what had happened, it was too late. In less time than it took for him to draw in a breath, Amy had melted his cold heart, and there was no way he could undo the damage.

Oblivious to Ted's reaction, Amy only had eyes for the dog. Her happiness beamed from her face, and when she turned toward Ted and smiled, he felt as though he had been jolted with a bolt of lightening.

Ted didn't know how to react. Never had a woman had such an effect on him!

"What's his name?" Amy asked.

"Raphael."

"Like the archangel, Raphael?"

"Yes. When he was little, he always seemed to be guarding the other pups in the litter. Hence his name." Unable to take his eyes off Amy, Ted stood transfixed in awe. Then he grinned. "Now you have your own personal guardian angel to protect you." As soon as the words had left his mouth, he saw a strange expression cross Amy's face. It was if some unseen cloud had suddenly overshadowed the joy that had been radiating so strongly from her.

"I could really use a guardian angel." Amy spoke so softly only Ted's ears heard the whispered words, and then she buried her face in Raphael's fur, letting joy fill her heart with its magical spell.

Chapter 14

Edward stepped back a few feet from Amy and Ted to discreetly observe the interchange occurring between them. He had watched Ted closely as he had introduced him to Amy and he immediately suspected what had happened to his friend. Ted's reaction to Amy was as apparent as the joy on Amy's face as she excitedly wrapped her arms around Raphael's furry neck.

Edward grinned and then gently pulled Ellen by her hand into the hallway. He leaned close to his wife so no one else could hear and whispered, "Look at Ted's face. Didn't I tell you if I could ever get the two of them together this would happen?"

Ellen whispered back skeptically, "Well, I hope you haven't set your friend up for a heartbreak. You know your sister doesn't care much for dating. She isn't even aware he is standing there. Her eyes are looking down at Raphael, not up at Ted."

"Well, she has to look up sometime."

"But that's no guarantee she'll see him, at least not the way you're hoping."

"Ted will make sure she does," Edward said. "When he wants something, he usually finds a way to get it."

"I hope you know what you're doing," Ellen replied doubtfully. "Playing cupid really isn't one of your strong points."

"I know, but this isn't something I just planned on the spur of the moment. I've been trying to get those two together for months, but neither one would agree to it. Both of them kept telling me they were quite happy with their lives just as they were, and they didn't want to complicate things by getting involved with anyone."

"So, you decided to complicate their lives for them."

"Hey now, this isn't a bad thing. Ted is really a great guy. I would trust him with my life and most definitely with my sister's. Otherwise I wouldn't have done this. Amy needs someone and so does Ted, and I think they are perfect for each other." Edward pulled Ellen into his arms and then leaned over and kissed her. "Just like us."

Ellen playfully pushed her husband away. "I hope you're right. Even though your sister puts up a tough front, I think she's scared, but I don't understand why. Has something happened to her to make her avoid involvement?"

"I don't know for sure. She never did date much. She and Dad got into a terrible fight every time she went out with someone. He was totally against her having a boyfriend, and I think he scared off most of the boys that even thought about taking her out. He used to preach at her all the time about the sins of lust and how easy it would be for her to be disgraced. Maybe he just turned her off on dating all together."

"I've noticed your sister doesn't talk much about your father. It's like she wants to pretend that he didn't even exist."

"Their relationship was rather tense at times, and I think she's still angry with Dad over something. I just don't know what it is. I've tried to get her to talk about it, but she refuses to even to discuss it with me."

"Sometimes things can get pretty rough between a daughter and a father. I know there were times that Dad and I didn't agree on most things."

"I think it's something more than that."

"Well, maybe I can get her to talk to me about it. I'll take her to lunch next week and see if I can find out anything."

"I doubt if that will work. Amy isn't one to talk about her problems. When things go wrong, she tends to try to carry the burden all by herself; she has always been a loner. But then, so has Ted. That's why I'm hoping they will connect. They would be good for each other."

"Is Raphael one of Ted's collies? I remember you mentioned once that he raised them as a hobby."

"Yes. Ted had arranged to sell Raphael to someone else. But he discovered the man had a bad temper and refused to go through with the sale. It's against Ted's grain to allow any of his collies to go to someone who might mistreat a dog. And, of course, being the smart person that I am, I immediately realized this was the perfect opportunity to arrange a meeting between him and Amy. I talked him into selling me Raphael as a present for her and into personally delivering the dog to the party tonight."

"I hope you realize your plan isn't going to work unless your sister can pull herself away from that dog long enough to notice Ted." Ellen laid her hand on Edward's arm and smiled impishly. "I'd say this whole thing needs a little of my touch. Watch and learn, Sweetheart."

As Ellen walked toward Amy, she winked at Ted. "Amy, you know Raphael is a special breed. He isn't just another one of those all-American mutts. He'll have to have special treatment, special food, and such." She turned to Ted, grabbed his arm and pulled him closer to Amy. "Isn't that right Ted?"

"She's right," Ted agreed, quickly following Ellen's lead. "There's a lot to learn about caring for this breed of collie."

Ellen bent down and gently ran her hand over Raphael's soft mane. "Edward told me part of the deal he made with Ted was that Ted would personally work with you until you understood all you'd need to know about Raphael. You wouldn't want to make any mistakes which could hurt the dog."

"That's right," Ted agreed. "I promised your brother I would work with you no matter how long it takes."

Amy laughed. "I don't think it will take that long. I'm not exactly stupid."

Flustered, Ted blushed. "That's not what I meant. I just—"

"That's all right, I know what you meant." Amy's eyes lit with amusement at Ted's reaction.

"Well then, how about getting together Monday night after work? I'm free about seven," Ted said.

"That's great!" Amy gave Ted a quick friendly hug and was totally unaware of the devastating effect it had on him. "Is there anything special I need to do for Raphael this weekend?"

"Not really. I have enough dog food in the truck to hold you over until Monday."

Christi grabbed Amy's hand and pulled her away from Ted. "Now that's settled, let's get back to the real business at hand. Aren't we supposed to be having a party? I do believe my glass is empty, and I'm in desperate need of a refill."

"Depends," Edward asked, "are you the one driving home?"

"No, she isn't." Ellen's mother responded as she served herself another slice of Amy's birthday cake. "I promised to drive the girls home after the party so they could have a good time and not worry about drinking and driving."

"Sounds like a good plan to me." Edward glanced at Amy as he walked over to the bar. "What about you, Sis, do you want another drink?"

"No, I've had enough for tonight," Amy said, wary about drinking any more wine because of the strange experience earlier in the bathroom. She didn't want it to happen a second time. She was afraid she'd start seeing blood dripping off the walls again.

Edward held up a newly opened bottle of wine. "Ted, can I pour you a glass?"

Ted thought for a moment before answering. "I didn't really plan to stay. I wouldn't want to impose on your hospitality."

"Oh, please stay for a little while longer," Amy pleaded. "After all, it is my birthday, and it would make me sad if you left. You wouldn't want to make me sad, would you?"

No, Ted thought. *I definitely wouldn't want to make you sad. What I want to do is to kiss you all over...starting with your mouth, and then I want to work all the way down to your toes. I want to steal your heart and make it mine. I want— Oh God, I want you to look at me again and smile.*

Chapter 15

Ted nonchalantly leaned against the bar, slowly sipping his glass of wine as he watched Amy. She was sitting quietly on the couch and smiling with Raphael at her feet as she listened to her friends talking and giggling like school girls at a slumber party. Every once in a while Amy's eyes would drift his way, and each time it happened he felt his heart race. It took every bit of control he had not to cross the room and sweep her up into his arms.

Edward, with a cold beer in his hand, was perched on the barstool next to Ted. "Look at Amy's face; doesn't she look thrilled with Raphael? I haven't seen her this happy in a long time. I wish I had thought of getting her a collie before now."

Ted grinned at Edward's remark. He didn't need to be told to look at Amy. She was so beautiful; what man could keep from it? "Didn't you say she had a dog similar to Raphael when she was little?" he asked.

"Yes. His name was Thomas," Edward replied. "Amy was about seven when Dad gave her the dog, and she loved Thomas more than anything else in the world. Unfortunately, the dog disappeared on Amy's eleventh birthday. He just vanished without a trace, and we never did find out what happened to him. Losing that dog broke her heart, and she cried for months afterwards. It hurt her so much that she even gave up speaking for the longest time."

"I think Raphael will be good for her," Ted said, his gaze still locked onto Amy. "He's a gentle dog and loves to be pampered. The more someone spoils him the better he likes it."

"Amy needs someone to spoil her," Edward said very solemnly as he took another sip of his beer. "A man couldn't find a better person than Amy. And just in case you're interested, I know for a fact she's not dating anyone right now."

"Maybe I can do something about that," Ted said. "That is, if she'll let me."

"You won't know until you try. Good luck on Monday, but take some advice from someone who knows her—go slow. If you come on too strong she'll run fast, and she won't look back. She doesn't give guys second chances."

"Who doesn't give guys second chances?" Ellen joined the two men at the bar. "Can't be me you're talking about. I give Edward second chances all the time."

"Amy. Who else?" Edward tilted his glass back finishing his beer and then turned toward Ellen with an offended look on his face. "And what do you mean you give me second chances all the time?"

"Oh, let's see. This morning I gave you the chance to kiss me in the bedroom, then in the living room, and again in the hall. And if you want to meet me in the kitchen in the next couple of minutes, I'll give you another go at it." Ellen smiled seductively, picked up a couple of empty dishes and headed toward the kitchen.

"I think that's an invitation I'm not going to pass up," Edward rose from the barstool, grinned at Ted, and placed a fresh bottle of wine on the bar. "If you want another refill in the next few minutes, I'm afraid you're going to have to pour your own."

"No problem. I believe I can handle that, and if you want, I can man the bar for you so you don't have to hurry back." Ted said, refilling his wineglass while his eyes hungrily sought out Amy again.

+++++

For a half-hour, Ted took pleasure in filling wineglasses and watching the crowd. Amy and her friends were having a good time laughing and talking, and he enjoyed listening to them. Everyone at the party seemed to be having fun…except for one older woman, who didn't fit in with the rest of the people in the room. Ted couldn't decide why she was even there. She didn't appear to be celebrating Amy's birthday. In fact, she acted as though she found Amy's presence distasteful.

For some reason that really bothered him.

He just couldn't figure her out. She carried a vase of red roses with her wherever she went, and when she sat down she would start rearranging the flowers, like she was never satisfied with how they looked. A couple of times he actually thought he heard her talking to them.

With his attention focused on the woman, Ted didn't notice Amy heading toward the bar. When she tapped him on the shoulder, and he turned to find himself staring straight into her beautiful, hazel eyes, his heart actually felt like it skipped a couple of beats.

Ted couldn't believe the effect Amy had on him. He desperately wanted to pull her into his arms and let his lips taste every part of her body.

"Are you having a good time, Ted?" Amy asked, placing her hand on his. "You look lonely sitting over here by yourself."

"I'm not much of a mingler, but that doesn't mean I'm not enjoying myself. I'm just relaxing listening to you and your friends talk." *And waiting for you to smile at me again*, Ted thought, not wanting to move, afraid she might take her hand away, and he didn't want that to happen. Her touch was magic. For the first time in a long time he didn't feel lonely.

"I really want to thank you for letting me have Raphael," Amy said. "It must have been hard for you to give him up. I know it would have been for me."

"I raise the collies to sell. It's only hard to give them up if I don't know if they are going to a good home. I can tell by watching you that Raphael will be well treated. You seem like a very loving, caring person." Ted's eyes sought hers, and when he found them, he reached over and placed his other hand on top of hers, cupping it gently within his.

"Thank you." Amy blushed, her cheeks flushing a bright red. Ted's touch disturbed her, and she quickly pulled her hand away.

Amy's blush intrigued Ted as much as her smile. He found himself wanting to know everything he possibly could about her. But he couldn't find the words to ask. He felt as tongue-tied as a sixteen-year-old boy on his first date. While he was trying desperately to think of something...anything...to say to keep Amy at his side, the strange rose-lady appeared carrying her vase of flowers.

Over the top of the roses, Connie glared at Amy. "If you don't want these roses, Amy, I'm going to take them home with me," she said reproachfully.

Amy rolled her eyes, looking up at the ceiling for a fraction of a second, and then sighed. "Mom, you know I can't stand roses. Their fragrance always triggers a migraine."

"Well, I was only trying to make you happy. I thought the roses would be a nice reminder of your father. Since it is your birthday, you really should at least think about him. After all, he is the reason for your birth, you know."

"But, I'm allergic to roses. I can't take them home. Every year we go through the same thing. You bring the roses and I send them home with someone else. Get a clue, Mom, and stop wasting your money."

"It's not a waste of money if it makes you think of your father. He should be remembered, especially today."

"Remembering him isn't hard. How could I ever forget what he did to me?" Seeing the defensive look that appeared on her mother's face, Amy stopped. *It wasn't worth the trouble arguing with her*. "You can take the roses home with you or leave them here for Ellen to enjoy. I don't really care as long as I don't have to be around them."

"You're nothing but an ungrateful daughter. I'm thankful your father isn't here to see how you've turned out." Connie turned in a huff and stormed off carrying the roses with her. She angrily grabbed her coat and left Edward's house without even putting it on.

+++++

Ted was astonished when he heard Amy call the rose-lady "Mom." There was no way he would have placed that woman as being Amy and Edward's mother. He had known Edward for about five years, and that bitter old lady wasn't the type of person he would have imagined to be his friend's mother. Edward, a very sensible person, had his feet planted on solid ground. And from what he could tell about Amy, he suspected she acted the same way. But their mother didn't seem to have anything planted anywhere. If he were to guess, he would even say she was very disturbed, or maybe a better word would be psychotic.

After listening to Amy and her mother, he knew there definitely were some bad undercurrents flowing between them. Obviously their relationship wasn't ideal, and that made him curious to find out more.

Ted decided to take a chance to see if he could get Amy talking. "So that's your mother. I've been sitting here wondering who she was. I've been watching her carry those roses around for the past hour and couldn't figure out how she fit into this little group of yours. She seemed a little bit different than the rest of the people here."

"Different? I guess that would be one way to describe her," Amy replied cuttingly.

When Amy turned toward him, Ted was disappointed to see her smile had disappeared. *Would it be safe for me to pry?* he wondered. He got the distinct impression that Amy was feeling a bit downhearted, and he didn't know if it would help if she were to talk about it. He finally decided to give her the lead and let her set the direction she wanted to travel.

"There seemed to be a little tension between you and your mother. Do you need to talk about it?" He carefully searched her face for clues to determine if he had overstepped his boundaries and finding none, he continued. "I'm a good listener, and I don't lecture or give advice. That's better than having your own personal therapist. Plus, I don't take notes. What more could a woman ask for?"

Amy shrugged. "Mom and I don't get along. It's no big secret, but I don't like to talk about it."

"What about your father? Edward told me he died from a heart attack about eight years—." The look on Amy's face stopped him before he had a chance to complete his sentence. Something deep within warned him not to continue.

"Boring subject; one I'd rather not discuss. Let's just say my parents weren't the Ward and June Cleaver types and leave it at that."

Amy brushed a lock of hair away from her face and looked at Ted curiously. "What about your parents?"

In a way he was afraid to answer that question. His parents had been terrific. At least they had been in the short time he had been lucky enough to have them around, but he wasn't sure it would be a good idea to brag about them to Amy.

"It's all right to talk about them," she said, sensing his reluctance. "I'm not a fragile little flower that bends and breaks when it rains. Just because my parents were less than perfect doesn't mean I will fall apart when someone else talks about how great theirs were."

"I'm not sure—." Ted still felt hesitant about saying anything.

But then Amy leaned over and whispered in his ear. "I think I would really like to hear about your parents."

With that little gesture, he realized no matter what she wanted to know, he would tell her. It was a good thing he wasn't a secret agent because his country would be in big trouble. He would tell Amy anything she wanted to hear if she would just keep whispering in his ear.

Chapter 16

Ted pulled out a barstool for Amy and then took the one next to it. He picked up his wineglass and sat staring into it a few seconds before saying anything. Thinking about his parents always made him feel sad, and he had difficulty talking to others about them.

"My father died the year I turned eight," he finally said. "A drunk driver crossed the center line and hit him head on, killing him instantly. I can't believe how much I still miss him. Sometimes when I close my eyes I can see him standing out on our front lawn pitching baseballs, laughing, telling me I was the best ball player in town. By most men's standards he wouldn't have been considered to be a great man, but to me…well, he was the greatest."

Ted stopped for a moment. He could feel a familiar tightness encircling his throat making it hard for him to speak. It had been years since he had even mentioned his father to anyone, and he was having difficulty finding the words he wanted to say.

Amy realized that the silence between them wasn't an invitation for her to speak, so she quietly waited until he was ready to continue.

"In my bedroom closet, in a box high on the top shelf, is the baseball Dad gave me for my eighth birthday…the day before his accident. I remember sitting outside on the front porch steps tossing that baseball, waiting for him to come home from work. The night before, he had promised to take me to the park to practice. He was over two hours late, and I had begun to get worried. It was getting dark and I was afraid he wouldn't make it home on time. I heard a car pull up in the driveway and turned around expecting to see him. But instead, what I saw was a police car. I knew the officers; they were my Dad's friends. When they got out of their car, I yelled at them to catch the ball, and then threw it. But they didn't even try to catch it. The ball hit the side of their car and bounced off leaving a large dent. I thought they were mad at me from the awful look on their faces. But they didn't even say a word about the dent. They only asked if Mom was home. When they went into the house, I knew something was wrong. I just didn't know how wrong until I heard Mom scream." Ted paused for a second as he tried to calm the grief stabbing at his heart. "Every once in awhile I can still hear that scream in my dreams. I think it will haunt me until the day I die."

"Ted, I'm sorry. If it hurts to talk about your parents you don't have to go on. It's really none of my business. I didn't mean to dredge up bad memories."

"Sometimes it helps to tell someone about your pain. It can make the sharpness less intense."

Amy felt a slight twinge of jealously. *Yes*, she thought, *talking might help…if you're allowed to talk.*

Ted didn't notice the subtle shift in Amy's mood. He had become lost in the pain of his own memories. "After Dad died I didn't want to play baseball any more. So I gave all my equipment, except for that ball Dad had given me for my birthday, to a kid down the street. I just couldn't part with the ball, but I couldn't stand to look at it either. So I wrapped it in a newspaper, stuck it in an old shoebox, and sealed the box shut with duct tape. And that's where it has been for the past twenty years, buried in a shoe box, stuck in the back of a multitude of different closets. But the funny thing is—even though I never look at it or touch it, I always know exactly where it is."

"Do you think you'll ever take it out of that box?"

"Someday I'd like to give it to my own son. If I ever have one. Maybe for him I'll even play baseball again."

Amy wanted to cry as she thought about the sad little boy who had sealed his pain away in a shoebox. Ted's hurting expression touched Amy's heart, and the jealousy she'd experienced a few seconds earlier entirely disappeared.

"What about your mom? How did she handle your dad's death?" she asked, the grief in Ted's voice touching her more than any thoughts about herself.

"I think it turned out to be harder on Mom than me. Dad didn't have any life insurance, so she had to find work right away. Since she didn't have any skills, the only job she could find was as a waitress in an old run-down truck stop, working long hours late into the night. The job didn't pay much; we had to sell our home and move into a cheap apartment."

"It sounds like things got a little rough for both of you."

"It did. Especially for Mom. She missed him so much. That job sucked the life right out of her. She was always so tired. But she told me she wouldn't have done anything different if it would have meant she couldn't have had what little time she did have with Dad."

"She never remarried?"

"No. She said the love Dad gave her was enough to last her a lifetime." Ted looked at Amy and sighed. "You know, now when I look back, I can see our lives weren't nearly as bad as I thought they were. When the car broke down and there wasn't enough money to get it fixed, we had to walk everywhere. But walking didn't turn out to be a bad thing. Some of the best times I remember with Mom were when we were out walking."

"Where did you go?" Amy asked, really wanting to hear more.

"Sometimes we would take a picnic lunch and go to a small park by our apartment. While we ate, the ducks would crowd around us demanding to have their share of the food. It was fun watching them fight over each little scrap of bread. You knew it wasn't because they were hungry. Those ducks were the fattest birds you ever saw." A small, sad chuckle escaped Ted's lips as his thoughts took him backward in time.

"You were lucky to have a good relationship with your mother. It sounds like you had fun together." Amy's eyes dampened just a little. *My mother never took me to the park. She never took me anywhere.*

"She loved to take her shoes off and walk barefoot through the grass. Once, on a dare from me, she even waded barefoot into the pond. Those silly ducks thought she was going to feed them, so they swam over crowding around her. I thought they were going to push her over into the water. She started laughing so hard she almost did fall in." Wistfully, Ted stared into his wineglass. "That's the way I like to remember her. Standing in the water with her old, faded jeans rolled up to her knees, the wind blowing her hair, and the sunlight making her eyes sparkle. She was a beautiful lady."

"Was?" Amy asked.

"When I was sixteen she died from leukemia," Ted replied sadly.

"Oh, I'm so sorry Ted. From the way you talk about her, she must have been a wonderful woman."

"She was. One of the hardest things I've ever had to do was watch her waste away to nothing after she got sick. She had always been a strong person. When the illness took control it was a shock to see what it did to her. It started out with fatigue and weakness. Some days she would come home from work, collapse on the couch, and stay there until it was time to go back to work again. Next, large bruises appeared all over her body. The littlest taps would leave huge black and blue spots. Then she started having one cold after another. But she refused to see a doctor until it was too late. She thought it would cost too much. Finally, when pneumonia put her in the hospital, we found out how sick she really was. Within six months she was dead."

Amy didn't say anything. Somehow she was feeling Ted's pain as if it were her own. She wanted to wrap her arms around him and hold him until the ache in his heart went away.

Suddenly Ted realized he was doing all the talking. The sadness showing in Amy's eyes was not what he wanted to see. *This is not the way to impress a woman,* he thought, mentally kicking himself for even starting the conversation. "Hey, I didn't mean to tell you my whole life story. My problems aren't exactly a good topic for a birthday celebration. You should be over there with your friends laughing and joking, not sitting here listening to me cry on your shoulder."

"If I hadn't wanted to listen, I wouldn't have asked any questions," Amy said sincerely.

"I think you'd make a good bartender. You listen without saying a word."

"Well, I'm not going to pour you another glass of wine if that's what you're hinting at. It's time for everyone to head home." Amy glanced around the room. "Look, everyone is starting to pack up their things."

"I guess I've taken up enough of your time," Ted smiled, letting the warmth that was filling his heart shine through his eyes. "Your other guests are waiting to say good-bye. They're going to think I'm very rude for taking you away from them."

"I don't think it bothered them very much. Now they will have something new to talk about at the office next week. I know they are all wondering what was going on over here." Amy laughed. "They probably thought you were trying to seduce me. All they ever think about is sex."

"Here, let's give them something else to talk about," Ted grabbed a napkin off the bar and quickly wrote his phone number on it. "Call me anytime, about anything. It doesn't matter what." He pressed the napkin into her hand, their fingers touching for only a brief second.

Amy felt another blush coming on, so she immediately turned away. But not before her friends noticed her reaction, and as they giggled, a beet-red flush spread across her face.

+++++

Reluctant to leave Amy's presence, Ted stayed by her side until it was time for her to leave. He even helped her get Raphael situated in the back seat of her car. "Now remember, I'll be over at seven on Monday to help you with Raphael," he said, trying to delay her parting as long as he could.

Amy smiled. Then she unexpectedly stood on her tiptoes and planted a kiss on his cheek. "I'll remember. Don't worry." As she climbed into her car she realized that she actually felt good, the best

139

she had felt in years. When she pulled out of Edward's driveway, she saw Ted in the rearview mirror standing in the cold watching her and was surprised by the strange look on his face. *Was he worrying about Raphael?* she wondered, and with that thought, she became determined to prove to him she would take good care of his dog.

However, once she was out on the road and heading for home, all thoughts of Ted vanished into the darkness of the night. All she wanted to do was to get Raphael to his new home. Edward had been right—the painting had been a sensational gift, but Raphael had turned out to be an even better one.

Chapter 17

While Amy and Ted were outside saying their good-byes, Edward decided it would be best if he stayed in the house. He figured Ted would have a better chance of connecting with Amy if there were fewer distractions. Resisting the urge to spy on them, he crossed his fingers and silently wished his friend good luck.

"Ellen, do you really think Ted might have a chance with Amy," Edward asked. When Ellen didn't answer, he turned toward her and found her at the living room window peeking through the curtains at Amy and Ted.

"Hey, give them some privacy," Edward said seriously. "Don't you remember how much you hated it when your family watched us out on the front porch saying goodbye?"

"Oh hush, I'm not hurting anyone," Ellen replied, closing the curtain only a tiny bit.

Edward grinned. Ellen's pregnant belly kept her from getting too close to the window without leaning over. "I guess not. In fact you are actually doing me a world of good. You're looking awfully cute from over here." Edward walked up behind Ellen and playfully placed his hands on her buttocks.

"Not now. Can't you see I'm busy?" Ellen said, brushing Edward's hands away without losing her position at the window. "I don't want to miss a thing."

"Well, is anything going on?"

"I thought you didn't want me watching."

"Let's not get technical here. If you're going to watch, you have to give a report."

"Oh…she just kissed him! I can't believe it. You should see the look on his face."

"You've got to be kidding. Amy doesn't even hold hands on a first date, and this wasn't even a date."

"Well, it was only a kiss on the cheek. But that's pretty good for a start, don't you think? That's the closest I've seen Amy get to a guy in a long time. Usually she stands on the other side of the room from them." Suddenly Ellen jumped back and let the curtain fall back in place. "Ted's coming in."

By the time Ted opened the door, Edward and Ellen were innocently working together cleaning up the room.

"Here, let me help you before I go," Ted said, walking into the living room and picking up a couple of empty wineglasses. "Since I was an uninvited guest the least I can do is to clean up after myself."

"Don't worry about it," Edward said. "We've got all day tomorrow to tidy this mess up."

"I don't mind helping you. Besides, I don't have any reason to hurry home. No one is waiting for me there." With a serious look Ted glanced at Edward. "At least not yet."

Ellen smiled at Edward. *Maybe one of Edward's talents is matchmaking after all,* she thought cheerfully while she gathered up a stack of dirty dishes and began placing them into the dishwasher. "Ted, how did you get into raising collies? It's a strange hobby for an engineer."

"It's a long story—"

"We've got all the time in the world," Edward quickly interrupted. "Besides, I'm kind of curious myself. Why do you raise dogs?"

Ted looked at Edward and Ellen and realized that he felt comfortable in talking with them about his previous marriage. "I had originally bought my ranch as a wedding present for my ex-wife, Kathy, but it wasn't good enough for her. She couldn't stand the isolation out in the country. After a year she left me and moved back to New York. I turned into a workaholic, leaving home at dawn and returning only to fall into an exhausted sleep at night. Then the strangest thing happened. One night when I got home from work, the filthiest looking mutt you could ever imagine stood waiting by my back door. The poor thing was so weak it could hardly lift its head. I went into the house, but I just couldn't get that dog out of my mind. He looked so pathetic and thin. I knew he had to be hungry, so I heated up a bowl of milk and practically spoon-fed him. I can still see him looking up with those big eyes of his and pitifully wagging his tail as if to say thank you."

"There was a hamburger in the refrigerator that had been left over from supper the night before, and I figured he needed it more than I did. So I left it out on the steps for him. I really didn't expect to find the dog hanging around the next morning, but there he was, bright and early, standing eagerly by the back door waiting for me to feed him again."

"I couldn't leave for work knowing that the dog was hungry. I scrounged around in the kitchen, found a can of hash, and dumped it into a cereal bowl. When I walked out the door I expected him to jump all over me, but he waited quietly, almost at attention, for me to give him the food. While he was wolfing it down, I noticed a collar buried under the mud in his thick fur. Somehow, I had missed it in the darkness the night before. A brass nameplate was attached to the collar with a name and phone number engraved on it. I immediately called the number, and that phone call changed my whole life."

"What do you mean?" Ellen asked, as she finished putting the last of the dishes into the dishwasher. "Was there a reward for finding the dog?"

"In a way," Ted smiled. "I was rewarded by meeting the most impressive man I would ever have the privilege of knowing...Mr. Conley Taylor."

"I don't think I've ever heard of him," Edward said.

"Probably not. He was simply a good man, who worked hard at living. That's what impressed me about him so much." Ted pulled

144

out a barstool and sat down. "It turned out the dog was a purebred collie. The dog, whose name was Rancher, had been a present to Conley from his wife just before she died from breast cancer. About six weeks before the dog showed up at my place, Conley had been camping with his son, and somehow Rancher had gotten lost. It had devastated him. Losing Rancher had made him feel like he had somehow failed his wife. When I told him I had found the dog, I actually felt his excitement come across the phone lines."

"He wanted to pick Rancher up right away, but he lived two hours away. I didn't want to leave the dog at the house by himself for those two hours. I was afraid he might wander off again. So I called work and took the day off. The dog was in such a pathetic mess that I got brave and gave him a bath. You should have seen my bathroom by the time I finished. Rancher thought we were playing and water ended up everywhere. By the time it was over, I had more mud on me than the dog had to start with."

"I can just see you trying to stick a dog the size of Raphael into a tub." Ellen chuckled, imagining the chaos that had gone on in that bathroom.

"Not just a regular tub, but one of those huge sunken ones," Ted replied and then laughed. "In fact, I almost fell into it a couple of times."

"What happened when Conley picked up Rancher?" Edward asked, sitting down at the bar next to Ted.

"When Conley drove his truck into the driveway, Rancher knew immediately who it was. That was one smart dog. He might have been weak from his ordeal, but he shot out to that truck before Conley even had a chance to open the door. From the way the two of them acted, you would have thought Rancher had been a lost kid instead of a dog. Of course, now that I've raised dogs myself for a few years, I can understand the feeling. If I ever lost one of my collies I would act the same way."

"So how did all of this change your life?" Ellen asked.

"Conley and I were friends from the moment we met. I kept in close contact with him up until the day he died. In a way, he willed Rancher to me. Conley had a couple of strokes, one right after the other, and he couldn't care for the dog anymore. And his son couldn't do it either. One morning Conley's son showed up in my driveway with Rancher, a stack of books on dog care, and fifty pounds of food. I had no choice but to accept the collie. And in the end, it turned out to be the best thing that could have ever happened to me. Collies are very affectionate, and Rancher gave me back part of myself by showing me I could still care for something other than work. All my pups are Rancher's descendants, so you can understand why I am so particular about who I let have one of my collies."

"I'm just glad Amy got Raphael," Ellen said, cutting herself a small piece of Amy's birthday cake. "She loves him already, I can tell. She'll take very good care of him. You don't have to worry about that."

Ted didn't say a word. The only thing he was worrying about was if Amy would go out with him. He couldn't get the image of her face out of his mind. Somehow she had bewitched him with her magical smile, and he was completely spellbound. More than anything he wanted to be with her, feel the touch of her skin against his, and taste her lips as he kissed them time and time again.

Toni Auberry

Chapter 18

The drive home from Edward's turned out to be more dangerous than Amy had anticipated, and she was thankful she had chosen not to drink any more wine after supper. The freezing weather surprised her. She couldn't recall it ever being so bitterly cold on her birthday. The blustering winds and icy roads were proving to be a definite driving hazard. Only ten minutes out and she had already passed two cars that had somehow managed to slide off the road. Just attempting to keep her car from doing the same was turning out to be a nerve-wracking experience. She had such a tight grip on the steering wheel that her hands were becoming numb.

She had to concentrate solely on driving and totally forgot about Raphael in the back seat. When he placed his cold, moist nose against the back of her neck, she cried out in surprise. Her hands unexpectedly jerked the steering wheel sending the car into an uncontrolled spin. By the time the car finally came to a halt, it had gone through a complete three hundred and sixty-degree turn in the middle of the road.

"Wow, that was scary!" Amy drew in a couple of deep breaths in an attempt to relax. She slowly released her death grip on the steering wheel and waited as an adrenaline rush reached its peak and then subsided. Worried about Raphael, she turned to check on him and discovered he had come through the entire episode unscathed.

"Oh Raphael, look what you made me do! You need to stay on the seat. As soon as I can, I'm getting you some kind of restraint whether you want it or not."

Amy undid her seatbelt and practically crawled over the top of the seat to get to Raphael. The chore of persuading him to calm down took a couple of minutes. He thought Amy wanted to play and kept jumping up trying to lick her face.

"Now stop that! Lie down and behave yourself. I need to be able to concentrate on driving." Amy tried to sound strict, but Raphael looked so much like Thomas that she had trouble reprimanding him. In reality, all she actually wanted to do was hug him.

Finally, Raphael settled down. Lying in the back seat with his head dejectedly placed on top of his paws, he looked up at Amy with huge, brown eyes that seemed to say, "What did I do wrong? I only wanted to play."

"Now, Thomas...I mean Raphael, you have to learn to do what I tell you," she scolded him as a picture of Thomas filled her mind.

Not wanting to remain out in the middle of the road any longer, Amy situated herself back behind the steering wheel. As she moved her hand to shift the car out of park, she quickly scanned the roadway for any signs of traffic.

Suddenly a flicker of movement by the side of the road caught her attention. From behind a thicket of tangled brush, a shadowy figure appeared to be moving toward the car. Amy thought she saw the glint of cold, gray eyes piercing the darkness. Her throat muscles clinched tightly, and she choked back a scream. She quickly fumbled for the locks and secured all the doors. Too frightened to think, she stared out into the darkness searching for the beast she knew must be lurking nearby.

Then when a blustery gust of wind wildly shook the nearby brush, she realized it had only been her own vivid imagination stalking her in the night.

"You'd think I'd know better than to let such things scare me," Amy said aloud as she reached for the gearshift again. "Twenty-six-years-old and I'm still acting like a frightened seven-year-old."

But Amy's self-chastisement quickly ended when a terrified child's voice arose over the roaring of the wind...a voice that froze her blood as cold as the icy windows she was staring out of.

"No, please don't...please...please...no—" the child's voice begged frantically until the words became barely audible. It was almost as if someone had placed a hand over the child's mouth to stifle her pathetic pleading. And then the crying started.

As Amy anxiously scanned the area around the car for the child, she shivered violently from a drenching, cold sweat. Her eyes darted quickly from one side of the road to the other and then across the empty, frozen grounds surrounding her. Unable to determine where the sounds were coming from, she hurriedly opened the car door with trembling hands. Taking a deep breath, she forced herself to step into the freezing weather. She listened intently trying to hear beyond the sound of the howling wind. *The child had to be near,* she thought uneasily. *Her cries seemed so close. But where is she?*

Amy couldn't tell which direction to go. Frustration tugged at her mind. How could she help if she couldn't tell what needed to be done?

The muffled crying continued incessantly. It came from everywhere and from nowhere, floating in on the gusting, frigid winds.

Visibly shaken by the strangeness of the situation, Amy felt her own tears trailing in a stream down her cheeks. "Please stop crying," she begged, "and tell me where you are, and I'll help. I promise, I'll help."

But the child didn't answer. Amy listened as the crying slowly faded only to be replaced by a new sound, a terrifying sound— the heated, irregular breathing of a man caught up in the throes of passion.

"No! No!" Amy held her hands tightly over her ears trying to shut out the obscene, grunting noises. "Ohhhhhh!" she moaned as if in pain. "No! Stop it! Stop it!"

And it did stop…with a final sickening, fervent, groan filling the air. Then the child's crying returned even louder than before.

"You stupid little slut be quiet," a malicious voice growled. "If you wake anyone up, you know what will happen. Stop that whimpering. You only got what you asked for." The man seemed to be whispering directly into Amy's ear. Distraught, Amy searched all around the car, but saw absolutely nothing. Frightened beyond reason, she leaped back into the car and sat huddled in terror behind the steering wheel.

What had just taken place?

She couldn't account for what she had just heard. There wasn't a sign anywhere of a child or a man. Only a black nothingness surrounded the car. "Raphael, what is going on? Can't you hear it?" Amy looked back at the dog and saw he was obediently lying on the back seat.

Raphael gazed up at Amy expectantly waiting for a command. He didn't appear the least bit ruffled by the bizarre happenings. In fact, his calm appearance saved Amy from the paralyzing fear that threatened to immobilize her.

She reached over to shift the car out of park, and in her haste she accidentally shifted the car into neutral instead of drive. Panic struck again when she thrust her foot down on the gas pedal and the car didn't move.

What is happening? Amy's mind screamed in alarm. *Why isn't the car going anywhere?*

When she realized her mistake, she jerked the shift stick into drive and took off with the car fishtailing on the ice. Tremors shook through her so severely that she couldn't keep an even pressure on the gas pedal. The car would surge forward, then slow down to a crawl, only to surge forward again. All the while, she kept looking in the rearview mirror as if expecting some horrifying creature to suddenly loom up from behind and sweep the car off into oblivion.

Fear sent her heart pounding furiously. Sweat poured off her forehead, and her hands grew moist and clammy under her leather driving gloves. She didn't understand what had just occurred, and she was too scared to think about it, so she tried to concentrate only on navigating the dangerous, icy roads. But the harder she tried to ignore thoughts of the weeping child, the stronger the cries echoed through her mind.

When she finally pulled into her driveway, she let out a big sigh of relief. "Thank goodness, Raphael, we're home. I was really beginning to wonder if we would make it." She looked over her shoulder at the dog sitting so nonchalantly in the back seat and protested, "You know, if you're supposed to be my guardian angel, you're going to have to be a little more alert than that."

She was feeling paranoid and suspiciously glanced around the drive and the front of the house, carefully checking for signs of anything out of the ordinary. When she saw nothing unusual she took the keys out of the ignition, pulled her coat snugly around her neck, and got out of the car. She paused for a second when her feet touched the ground as she listened carefully for sounds other than the wind stirring about. She heard nothing; all was quiet. No strange voices drifted in from unseen persons in the night as she opened the back car door for Raphael.

The instant the door opened Raphael bounded out in sheer joy at being set free and took off across the yard.

"Raphael! Come back here," Amy demanded immediately.

He turned abruptly at the command and reluctantly trotted back toward Amy, tail wagging, apparently oblivious to the freezing weather.

"Come on, let's go inside where it's warm." She unlocked the front door and entered the house with Raphael following obediently behind. "Welcome to your new home, my friend," she whispered, kneeling down and hugging Raphael. "I'm so very glad you are here. With all of the strange things that happened today I really don't want to be alone tonight."

Since it was late, she headed straight for the bedroom. After changing into a long, woolen nightgown, she fixed Raphael a place to sleep on the floor using a couple of old covers. "This is your bed, and it will just have to do till I can get something better fixed up," she said, ordering Raphael to lie down. Then she climbed into her bed and crawled underneath the covers.

Raphael lay upon his bed and looked up at Amy with such sad, pleading eyes that she didn't have the heart to make him stay there. "Oh all right, you can sleep up here with me," she finally said, "but only for tonight."

Raphael leaped onto bed, apparently very happy for the special privilege. Then he curled up at Amy's feet and contentedly lay watching her until she fell asleep.

With her new guardian angel sleeping snuggly at her feet, Amy's night passed quickly and peaceably. No nightmares cast their evil images. No strange voices spoke from unseen faces, and no blood flowed from dark red roses.

+++++

Early the next morning Raphael eagerly inspected his new home. Amy took him from room to room letting him sniff every corner of the house. His curiosity was immense. He had to poke his nose into every nook-and-cranny. And as she watched each quizzical turn of Raphael's head, a tiny fire within her soul began burning brighter and brighter. The simple joy flowing from Raphael as he moved from room to room inspecting his new domain amazed her.

Somewhere in time, as a small child, she had felt simple joy. But it had been so long ago she had forgotten such a thing even existed. Watching Raphael made her wonder if somehow it might be possible to get such pleasures out of life again. Smiling, she thought about her birthday party. She realized that for a short time she had been happy. For awhile, she had felt as though she had belonged to a real family, instead of being an outcast.

Maybe things are going to be different from now on, she thought hopefully. *I'm so tired of being lonely.*

The morning hours passed quickly. The peacefulness sweeping over her was so intense she didn't want the day to end. It felt good just sitting back and laughing at Raphael's antics as he explored his new world. When they went outside she felt warm despite the chilling winds.

As she sat on the porch steps leading up to her back door, she laughed whole-heartedly when Raphael grabbed her coat with his teeth and tried to pull her off the steps.

Suddenly, she wasn't twenty-six any more. She was seven, laughing and playing with Thomas in the backyard of her old home, and like a child she ran across the yard chasing Raphael...playing catch with an old rubber ball he had found in the yard...hiding behind a tree and jumping out to surprise him. She laughed and giggled, just as she had done with Thomas all those many years ago, and it felt wonderful.

"Oh, Raphael, what a joy you are to me," Amy said. "You've stolen my heart, and already I love you as much as I loved Thomas."

Amy felt marvelous. In less than one day, her life had taken on new meaning. Only yesterday she had been as sad and lonely as any young woman could possibly be, and now...everything was totally different. She also discovered that her newly found happiness only reinforced her decision concerning law school. She had found, through Raphael, that there could be new life after the death of one's spirit, and she desperately wanted to help show others like herself how to find it.

Toni Auberry

Chapter 19

Later that evening, Amy realized she didn't know if Raphael could be left home alone when she went to work in the morning. Comtec had just installed a new computer system, and as the office manager she had to help with the training. She knew it was essential that she go into the office even though she didn't want to.

She searched through her purse and found the napkin Ted had hastily scribbled his phone number on. She thoughtfully held the rumpled napkin in her fingers and wondered whether it would be all right to call to find out if Raphael could safely be left home alone.

An image of Ted's face innocently played through her mind. *He had looked so handsome last night sitting at Edward's bar. His blond hair had been slightly mussed, and he hadn't even bothered to comb it back in place. For some reason it had made him seem real, more human. And his smile, it had literally beamed from his face lighting up his blue eyes like diamonds.*

She finally decided Ted would want her to call so she reached for the phone. She'd seen how concerned Ted had been about Raphael, and he wouldn't want her to do something wrong that might hurt the collie.

Her fingers nervously dialed Ted's home phone number, and when his answering machine picked up the call, she felt an odd sense of disappointment.

"Ted, this is Amy Tedrow, Edward's sister—" she paused and almost hung up, but after a few seconds she decided to continue. "I just wanted to ask you something about Raphael. Could you call me back this evening when you have time?"

+++++

Ted was at his desk diligently working on one of his engineering projects when the phone rang. Not wanting to be bothered, he let the answering machine do its job. However, the moment he heard Amy's voice, he jumped up and ran to the phone. In his mad dash to talk to her, he managed to knock all his paperwork off the desk onto the floor, but he didn't even realize it had happened. His thoughts were only on Amy.

"Amy! Don't hang up!" Ted almost shouted as he picked up the receiver.

"Hi Ted," Amy's voice quivered slightly from an uneasiness that had suddenly appeared from out of nowhere. "I...I was hoping you'd be home. I needed to ask a question about Raphael."

"What can I help you with?" Ted felt disappointment settle heavily across his shoulders because Amy hadn't called just to talk.

"I forgot to ask if I could leave Raphael alone in the house tomorrow when I go to work."

"He has been trained as a house dog and will do all right if you don't leave him alone for long periods. Just be sure you take him outside right before you go to work and as soon as you get home. Unless, of course, you want a mess in your house. Oh, and be sure he has plenty of food and water, and remember to close the doors to any of the rooms you don't want him wandering into."

As Amy intently listened to Ted's instructions, she became vaguely aware of a strange sensation spreading through her body. The moment she had heard his voice, a rush of warmth had quickly moved from her face all the way down to her toes. Flustered by the unusual feelings, she wished she hadn't called. "Thanks for the instructions, Ted. I really appreciate you taking the time to talk with me. I know you're busy—"

"So, where do you work?" he asked, hoping to keep her on the line. Listening to the softness in her voice was like listening to a flute playing a baby's lullaby, and he wanted to hear more of it.

"At Comtec, a computer development company. I manage the main office. We just installed a new computer system, and tomorrow I will be assisting in instructing the other office employees on operating procedures. That's why I can't stay home with Raphael," she said apologetically, not wanting Ted to think she was going to leave the collie alone so soon for no good reason.

"You're still going to be able to meet with me at seven, aren't you?" Ted hopefully asked.

"Yes. If my plans change, I'll call and let you know." Amy felt apprehensive as her stomach began twisting itself into a thousand knots. Wary of the way she was feeling, she lied to get Ted off the phone. "Someone's at the front door, and I've got to go," she suddenly declared, saying goodbye and slamming the phone receiver back into its cradle before Ted had time to object.

What is going on? Amy fought back the panicky sensation that was threatening to overwhelm her. *Why does the simple act of talking to Ted make me feel so strange?*

Ted stared at the silent phone in his hand. *Why had Amy hung up before we even got the chance to say anything? Why doesn't she want to talk to me?*

Frustrated almost beyond control, Ted couldn't force himself to return to his work. Instead he took two of his collies out for a run hoping it would help take his mind off Amy. But it didn't help because she was all he could think about.

+++++

As Amy was getting ready for bed Sunday night, she glanced at the now cherished painting that was hanging above her headboard. *Had that little girl loved her collie as much as I loved Thomas when I was her age?* she wondered for just a second before her thoughts turned toward Raphael.

Amy glanced around her bedroom, but the collie wasn't anywhere in sight. "Raphael, come here," she called. "It's time for me to go to bed, and that means you have to lie down too." She stood by the side of the bed, reached over to pull back the covers, but then stopped as she listened intently for the sound of Raphael's footsteps. When she didn't hear them, she turned toward the door and started to call for him again.

The strange sight she beheld at that moment sent waves of shocking surprise washing over her.

Raphael was sitting motionless right inside her bedroom door, but he wasn't alone. A young girl with long, brown hair and dressed in a blue nightgown stood beside him. Her hand rested possessively upon Raphael's back. The child's huge, hazel eyes were looking straight into Amy's with such an expression of complete misery that Amy instinctively wanted to wrap her arms protectively around the child. A feeling of overpowering grief and pain filled the room. For one full minute, time hung suspended. The girl didn't move, and neither did Raphael or Amy.

Then a single tear from the girl's sorrowful, hazel eyes slowly began to travel down one of her cheeks.

Amy watched in amazement as the girl bent over and whispered secretively into Raphael's ear. She couldn't hear what had been said, but afterwards the girl wrapped her tiny arms around Raphael's neck, buried her face in his fur, and started crying silent tears.

The blue nightgown, the long brown hair, the sad eyes, Amy shifted her glance upward to the painting above her bed. She couldn't believe it. The girl standing next to Raphael was the same girl in the painting!

Amy's eyes darted back to Raphael, and another surprise awaited her. The strange apparition instantly vanished, melting into the shadows of the room without leaving a trace. Amy glanced furtively around the room searching for an explanation, but couldn't find one. Only Raphael remained, patiently waiting for Amy, his tail wagging, and adoration shinning in his eyes. Astonished, Amy looked bewilderedly at the portrait over the bed. *What had just happened?*

Slowly realization set in. The impact literally left her weak and unable to stand. Immersed in total confusion Amy ungracefully lowered herself onto the edge of the bed. Her right hand went up to her chest, and she could feel her heart racing as fast as her thoughts. *How could it possible be true? The hair, the dress, those eyes. The little girl in the doorway was the same girl in the painting, right down to the haunting look in her sad, hazel eyes.*

Amy's heart increased its pounding beat. *The girl had to be a ghost! There could be no other logical explanation.* Her eyes fixed on the painting as she searched for any possible clue that would explain the strange event that had just occurred. She hadn't imagined the child standing by the door. She had sense enough to know if what she was seeing was real…and the girl had been real! She would bet her life on it. She could still feel the child's oppressive grief lying heavy on the air. It had saturated the room so strongly that she believed she could almost reach out and touch it.

"What do you want?" Amy asked, her mind full of tangled half-finished thoughts. "Why are you here?"

164

She took the painting down off of the wall and held it tightly in her hands. Her eyes stared into the girl's as though she might find an answer painted in them. Supposedly spirits stayed on earth because they had unfinished business. At least that's what she had heard. Ghosts were only spirits that couldn't rest in peace.

So why couldn't the girl's spirit find peace?

A sense of determination overcame Amy. She had absolutely no idea what she would have to do to help the child, but whatever it would take she would do it. And with making that decision, Amy suddenly felt relieved. The pleas for help she had heard yesterday afternoon before falling asleep, the muffled crying last night out of the road, both had been real. She hadn't been losing her mind after all. Maybe even the bloody roses were images sent to her by the child.

Amy's heart ached for the mournful, little girl, who had somehow found a way to speak from the grave. Something had kept the poor thing from moving on to the next level after death. Her job would be to find out what that something was and then discover a way to help.

She hung the painting back up above her bed, curled up under her covers with Raphael snuggled up at her feet, and made plans to try to discover the origin of the painting. *Somehow the ghost and the painting were linked,* she thought, *and my only chance of finding what that link might be is to discover who the child in the painting had been. In the morning I'm going to call Edward and find out what he knows concerning the little girl's portrait.*

With that very important decision made, Amy allowed herself to drift off into a restless sleep.

Chapter 20

Startled awake from the depths of a dreamless sleep, Amy opened her eyes to a lightless world. Burrowed deep beneath her grandmother's quilt, all she could see was the intense blackness that had cloaked her face with its heavy weight, and the only sound she could hear was the noise of her own breathing echoing loudly in her ears.

She had no idea what had awakened her.

She listened intently, even holding her breath so she could focus on any sounds that might occur on the other side of the quilt. *How could silence sound so loud?* Amy wondered. *Is that what woke me…the empty sounds of silence? Shouldn't I at least be hearing Raphael's steady breathing?*

She wiggled her toes, expecting to feel Raphael curled up and asleep at her feet. But he wasn't there.

Finally her lungs demanded that she exhale, and she slowly let the air escape quietly through her mouth. She didn't want to make a single noise because she knew something might be waiting, listening, on the other side of the covers.

She lay motionless, her muscle taut and ready to spring into action. Two minutes went by, then five, and nothing happened. The heavy weight of the covers pressing down upon her face was suffocating, and she wanted to throw them off. Except, she knew something could be in her bedroom quietly waiting for her to show herself, and she was afraid.

Six, then seven minutes passed, and still nothing moved...not Amy...or anything else.

Maybe it was only a noise from out on the street that had jarred me awake, Amy reasoned. *Maybe I was only dreaming. She allowed her aching, tense muscles to slowly relax. Surely it's safe for me to move now.*

Cautiously she inched the quilt back from her face far enough for her to peek out into the dark night. Bright moonlight was streaming in from the bedroom window, and she could see the stars twinkling in their brilliance in the night sky.

All seemed quiet; there had been no need for her to be frightened.

Foolish fears, that's all it was, Amy scolded herself as she started to snuggle back under the covers. But her vanishing fears instantly returned when the stars suddenly disappeared, blotted out by a huge menacing shadow, a shadow that looked at the world through gray eyes glistening like polished marble, eyes filled with anger and malice, and something else...something more dangerous.

They were the hungry eyes of the beast.

No. No. No, her mind screamed. *Not again. God, no. Please not again.* Amy jerked the quilt back over her head and tried to escape by burying herself deeper under the bed covers. But there was no escape…just like all the other times when God had let her down.

The beast reached out with its hairy hands and ripped the quilt from the bed. Amy watched in horror as the creature flung her only source of protection across the room and left nothing between her and its cruel, hungry eyes.

The beast's weight fell heavily upon her, trapping her beneath its repulsive body. She squeezed her eyes tightly shut; she wasn't brave enough to look fully upon its face. The menacing hate shinning from its eyes was always the only thing she would allow herself to see. Her mind couldn't take anymore than that terrible sight.

Grotesque, misshapen hands painfully twisted her arms far above her head. The crushing weight of the beast pressed her into the bed making it impossible to breathe, and her lungs cried out for air. Struggling, she twisted and turned. She needed to breathe, but the creature wouldn't move. Finally, after what seemed to be an eternity, the beast shifted its weight, allowing her to suck in a single breath of precious air.

But, she still couldn't get free. It continued to hold her arms captive above her head. She wanted to scream, but could force no sounds from her mouth; terror had somehow made her mute.

One of the beast's hands reached down and yanked her nightgown up past her waist. It's fingers, coarse and rough, tore at her delicate skin as they moved down across her belly. Sharp fingernails cut into her thighs as the beast pried her legs apart. Then its full weight fell upon her again.

She tried to call out for help, but a hand suddenly clamped over her mouth sealing the sounds within her.

An intense pain originating down deep below the pit of her stomach enveloped her entire body, a pain that seemed to have no end.

God, why don't You help me! Amy pleaded. *Why can't You stop it?*

Tears squeezed passed her tightly clamped eyelids.

Disgusting, grunting, groaning noises reached her ears as the beast moved in a heated rhythm, pushing, slamming her body harder and faster into the bed.

Finally, she did scream.

+++++

Awakened abruptly by the sound of her own screaming, Amy jolted up in bed, gasping for breath as if she were suffocating. *A dream. It had only been another dream.* Yet the weight of the beast seemed to still be resting upon her chest.

An immense shadow suddenly materialized at the foot of her bed. A sharp cry of fear emerged from her lips, but then she realized it was only Raphael.

She reached up to wipe away the tears she had cried while she had been dreaming. She felt terrible…a dull, nagging ache cramped within her belly, and a pounding migraine had started its unmerciful throbbing at the base of her skull.

How I hate those nightmares of that faceless beast, she thought as her hands weakly massaged her temples. *They always leave me weak and feeling totally defenseless in their aftermath.*

+++++

More times than she could possibly count over the past eight years, Amy had escaped from the lingering terrors of her nightmares by retreating into the living room and trying to resume sleep on the couch.

This time was no different. Knowing she wouldn't be able to rest peacefully in bed, she picked up a pillow, a couple of blankets, and reluctantly headed toward the living room.

"Come on Raphael, we're moving into the other room for the night." With a quiet sigh of resignation, Amy put together a makeshift bed on the couch. She crawled under the covers and pulled the blankets up around her neck. She tried to relax, but her mind wouldn't shut down.

For some strange reason she felt as though she were guilty of some great sin. Yet she knew that wasn't true.

Why did those accursed nightmares always make her feel as though she had done something wrong?

A look of resignation came over her face. No matter how much she tried, she could never answer that question. Every time she attempted to reason through the dreams, she hit a mental blockade…one she couldn't get past.

She supposed some things were better off if they weren't really understood, and in the back of her mind she knew this was one of them.

Chapter 21

By six o'clock Monday morning Amy was out of bed and getting ready for work. For the first time in years she was dreading going into the office, and it wasn't due to the mass confusion with the new computer system, but because of the computer consultant, Gary Steiner, who had been hired to assist with the company's transition to the new system.

I don't like that man at all, she thought. *Gary acts just like my father did—as though the world owes him something. He can be nice, I know, but I've watched him when he wasn't aware that I was there, and I've seen his true colors, especially when he is around the younger women. That's when he looks like a hungry dog staring longingly at a fresh piece of meat dangling just out of his reach.*

I remember seeing that same look on my father's face, and it always made my skin crawl. What I don't understand is why no one else ever noticed. How had my father fooled everyone for so long?

+++++

In preparation for her shower, Amy quickly disrobed and tossed her nightclothes into a pile to be picked up later. She always hurried when she was bathing because of the uncomfortable feeling she constantly had of being watched. She hastened into the shower stall and yanked the shower curtain closed with a quick flick of her wrist.

As the first wave of water washed over her body, a sudden chill sent a ripple of tremors throughout her entire body. And it wasn't because the water was cold; it was due to the fact that she always felt completely defenseless when she was naked.

Dealing with nudity had always been difficult for her for as far back as she could remember. For some reason, she simply felt much safer with her clothes on. Even as a child she had hated to undress, and more than once she had infuriated her mother by refusing to take her clothes off for her bath.

One of the worst beatings she had ever received took place after her mother had tried to force her into undressing for a bath while her father had been in the room shaving. She was ten then and had felt she was too old to take her clothes off with him present. She and her mother had heatedly argued, and the fighting had enraged her father so much that he had almost beaten her to death.

Amy closed her eyes and stood in the shower letting the hot water flow over her body. Without difficulty she could still picture the rage on her father's face that morning when he yanked her out of the bathroom and dragged her into the hallway. Shaving cream had covered half his face and had reminded her of a rabid dog foaming at the mouth. And when he had pulled his belt from his pants, he had seemed like a knight drawing his sword from its scabbard. She could still remember how he had used the belt as though it was a weapon against some ferocious enemy instead of against his young daughter.

She also very clearly remembers how he had held both of her small wrists in one of his huge hands and had ripped off her clothes, and then had savagely beaten her until blood poured from the welts crisscrossing her back and legs. As the lashing took place, he had bellowed like a mad bull. "The next time you are told to do something, you will do so without arguing. Do you understand me, young lady? Always remember who you are and that you are only allowed to stay here in this house if you obey the rules."

After the first few belt strikes had slashed across her tender skin, she had tried to tell him she understood and would do whatever he asked. But he had refused to listen. Rage had flowed from him like a sick madness. She had begged and pleaded for him to stop, but to no avail.

"Just shut up," he had roared. "You asked for this, so now you are going to get it."

And she had been powerless to escape the pain and incapable of doing anything but cry.

After his rage had depleted itself, he had left her lying in the hallway in a bloody heap on the floor. He had walked away as if she were nothing but a piece of worthless trash he was able to discard without a second thought. Then he had finished shaving and left for work without even acknowledging her pain or even saying a single word.

After that beating, Amy had never argued with her mother again, at least not where her father could hear.

+++++

As Amy showered, she thought of another of her childhood fears—how she had hated the night with its dark shadows that had imprisoned her in the bedroom. When she was young, night had held a special terror for her and had brought with it a deep, penetrating coldness that still had the power to chill her to the bone.

Amy allowed her thoughts to drift toward her father. *Maybe if my father's heart hadn't been so cold toward me, I wouldn't feel this way now. Maybe if he had protected me when the nightmares came and had offered me some kind of comfort from the terrors that had haunted me in the dark, I wouldn't have been so afraid.*

But he never tried to console me. He—

Amy suddenly remembered what had happened late one night when she had finally worked up enough courage to attempt the long trip from her bedroom to the bathroom. She had walked on tiptoes, oh so quietly, not wanting to disturb her father, when he had unexpectedly appeared at his bedroom door. She could still see the strange expression he had on his face and could clearly remember how his eyes had spoken of the hate he had for her. But there had also been something else in his eyes that night—underneath that hate had lain another emotion she hadn't been able to interpret, and she had felt naked and powerless under his critical gaze. Like a frightened rabbit, she had scurried back to her bedroom, and she had felt his eyes following her all the way.

After she had reached her room she had quickly closed the door and waited in quiet terror for something to happen. She had stood with her ear to the door listening for her father's footsteps, all the while praying he would go back into his own room. After what had seemed like an eternity, she finally heard him head downstairs to the kitchen. When she had been sure he was no longer a threat, she had gathered her pillow and a blanket and had made a bed on the floor right in front of the door. She had wanted to be sure no one could sneak into the room in the middle of the night.

Foolishness of course, Amy thought, *for who would have came into my bedroom except for Mom?*

Amy thought about one strange thing she used to do to help quiet her night fears—after she turned thirteen, she used to wear her regular clothes to bed every night, right down to her old, ratty sneakers. Somehow having her clothes on when she was in bed made her feel more secure. She had wanted to be prepared for anything. The way she had it figured, if for some reason she had to get up and run, she had to be ready…although she couldn't remember what she had wanted to run from.

Of course, Amy thought, *I don't do such absurd things now. I don't wear my shoes to bed or sleep on the floor by the bedroom door for protection.*

But at night she did lock every door and window in the house. Plus she had an elaborate alarm system that automatically placed a call into the police if anyone set it off.

Maybe the nightmares could sneak into the house to terrorize her during the night, but no person would be able to. And if they did, she kept a loaded gun in her bedroom dresser…a gun she had been expertly trained to use.

Chapter 22

The childhood scenes playing through Amy's mind were disturbing reminders of a life she preferred to forget. The terrible memories made her shiver despite the warmth of the hot water cascading down upon her shoulders. She reached for the shower controls and increased the temperature of the water until the heat became almost unbearable.

The air in the shower became misty and humid. Steam rolled up from the shower floor sending a warm, moist haze throughout the entire bathroom. The full-length mirror attached to the back of the bathroom door clouded over as a million minuscule particles of water settled upon it.

Amy glanced down at her breasts which were blushing a deep rose under the shower's sweltering touch, and she suddenly felt dirty, as though tainted by some filthy source that she couldn't describe. She quickly soaped up the washcloth and began to aggressively scrub every part of her body.

Why do I always feel as though I've been contaminated in some way? Amy felt tears gathering in her eyes as her hands scoured at her skin leaving painful redden areas upon her chest. *It seems no matter how hard I rub that unclean feeling never goes away.*

As the stifling heat from the shower increased, Amy slowly became aware of the nagging presence of a migraine that had begun to unfurl its painful tentacles. The appendages of pain were spreading out, wrapping themselves around her brain and squeezing, making her faint and weak-kneed.

She leaned unsteadily against the side of the shower stall for support and let the hot water wash over her in a vain attempt at cleansing her body and her soul. She began to hear a strange rumbling in her ears like the hum of a faraway crowd. She listened closely, trying to decipher the strange sound, but couldn't hear clearly over the noise of the shower as it rained down upon the plastic shower curtain next to her. Her hand reached up and slowly turned the water off. As she heard the last of the water swirl down the drain, she realized that the rumbling had faded away—only to be replaced by the solitary voice of a young girl.

At first the child's words were jumbled and incoherent, but gradually they became clearer as Amy stood shivering in the shower stall from something more than the cold.

"Mommy will make me leave if she finds out," the voice softly whispered. *"I know she will, and I don't have anywhere else to go. No one wants me."*

Amy felt her throbbing migraine tighten its hold with each word the child spoke.

"Dad says everything is my fault. He says I'm bad, and no one wants a bad little girl in his house."

The pain surging through Amy's head made her dizzy, and she swayed slightly, holding onto the rail in the shower for support.

"But I'm not bad...really I'm not. None of it's my fault, I swear. I didn't want to do it. He made me."

"Who are you?" Amy finally asked in a quiet whisper that barely brushed across her lips. "Are you the girl in the painting?"

Only a muffled sobbing answered.

Amy threw back the shower curtain, grabbed a towel, and quickly wrapped it around her body. When she stepped out of the shower, she gasped in surprise—in the mist-covered mirror hanging on the back of the bathroom door, she saw the shadowy outline of an unknown form. Then as she stared wide-eyed and bewildered, an eerie glow began to radiate from beyond the strange image in the mirror. Slowly the figure in the polished glass grew more defined. And then in less time than it took for her heart to beat twice, she saw the ghost of the little girl from the painting emerge from behind the steamy translucent droplets of water that had coated the mirror while she had showered.

She warily watched the child scan the room in a desperate search that ended the very instant the girl's eyes turned upon her, and she saw that the eyes were brimming with a flood of tears that was overflowing and streaming down the girl's face.

An overwhelming compassion for the innocent in the mirror swelled in Amy's heart. She wanted to reach out to comfort the girl, but she was afraid to move. She was fearful that any movement might cause the child to vanish again, and she definitely didn't want that to happen. So she only stood quietly and watched as the weeping child looked despairingly down at her hands and then raised them palm-up as if to show Amy something.

Amy glanced at the open palms and felt horror take hold as she watched bright red blood start pouring from the girl's hands. The blood flowed from the girl's palms, ran down her fingertips, and then surged in a torrent that streamed down the mirror. Within a matter of seconds, before Amy even had the time to blink, an immense pool of blood had formed on the bathroom floor right at the base of the mirror. The blood started spreading across the tiled floor toward Amy's bare feet.

She stood spellbound, shocked by the sight of the blood and by the look of hopelessness on the girl's face. But then something else happened…suddenly she wasn't afraid any longer. Somehow she knew that the girl wasn't trying to scare or hurt her, but was instead, trying to tell her something.

What do you want from me? Amy thought, her heart bursting with the need to pull the girl into her comforting embrace. *What can I do to help you find peace? Because that's what you need isn't it? To find peace so you can leave this world and move on to the next.*

But before Amy had the chance to find out the answers to her questions, she saw the bathroom door inch forward, pushed open by Raphael's shiny, black nose.

And as soon as the door moved, the girl and the blood instantaneously disappeared, leaving only Amy and Raphael alone in the spotlessly clean bathroom.

When Raphael spied Amy, he bounded joyfully into the room, apparently oblivious to the unusual happening that had just occurred. All he wanted to do was play. He tugged at Amy's towel trying to pull her toward the bedroom.

Thankful to escape the confines of the bathroom, Amy followed Raphael without protesting. She exited with a feeling of great relief, carefully placing her feet upon the tile floor so as not to step in the spot where the blood had coated the floor only moments before.

Once Amy was in her bedroom, she noticed that the painting seemed to be the dominant force in the room, so she knew that the child's presence still remained even though she could no longer see her. She also knew what she was going to have to do. The girl obviously needed her help, and she couldn't turn away without doing all she could to end the poor thing's misery. It didn't matter that other people would think she was crazy. What would they know about it anyway? No one else had seen or heard the girl's heartbreaking sobs or had seen the sad, pitiful eyes brimmed with tears. She'd been the only one the child had shown herself to, and she was the only one who could help.

Toni Auberry

Chapter 23

Amy skillfully threaded her car through the morning traffic as she headed toward the office. While she drove she allowed her thoughts to drift toward Gary Steiner, the new computer consultant. By most women's standards he would be considered an attractive man. Thirty-years-old, six feet tall, he had a slick lean look. She believed that he probably worked out with weights regularly because even under his business suit his taut muscles were clearly visible. His short black hair gave the impression of a dependable, hardworking man. But she knew that impressions could be deceiving, and she didn't think the term *hardworking* could be applied to any accurate description of Gary.

The first couple of days after Gary had arrived at the office some of the women had subtly flirted with him. But when he had blatantly taken the flirting as outright invitations for sex, the women had quickly backed off. Unfortunately, he didn't appear to know what the word *no* meant.

185

When Amy pulled into Comtec's parking lot, her animosity toward Gary instantly increased when she realized that he had parked his sonic-blue Mustang in her parking space again. Last Friday she had specifically requested that he not park his car there, and apparently, he had blatantly ignored that request.

Already angry, Amy felt her frustration flare even more when she exited the elevator and saw Gary hovering like a hawk over Susan, her secretary.

More than a little annoyed, Amy headed toward them. *Today is definitely going to be a long one*, she thought peevishly. *It isn't even eight o'clock and that man has already set my nerves on edge.* She looked at Susan sitting at her desk working on the new computer program and at Gary standing next to her with his body almost plastered against her side as he issued instructions. She watched as Gary leaned over Susan and placed one of his hands over hers on the computer's mouse and then put his other hand possessively on her shoulder.

"Honey, this is what you need to do with your hands now," Gary said, his voice flowing with sexual overtones as he moved the mouse under Susan's captured hand. "You need to hold firm and use short quick movements to get the results you want." And as he spoke his other hand moved in a caressing motion from Susan's shoulder down her back. "That perfume you're wearing is something special," he said, drawing in a deep breath. "It sure gets to a man."

"I think you'd better stop—right now," Susan angrily retorted, trying to free her hand from under his on the mouse. But Gary's grip tightened, and she couldn't break his hold. She attempted to stand, but he brought his hand back up to her shoulder and dug his fingers in, preventing her from rising from the chair.

"I'd better stop what?" Gary replied smugly. "I'm only doing my job."

"Susan—is there a problem?" Amy hurried over to intervene before the situation escalated.

"Nothing I can't handle." Susan glared at Gary as he backed away from her chair a couple of steps.

"Are you sure?" Amy asked doubtfully.

"Of course she's sure," Gary spat out. "Why would you even think she had a problem?"

"Susan, I need to see you in my office." Amy said, turning away without acknowledging Gary's statement. "Please bring that packet from Thompson's Supply with you. We need to work on their account this morning."

"You really think you're hot stuff, don't you?" Gary spoke under his breath loud enough for only Amy to hear.

Amy glanced back at Gary and saw the raw contempt he felt toward her showing in the sneer on his face. Her whole body started trembling as she remembered seeing that very same look before...on her father's face just before his foot had found its mark upon her ribs.

She quickly averted her eyes, feeling like a helpless child. But a second later, anger took control and she used that anger to give her the strength to lift her gaze upward to look at Gary again.

"Guess I'd better get back to work," Gary said smugly. "Wouldn't want you to think I'm wasting your company's precious time." Smiling, he looked down at Susan. "I'll get with you later."

"I think Susan will be busy the rest of the day," Amy replied with a forced smile. "And so will you. We need to have the system up and running by Friday."

"All right, Little Lady, I'll get started on that right away," Gary condescendingly replied. Nonchalantly, he stuck his hands in his pockets, turned his back on Susan and Amy, and then headed across the room.

Extremely annoyed by Gary's behavior, Amy came up behind him and grabbed his arm. "Wait, Mr. Steiner. I need to have a word with you…in private…in my office." Amy opened her office door and stepped aside, letting Gary enter first. After they were both inside the room, Amy had to use every ounce of her self-control to keep from slamming the door in frustration—Gary had made her that angry.

"Mr. Steiner," Amy said sharply, "there are two things you are going to have to understand."

"Oh, and what's that?" Gary replied, letting a cynical smirk cross his face.

"First…my name is Ms. Tedrow, not Little Lady! And I expect to be addressed as such."

"Excuse me," Gary sarcastically apologized. "I didn't mean to upset you—Ms. Tedrow."

Ignoring the lack of sincerity in his voice, Amy continued, "Second…in this office we treat everyone with equal consideration and respect. This includes respecting others' private space. Which means you need to keep your hands off the women in this office. Am I making myself clear on this point?"

"You're making a big deal out of nothing," Gary angrily snapped. "I don't think I've done one thing wrong."

"I don't care what you think. I expect you to keep your hands to yourself, and if you don't, I will report you to my supervisor. I don't want to see another scene like the one I just saw between you and Susan. I won't give you a second chance if you do it again. Do you understand?"

"Sure. Every little word." Gary glared hatefully at Amy. "But maybe you'd better warn Susan too. I don't want to get into trouble because some stupid woman can't keep her hands off me." Then Gary spun on his heels, turned his back on Amy, and stormed out of the office, slamming the door as he left.

Shaken by the confrontation, Amy collapsed into her chair. "What an idiot!" *How I hate men with sexist attitudes,* she thought resentfully. *They make me want to run screaming from the room. Except if I were to do that it would only reinforce their idiotic opinion that women are somehow emotionally impaired.*

+++++

Years ago, Amy had promised herself that she'd never allow a man to control her in any manner, and she especially took offense if a man tried to make her feel inferior through the use of words as weapons. So for the sake of self-protection, she had taught herself how to be strong and how to stand up and fight back. And it hadn't been easy. The emotional scars left by her tyrannical father had been very difficult to contend with. But deep inside she had a strong will...a bequeath passed to her from her childhood. A lot of kids would have given up and crawled into a hole somewhere never to be seen again in the light of day, but not her. After her father's death, she had sworn that she'd never allow a man to abuse her again, and every day since that day she had done her best not to let that happen. In college she took classes on assertiveness to learn how to stand up for herself and psychology classes to understand why people acted like they did. She figured the more she knew about people the easier it would be to deal with them. And she had been right.

Through her studies, she discovered that most behaviors were learned behaviors. So she decided in her first year of college to learn how to change herself from a scared, little girl into a woman who wouldn't run and hide when things went wrong.

Realizing that knowledge formed the foundation for surviving any situation, she went about gaining knowledge any way possible. She wanted to survive, so therefore, she put her whole heart into it. Over the last eight years she had managed to reshape her behavior by taking classes, reading, and studying.

Men like Gary Steiner would never have the opportunity to destroy all she had worked so hard to build. She absolutely refused to allow it to happen.

Amy sat at her desk, surrounded by piles of paperwork, and smiled thinking about the karate school she had been attending two days a week for the past five years—Terry Juan's Academy of the

Defensive Arts. A small school, but one with a big message. Terry Juan, her Sensei, didn't believe that survival was solely based on being the biggest or the strongest. In her classes, Terry frequently focused on helping her students find the guiding spirit that dwelled within their own hearts, the spirit that gave them the strength to survive against the odds.

While working out with Terry and the other martial arts students, Amy had discovered that there were more ways to fight than just with fists...knowing how to use her brain and her heart had proven to be as equally important.

She realized that her Sensei had helped make a big difference in her self-confidence. For one thing: Terry hadn't laughed at her the first day she had entered the dojo looking like a timid, lost mouse. Instead, she had offered encouragement, pushed toward achievement, and had given her friendship willingly.

In the beginning Amy knew that she had looked ridiculous compared to the other students. Each one of them had moved so gracefully and easily through their katas, while she had somehow managed to trip over her own feet most of the time. Yet she had endured and worked on mastering the katas, learned the power of mediation and self-control, and found strength within herself that she hadn't known existed. And it all paid off. Over the past five years, she had slowly become less afraid of the little things—like walking alone down a deserted street, or hearing strange noises outside the house at night.

Amy chuckled, lighting a tiny spark in her eyes as she remembered what had happened at class the prior week when one arrogant young man had tried to best her. She had effortlessly tossed him to the floor before he even had the chance to realize what was happening. *Good old hands-on experience*, she thought, *has always helped me learn better than anything else.*

From the very first, the karate lessons have been good for her. They have allowed her the chance to learn how to protect herself and taught her how to fight back when she had to. In addition, during class she got the chance to expend energy physically, which helped purge a lot of repressed anger.

A few times her sparring partners actually laughed over the wholehearted way she practiced the self-defense maneuvers. Once, two black belts had even jokingly commented that they never wanted to unexpectedly meet her in the middle of the night in a dark alley. They had figured she would fight first and ask questions later. And they had been right. She would never give anyone the opportunity to do to her what her father had done. She would fight if she had to, even if she knew there would be no chance of winning. Fear would not control her life again. She had sworn she would die first and she had meant it.

Amy knew that there were times when Terry had wanted to ask what drove her so hard, but not once had her Sensei tried to pry into her private affairs. Besides, even if Terry had asked she wouldn't have been able to explain to her the night terrors or the feelings of helplessness that always seemed to be lurking around every corner waiting for the chance to swoop in and destroy her.

How could she tell anyone about the beast that invaded her dreams in the middle of the night and ripped apart her heart and soul while she slept?

No one would believe her, and they just might think she was crazy.

She had learned a long time ago that there were some secrets she just couldn't tell anyone. Not if she wanted to survive in a world where she had to prove she was strong.

Toni Auberry

Chapter 24

Susan knocked softly on Amy's office door, then opened it just wide enough to peek in. "Are you all right? Gary was really upset when he left here. I heard him ranting all the way down the hall, swearing with each step and mumbling something about damn pushy women."

"We had a little talk about allowing people to have their personal space." Amy said, motioning Susan to enter the room.

"Well, I hope he listened," Susan replied. "Before you showed up, I was seriously contemplating stapling his hands to the desk to keep them off me."

"I don't think you'll have to do that." Amy smiled at the mental picture that Susan's statement brought to mind. *Maybe someone should staple Gary's hands to a desk,* she thought, remembering Gary's behavior. *Then he'd learn to keep them where they belong.* "The problem with Gary should be cleared up now," she said, "but if not, just bring it to my attention, and I'll take care of it."

"I really don't expect anything else to happen," Susan said. "At least not while you're at the office. Usually when you're nearby he doesn't try any of his little tricks. I think you scare him a little."

"Guys like Gary scare me more than just a little, but I wouldn't let him know that. He'd use it like a weapon against me."

"He does seem like the type that could get vicious."

"That's the impression I get too. Which of course is the reason why it was extremely hard for me to say anything to him. But I made myself do it anyway. And I'm glad I did. At least now I think we've reached an understanding about one thing—he knows to keep his hands to himself."

"Maybe…but I wouldn't bet on it. His hands have a tendency to go places where they shouldn't go. From the way he acts, I'd say it is second nature for him."

"Has this happened before?" Amy asked with concern. "If it has…you haven't said anything to me about it."

"I didn't want to bother you. I was afraid I was overreacting. But this morning, his hands did wander a little too far. I was considering placing an elbow into his crotch when you showed up. Too bad I didn't get the chance. That would have gotten his attention better than any lecture."

"Do you want to fill out a written complaint? I don't have any problem with that."

"No, not this time. But if it happens again I will." Susan looked down at the packet containing the information from

Thompson's Supply that Amy had requested earlier. "Are you ready to start on this now, or would you prefer I come back later?"

"Let's do it later," Amy said. "I've decided to work on a couple of other things first. I'll let you know when I'm ready."

+++++

As soon as Susan left the room, Amy called Edward. She wanted to find out what information he had on the painting of the little girl. She knew she had to phrase her questions carefully so he wouldn't start an unwelcome interrogation.

Edward answered his phone after the first ring. "Hi, Amy."

"How did you know it was me?" she asked.

"Caller ID. Remember I had it installed last month so I could screen my calls."

Amy didn't want to waste time on small talk, so she didn't comment on his statement. Instead, she asked about the painting. "Do you remember the name of the antique shop where you found that precious painting you gave me? I'd really like to try to trace it back to its original owner." Amy crossed her fingers, waiting anxiously for Edward's reply. *He had to remember. If he didn't—*

"Why? That sounds like a lot of trouble to me."

"When I described it to someone at work they thought the painting might be valuable. So I thought I would try to find some information about where it came from."

"Really?" Edward chuckled. "If it turns out to be worth a million dollars you won't forget about me, will you? I should be entitled to at least half. After all, I did buy it for you."

"Oh, I'll think about it if you promise to behave yourself."

"I don't know what you're talking about. I'm always on my best behavior. Just ask Ellen, she'll tell you."

"You might be surprised at her response. Some days you can get awful bossy with her. You know, if you really want to keep her happy you need to quit trying to control her."

"What in the world are you talking about?" Edward paused for a moment, thinking over what Amy had just said. "I don't really do that, do I?"

"Yes, you do. Just like Dad used to do with Mom. But that's not what I wanted to talk with you about right now."

"You can't just drop a statement like that in my lap and then back off without explaining yourself. I don't act like Dad. He bullied Mom all the time, and I don't do that to Ellen."

"Maybe you should stop and listen to the way you talk to her. You're not nearly as bad as Dad, but you could get that way if you're not careful. As long as Ellen agrees with you then everything goes smoothly. But if she wants to do things a little bit differently than you do, I can tell you exactly what happens. It gets done your way or not at all."

"Now Amy, I think you're exaggerating just a little."

"Like I said…you need to pay attention to the way you treat your wife. You might be surprised by what you find."

"I doubt it," Edward replied sharply, a little annoyed by Amy's statements.

"I'll make you a deal," Amy said. "For one week I want you to be very attentive to everything you say to Ellen, especially when she disagrees with you. And I want you to think about the times over the last six months that you and Ellen have had conflicts and how those disagreements were settled. You might be a little shocked by what you discover."

"If I'm that bad, why hasn't Ellen said something about it?"

"She loves you too much to say anything. She goes along with what you say because she doesn't want to cause any problems. But, sooner or later she's going to get fed up with it. I'm warning you…if you want to keep her happy you really need to start letting her have more say in your marriage."

"Maybe you're just putting some of your bad feelings toward Dad on to me."

"That's a possibility, but still, what's it going to hurt if you just take note of how you're acting around Ellen?"

"All right, you've made your point. I'll do it for one week, but I still think you're wrong."

"We'll see," Amy said. "Now back to the reason I called. What about the painting?"

"If you think the painting might be worth something, why don't you take it to a reputable art dealer and have him give you an appraisal? That would be the smartest thing to do."

"Maybe later. Right now I only want to do a little research on my own. I doubt if it's really worth much. I'm just curious for my own personal reasons."

For a few seconds only silence came across the line. Amy felt her heart racing, as though she was waiting to hear if she had won the lottery.

"I believe the name of the shop was Cherished Treasures," Edward finally replied. "It's located over near Sixth and Jefferson. You could call first to see if that's the place. The number should be in the phone book."

"Thanks, I'll let you know if I find out anything interesting."

"Especially if it involves a lot of money."

"I promise," Amy laughed, "you'll be the first one I'll tell."

+++++

"A painting with a girl and dog?" the owner of Cherished Treasures asked. "I think I know which one you mean. Some guy in a fancy suit came in this morning asking about that same painting. He said it used to be his grandmother's and that it had been auctioned off by mistake. He was very insistent about trying to locate it. He wanted to buy it back."

"Did he leave his name?" Amy asked hopefully, her mind flooding with excitement.

"Yes, and a phone number. He wanted me to call if I remembered anything about the person who had bought the painting. I told him it would be very unlikely since I'm not one for details. I just buy and sell. I don't keep track of everyone that comes into the shop."

"Do you still have that information?" Amy asked, her heart suddenly fluttering like a butterfly in her chest. *He had to still have that name and phone number.*

"Hang on a minute. I'll have to check. I had it written down on a scrap of paper, but I threw it away this morning. Didn't think I would have any cause to use it. Fortunately for you I haven't emptied the trash yet, so it should still be there."

Before Amy had the chance to respond, she heard the phone at the other end being not so gently laid down, and then silence came over the line. As she impatiently waited for the owner of the store to return, her fingers unbiddenly wrapped themselves tighter around the receiver. *What if he couldn't find that piece of paper?*

But he had to have it, Amy thought anxiously. He had to. Everything depends on it.

At that very moment, she needed that name more than she needed to breathe. She clutched the phone, her fingers attempting to imprint their image on the receiver. *Who would have ever thought that my whole life would suddenly revolve around one small scrap of paper lying at the bottom of a stranger's wastebasket?*

Finally after several long, suspense-filled minutes, the shop owner's voice came back on the line. "You're one lucky lady. I found it—Mr. James Perry...555-1212."

"Thank you for going to all this trouble." Amy said, hastily scribbling the information down on her notepad. "You have no idea how much you have helped me."

"No problem. Come by my shop any time and look the place over. We get new stuff in every day. If you come in this week I'll give you a great deal on a beautiful landscape painting I got in only this week."

"I may just do that. Thanks again for your help." Amy placed the receiver down and instantly felt like laughing. It was too good to be true. How could she have gotten this lucky this fast? Maybe fate really meant for her to help that poor child.

Amy wondered what would be in store for her next. She thought about some of the strange twists of fate that had already happened to her over the years. Though there had been plenty, none of them had seemed as strange as this one.

Who would have ever thought she'd be ghost hunting?

Not sure what to think of the new development, Amy carefully contemplated what to do next. If this Perry guy really wanted his painting back, she might have a big problem on her hands. She wasn't going to give it up without a fight. The painting was the link that drew the child to her, and if she lost it, she might lose that connection. Then it would be impossible for her to help. And for some reason, there was an urgency in her need to help the girl…an urgency even she didn't understand.

After much deliberation, Amy finally picked up the phone and dialed Mr. Perry's number. She really didn't have a choice. Unless she could find some information on the child in the painting, it would be impossible to unravel the mystery of the sorrowful spirit that had stolen her heart.

As she nervously waited for Mr. Perry to answer his phone, she frantically tried to think of what she wanted to say. Telling a perfect stranger she was seeing and hearing ghosts really wouldn't be the smartest thing for her to do.

Amy felt breathless. After each unanswered ring echoed in her ear, she became more and more tense. Just as she was about to hang up, a man's deep voice came across the phone line.

"Hello. James Perry speaking."

Not knowing what to say Amy remained silent.

"Hello...anyone there...hello."

"Mr. Perry," she finally nervously replied, "I'm Amy Tedrow. Someone informed me you were trying to find a particular painting."

"Yes, that's right. I hope you are talking about the painting from Cherished Treasures. The one with the girl and the collie."

"Well, yes...that's the one...but I had better tell you the painting was a special gift from my brother, and I'm not interested in selling. I'm just calling because I wanted to see if you know anything about the little girl in the painting. It is really important to me to find out who she was."

"Oh, are you sure you wouldn't consider letting me buy it from you?" James replied unhappily, disappointed over her response. "Someone made a huge mistake including it in the auction. The painting means something very special to me, and I would love to have it back. I promise I would give you a very fair price for it."

"It's not the price that's important," Amy said.

"I can understand how you feel. The money isn't important to me either. There's a lot of sentimental value attached to that painting. It's been in my family for years, and I hate the thought of losing it." James' voice took on a slightly pleading tone. "Are you positive you wouldn't consider selling?"

"I might think about it," Amy responded. "If you will tell me what you know about the girl in the painting."

"Why is that so important?"

"It's hard to explain, especially over the phone."

"Now you've piqued my curiosity." James replied, his interest aroused by the strange request. "If you will tell me why it's so important to know about the girl, I will give you what information I have. That is, if you also will give me the option to buy the portrait back if you change your mind about keeping it."

"I guess I don't have any choice, do I?" Amy reluctantly agreed.

"Not really. We're kind of in a stalemate, aren't we? Listen, right now I'm in the middle of an important business matter, so I really don't have time to get into this. Could we meet for lunch tomorrow?"

"I think it could be arranged. How about meeting me at the Outcast over on Main at twelve-thirty?"

"Sure, I know where that is. I'll be wearing a navy-blue suit with a white carnation in my lapel, just like those gangsters in the movies. But I promise I won't be carrying a gun in my briefcase."

Amy laughed. "I'll be the harried-looking woman in a red pantsuit. We're installing a new computer system at work so I'm afraid you're going to find me a little stressed out."

"I promise not to make it any worse on you. I want to get on your good side. I really would like to talk you into selling me that painting."

"I don't think you're going to be able to do that, but we can talk about it tomorrow at lunch."

"Deal—tomorrow at lunch. See you there."

+++++

Amy placed the receiver down in its cradle, but before her hand had released its hold, the phone rang.

"You have a call on line two," Susan said.

"Do you know who it is?" Amy didn't really feel like talking right now. She had too much to think about.

"Some guy with a very sexy voice. He must be pretty determined to talk with you. I put him on hold over five minutes ago, and he's still there."

"Well, if he's that determined, I wouldn't want to disappoint him. I'll take the call in here."

Punching the button for line two, Amy wondered who could possible be calling. It couldn't be Edward; Susan would have recognized his voice.

"Hello, this is Amy Tedrow. How may I be of assistance?"

"Oh, I can think of several ways," Ted's husky voice answered her.

"Ted! Why are you calling? Do you have to cancel for tonight?" She hoped not. She really wanted to see him. Because of Raphael of course. There were a million questions she needed to ask him.

"I'm impressed. You recognized my voice."

"I did just talk to you yesterday," she replied a little snappishly. The sound of his voice had sent a warm flush all the way through her body, and it irritated her.

"But you didn't talk nearly long enough. Remember, you hung up on me after only a few minutes."

"I didn't hang up on you. There was someone knocking at my door, and I couldn't talk," Amy defensively replied. "And right now I'm in the middle of an important business matter and can't talk either." She didn't understand what was happening. Just the sound of Ted's voice had sent strange tingles through her body; even her toes were feeling it.

"How can I get to know you if you can't take the time to talk to me?" Ted asked, his voice soft and sensuous. "And I do want us to get to know each other."

"I'm...I'm busy right now," Amy quickly replied, her voice suddenly acquiring a little tremor. "Tonight. We'll talk tonight when you come over."

"So, the date is still on then?"

Amy almost dropped the phone. *Date? What date?* She hadn't made any date! He was only supposed to be coming over to talk about Raphael. Nothing had been said about the meeting being more than that. Flustered, she began to stammer over her words. "I didn't...I mean...its not...well, it's not exactly a date."

Hearing the change in Amy's voice, Ted realized he had somehow upset her. Not wanting to cause any further damage he quickly changed the subject. "Since we're both working so late this evening why don't I stop and pick up some Chinese for supper? We'll both feel better after we eat something, and then we can relax a little while we talk about Raphael."

"I...I...don't know," Amy said.

"I'll bring the food, and you can supply the dishes," Ted hastily replied. "See you tonight at seven." He didn't want to give Amy the chance to decline, so he hurriedly said good-bye and hung up.

Sitting at the desk with the phone still in her hand, Amy thought about calling Ted back and canceling. All of a sudden it didn't seem like such a good idea to have a man she didn't really know come to the house when there wouldn't be anyone else around. She had no idea if Ted could really be trusted

Unfortunately the last man she had trusted enough to go out on a date with had turned out to be totally untrustworthy. That awful experience had happened over two years ago, and she still hadn't forgotten about it. It had been a total fiasco...the original date from hell.

Amy sighed heavily and leaned back in her chair as another of her memories took control of her mind.

The date had started out innocently enough, she thought, *but then, most dates generally do.*

The danger in dating usually occurs after the crowds are gone and couples are alone. Private moments of togetherness have led to years of secret pain for many women. Unfortunately, date rape is very real and happens more often than most people can imagine. Each year its terrible impact destroys the confidence and self-esteem of countless women. The trouble is most people aren't aware of how frequently it really does occur because so few women actually report it.

She had heard stories and read the statistics about date rape, but had foolishly thought nothing like that would ever happen to her. There had been enough pain in her life without the pain of that type of betrayal. She had sense enough to choose her dates carefully...or at least she had thought she had. But just like her father's destructive nature had been expertly hidden behind his political image, Billy's violent temperament had been hidden behind sweet smiles and gentle caresses.

She and Billy had gone on three dates before he finally showed his true colors. Twice they had gone to supper and then a movie, and once they had gone to a concert. Afterwards there had been a few goodnight kisses in the front seat of his car. Nothing serious ever happened, no fighting off unwanted touches, nothing to indicate that Billy couldn't be trusted. In fact, she had actually begun to feel fairly comfortable in his presence.

She should have been smart enough not to do that!

Chapter 25

August 13, 1996
6:30 PM

Billy arrived for their date driving a brand-new, blazing-red Corvette with black leather seats. His blond, shoulder-length hair was pulled back and tied in a ponytail, showing off the solitary diamond stud in his left ear. He wore a tight, black T-shirt that outlined his biceps and black jeans that hugged his hips perfectly.

"What do you think about this beauty?" Billy asked, his eyes lovingly glancing at his new acquisition. "Isn't she the most perfect thing you've ever seen?"

"Well, it certainly is...*red,*" Amy replied, her eyes squinting against the glare of the afternoon sun as it radiated off the car's brightly polished finish.

"Is that all you can say? This car is one of the sleekest vehicles made for the road today. I'd think you'd be able to say something more about it than to just say it's red. In fact, the odometer has only got twenty-five miles on it and half of that I put on driving it over here to show you. That makes her a virgin to the highway and makes me the lucky one who gets to break her in." Billy grinned and placed an arm around Amy's waist pulling her close to his side. "I love breaking in new things."

Amy artfully avoided a kiss as she slipped out of Billy's possessive hold. "It must have cost a fortune. Where in the world did you get that kind of money? Only last month you were complaining about not having enough cash to pay your rent. Remember…that's why your brother moved into your apartment…to help share expenses."

"When I want something bad enough I can always find a way to get it," Billy said, locking his fingers around Amy's wrist in an attempt to drag her back into his embrace. "And what I want right now is you sitting beside me as we do some serious cruising."

"We're not going anywhere if you don't release my arm." Amy replied angrily, as she attempted to break from Billy's tight grasp. When she finally was able to pull away, she accidentally stumbled and fell against his Corvette, and in the process she left an almost indistinguishable handprint on the car's shiny, perfectly-polished hood.

"Damn it!" Billy shouted. "Watch what you're doing." He immediately took a handkerchief from the back pocket of his jeans and wiped the print away, buffing the hood until it gleamed spotlessly again.

"What in the world is your problem?" Amy asked, her eyes growing wide with astonishment over Billy's bizarre reaction to the incident. "It's only a little smudge for goodness sake."

Billy didn't respond to Amy's question. Instead he stuffed his handkerchief into his pocket and got back into the Corvette. "Are you coming or not?" he finally asked.

Amy hesitated for a moment, then opened the car door and joined Billy without saying a word.

+++++

Five miles down the road, Amy could tell that Billy was still angry. His lips were pursed tightly together, a strange glint was flashing from his eyes, and he hadn't spoken a single word.

"Billy, if you don't stop acting like this, you can take me back home," Amy said, nervously clutching the small black purse she was carrying.

"Acting like what? All I'm doing is driving." Billy retorted with a sharp bite to his words. Then before Amy had the chance to respond he suddenly turned off the street and whipped the Corvette into the parking lot of a seedy-looking apartment complex.

"Hey, I thought we were going to a party at Andria's," Amy said. "Why are you stopping here?" She anxiously glanced out the window and was surprised by the height of the weed patches that were growing from multiple cracks in the poorly paved lot. She also saw several older cars with dented scratched fenders and quickly realized that the Corvette didn't belong among them.

Without warning a prickly sensation tingled at the back of Amy's neck, and she realized that something just didn't seem right.

"I have to pick up some supplies for the party," Billy answered nonchalantly. Avoiding the questioning look lingering in Amy's eyes, he carefully backed the Corvette into a parking space near the front of the building. "Tim left his stuff here and didn't have time to come back and get it, so I told him I would pick it up."

"I thought Tim was supposed to be out of town all week."

"Well, you thought wrong," Billy replied crossly.

Amy wasn't sure exactly how to respond to Billy's churlish statement, so she just didn't say anything. Instead, she warily scanned the area around the car. Finally she said, "I'm really surprised that you'd even consider parking this car here. Especially after the way you reacted earlier today."

Billy glanced oddly at Amy before he reached down and turned the engine off. The strange look in his eyes made Amy feel even more apprehensive, although she didn't exactly know why.

"Tim got back in town earlier then he had planned," Billy said, ignoring Amy's remark about the car. "Which means he gets to party with us tonight, but you know how he is. He's lucky he remembers his own name some days. He forgot to bring his stuff over to Andria's, so I told him I would help him out and stop by his apartment and get it."

Billy stepped from the Corvette and finally smiled, his anger apparently fading from his mind. "You might as well come in and wait. I have to make an important phone call while I'm here, and it might take some time. No sense in staying out here by yourself." He pulled a set of apartment keys from his pocket and stood by the car door waiting expectantly for Amy to follow.

As Amy reluctantly climbed the rusty, metal steps on the outside of the building to reach the entrance to Tim's apartment, she looked with dismay at the peeling paint on all the doors. The sordid condition of the building reminded her of the apartment complex she had to live in when she attended college. She had never felt safe there. And as they walked through Tim's front door, that same uncomfortable feeling from years ago began churning in the pit of her stomach.

"At least it doesn't look as bad inside," she said, quickly glancing around the living room. "I don't see any cockroaches crawling up the walls."

"Not everyone has a cushy job like yours and can afford to live like you do," Billy replied sharply. "Some men have to work their asses off to even have enough money for a place like this. Tim is doing the best he can."

"I'm sorry. I didn't mean to sound offensive." Amy suddenly remembered Billy had once told her that as a child he had been homeless on more than one occasion because of his father's explosive temper. Apparently he had spent a good deal of time in domestic violence shelters with his mother and younger brother, Steve, while they waited until it was for them to return home. Unfortunately, his home hadn't been a very nice place to go back to.

"Why don't you make yourself comfortable on the couch? You can take your shoes off and relax a little, and I'll join you when I get done." Billy went into the kitchen and rummaged through the refrigerator, found a beer, popped it open and took a couple of quick swigs from it. Then he picked up the portable phone lying on the kitchen counter and carried it into the bedroom to make his call in private.

Amy removed her shoes, curled up on the couch, and started thumbing through a magazine. But she had difficulty concentrating because her thoughts kept drifting elsewhere. She couldn't understand why Billy was so upset, and the uneasiness that was stalking her increased as she listened to Billy speaking on the phone in the other room. Although she wasn't trying to hear what was being said, she couldn't tune him out. He was talking too loudly for that.

She tried to concentrate on the magazine. After all, Billy's business was really no concern of hers. But when the tone in his voice changed, becoming louder and more forceful, she felt a tightness clutching at her chest that told her something was definitely wrong. The feeling continued to grow as she listened to Billy's footsteps pacing across the floor as he kept talking.

"Listen Tim," Billy almost shouted, "you promised me I could have the apartment all night. You know my brother has company over at my place tonight. What kind of a friend are you? Damn it, I have plans! You can't change your mind now. You'd better not show up here. I don't care if you don't have anywhere else to go. Stay away from here."

Amy heard Billy slam the phone down so hard that the noise echoed throughout the apartment

Feeling more and more troubled as each second passed, she closed the magazine and laid it down on the couch. *Why did he need the apartment all night?* Instinct told her something wasn't right, but unfortunately she didn't listen to the inner voice that had started whispering urgently in her ear telling her to get up and leave.

Billy strolled back into the room with a cocky smile plastered on his face. He popped open another can of beer and almost downed it in one swallow. Then he plopped down on the couch next to Amy and tried to put his arm around her shoulders.

But she wasn't in any mood to be touched. The moment his arm slide behind her she immediately stood up. When he grabbed her hand and forcibly pulled her back down beside him, she struggled to keep her fear under control.

"What's your hurry?" Billy said with a laugh. "We've got plenty of time yet. They're not expecting us at Andria's for an hour or so. Let's party a little bit here first." He shoved his can of beer in her face and grinned. "Here, have a drink. I think you need to loosen up a little bit."

The note of expectancy in Billy's voice disturbed Amy, but she tried not to let it bother her too much. *After all,* she thought, *I'm twenty-four, and surely I'm smart enough to handle him if the situation gets out of hand.* So instead of leaving the apartment...as instinct told her to...she took the beer from Billy's hand and reluctantly took a couple of small swallows.

"Come on Honey, relax a little," Billy whispered soft and sweet into Amy's ear. "I only want to spend some time alone with you. Isn't this much better than snuggling in the front seat of my car?"

The warmth of Billy's breath tickled against Amy's skin, and a pleasant, heated rush made her stomach flutter. Her nagging fears quickly melted away as he seductively pushed her hair away from the nape of her neck and placed tiny little kisses there. His gentle touch was pleasurable, so she didn't push him away. Those few little kisses weren't hurting anything, and it had been a long time since a man had touched her that way.

Billy turned Amy so they were face to face, and his lips moved slowly toward hers. Gently, he kissed her, their lips almost not even touching. His hand lightly traveled up her arm, his fingertips barely touching her skin, as he expertly stoked the fire building deep within her.

He made her forget that something had felt very wrong only minutes before. The annoying apprehension that had been lurking stealthy in the back of her mind quietly receded where it didn't bother her anymore. *I was only being foolish, there isn't anything to be afraid of,* she thought. *What could possibly happen?*

Billy sat back on the couch with one of his arms draped around Amy and pulled her up against him so her head rested on his shoulder. "Now, doesn't this feel nice," he said as they snuggled. "Just you and me, and nobody to bother us. We can do anything we like without worrying about someone watching."

They stayed that way for a few minutes. No words were spoken as Amy sat gently nestled within Billy's protective embrace. It was so quiet in the room that she heard a bird singing right outside of the apartment. The familiar sound made her feel even more secure, and she rested peacefully in what seemed like a sanctuary from the uncomfortable feeling that had flowed through her only a few minutes earlier.

She turned, looking into Billy's eyes for a sign of compassion and maybe even love, and she felt a need within her heart for tenderness, for comfort, for human contact. So she returned his kiss.

But the kiss quickly became something different than what she had intended. The moment her lips touched his, an unexpected sense of urgency arose from Billy, and his gentleness completely vanished. The sudden change overwhelmed her, and she tried to break away, but he wouldn't let go. He wouldn't let her end the kiss, and his arms instantly transformed from a place of comfort to one of entrapment.

Billy positioned one of his hands behind Amy's head so she couldn't pull away. His tongue forced its way into her mouth like a slithering snake. He actually pressed so hard with his mouth that her teeth cut into the backside of her lips, and the taste of her blood intermingled with the taste of fear.

Amy pushed with both of her hands forcefully against Billy's chest and finally broke free, but her freedom lasted only for a fraction of a second. He quickly grabbed her again and pulled her tightly up against his body. Then before she could utter one word of protest, his mouth covered hers again.

While one of Billy's hands continued to hold her head in place, Amy felt the other one move downward. Her alarm skyrocketed when she realized what he planned to do. When she felt his hand up under her skirt, she jerked her head back so sharply her neck twisted, sending sharp pains down her spine. But she didn't even acknowledge it. Her only thoughts were on getting free. She reached up to slap him, but wasn't quick enough.

He saw the movement and swiftly seized her hand, bending it backward at the wrist.

A deep moan escaped her lips as she cried out in pain.

A look of disgust instantly crossed Billy's face, and he shoved her away from him.

"What the hell was that all about?" Amy demanded to know, bounding off the couch the moment Billy released her. She reached for her shoes and as she bent down to pick them up, he leaped from the couch and knocked her down with a powerful push from behind. When she fell to the floor, her shoes flew from her hands and landed across the room. She lay sprawled on the floor like a tossed rag doll. Her eyes stared up at Billy in shock. "Keep away from me!" She cried out, her voice shaking from the fear controlling her mind. "Don't you dare come any closer!" she shouted. And for a moment she was seven years old again with her father standing like a towering giant over her small body.

But then she was brought back into the present by the fury in Billy's voice.

"You dumb cunt. What in the hell is your problem? What are you a lesbian or something?" Animosity shadowed Billy's face as he stood over Amy with his hands clutched in tight fists.

"Please, just let me leave," Amy pleaded. "I want to go home."

"Who do you think you are?" Billy asked angrily. "You can't throw yourself at me for weeks and then do nothing about it. You're nothing but a god-damn, prick-teasing whore."

"Please," Amy started to beg but then she looked at Billy and realized he hadn't heard a single word she had said. Her desperate pleas hadn't even reached his ears. Her eyes followed him as he took a step toward her, and she knew from the look on his face that he wouldn't stop. She had seen that same look upon her father's face enough times to know what would happen next.

She quickly recognized the disadvantage of being down on the floor and reacted more out of instinct than anything else. As soon as Billy stepped within the range of her feet, she immediately kicked up, aiming for a knee in hopes of breaking it. *If he can't walk, he can't chase me,* she thought as her foot made contact.

The kick didn't break anything, but it knocked him off balance, and he fell...except not in the direction she had expected him to. Instead of falling backward, he did a strange twist and toppled forward landing directly on top of her.

She flinched from the agonizing pain of his weight plummeting full force upon her right leg, but she didn't cry out. Her mind was too busy trying to find a way to escape. Pain took second place to fear.

For a moment, they lay on the floor side by side, each holding their own injured leg. Both were shocked by what had just happened—Amy by the suddenly brutal attack and Billy by the fact that Amy was fighting back.

Then fear sent Amy moving. Scooting back away from Billy, she used the couch to pull up. The front door was only a few feet away, and all she could think about was getting out of the apartment before he had a chance to stop her.

As she attempted to hobble past him, he reached over, grabbed her good leg at the ankle, and pulled. When she had to shift all of her weight on to the injured leg, she lost her balance and went down again.

Terrified, she lay on the floor trying not to let panic take over. She realized that to survive she was going to have to outthink Billy because it was definitely going to be too tough to outfight him.

Unfortunately Billy managed to get back up on his feet before she did.

"Damn it!" he shouted, "you just can't lead a man on and not expect to finish the job. You've been crawling all over me for weeks with all that kissing and hugging, and now you think you can walk away without doing anything." Infuriated he kicked out, planting his foot heavily into her ribs.

Painful spasms shot through Amy's chest making it almost impossible to breathe. Attempting to scream, the most she could accomplish was a weak whisper. "No! Don't!"

Billy reached down, grabbed her hair and wrapped it firmly around his fist. He yanked her up, spun her around, and locked her arm behind her back. Then he forced her into the bedroom where he angrily flung her down on the bed, tearing at her blouse as she went down. "You stupid bitch, you're going to pay for this! Who in the hell do you think you are treating me this way? Women beg me to fuck them; I don't have to take this kind of treatment from any whore like you."

Shocked, Amy stared down at her torn blouse. The buttons had been ripped off, and her breasts lay exposed under the ripped material. She shuddered; the black bra that had looked so sexy this morning suddenly didn't seem sexy any more. She started to pull the ripped pieces of her blouse back together, but then realized her skirt had gathered up around her hips. She didn't know which to cover up first.

She reached down to tug at her skirt, but before she had the chance to do anything, Billy slapped her hands away and shoved her down flat on the bed. Then he pulled her skirt up even higher and grabbed the edge of her new, black-lace panties and jerked hard.

"Did you buy this black underwear for me?" he asked, laughing cruelly as he dangled the torn lace in front of Amy's face. "Well, you did a good job picking it out. I'm really turned on by it."

The sound of the ripping material had almost made Amy faint, but she knew if that happened there would be no escaping her fate. So she struggled to keep her mind in control. Pushing and shoving with all of her strength, she finally managed to escape Billy's groping hands for a few seconds.

She started to scream, but before the sound even reached her lips, Billy backhanded her hard across the mouth. A trickle of blood formed at the corner of her lip where his college class ring had cut into it, and then a loud buzzing started ringing in her ears. She had to fight to keep from losing consciousness.

"Keep your fucking mouth shut, you bitch," he hissed in Amy's ear as he unbuckled his belt. "If you want to open it I've got something big to fill it with right here in my pants."

Amy knew she had to find a way to escape, and she desperately tried to remember some of the self-defense maneuvers from karate class. She could hear her Sensei's voice in her ear lecturing, "If you want to survive you have to be able to use your mind. Think, don't just react. Don't let fear do your thinking for you."

She reached backward to the bedside table, and her fingers found a heavy glass ashtray. Grasping it firmly, she waited for the right moment. As Billy unzipped his pants and started to pull them down, she went into action, kicking him in the stomach with every ounce of strength she had left. She visualized driving her foot straight through his body and sent all of her energy at him. When he doubled over from the pain of the impact, she hit him on the temple with the ashtray just as hard as she could.

Billy collapsed onto the floor moaning and cussing at the same time, and at that moment Amy vaulted off the bed. Without even thinking about her injured leg, she ran from the bedroom, out the front door, and down the apartment stairs. Leaving her shoes, the only thing she grabbed going out the door was the car keys lying on the bookcase by the front door.

She raced toward Billy's car, running barefoot and trying to hold her blouse together. She fumbled frantically with the keys and somehow managed to open the car door and get inside before she saw him charging out of the building. Shaken badly by what had just happened, she almost didn't react fast enough to lock the doors before he reached her.

Billy pounded on the windows of his car like a maniac as he screamed at her. "You god-damn fucking whore, get out of my car or I'm going to report you to the police! You can't take my car, it's mine!"

"Watch me!" she shouted. Ignoring his bellowing, she put the keys in the ignition, started the car, and pulled out of the parking lot.

Billy followed her cussing and screaming. "Damn it, I said get out of my car! I'll have you arrested for stealing, you stupid, dumb slut! Get out of my car right now!" He kept beating on the windows until he was no longer able to keep pace with the moving vehicle. "You have no right to do this!" he yelled as the car finally pulled away, leaving him standing all alone in the parking lot.

+++++

Shaken and still frightened, Amy somehow managed to drive to Edward's house without having an accident. From there, Ellen took her to the police station where she filed charges against Billy. This time she didn't sit back and remain silent. She stood her ground and fought back against the violence that had been forced upon her. Unfortunately, the rest of the day proved to be just about as traumatic as the battle with Billy. She had to go to the emergency room to be checked out by a physician, then return to the police station to fill out more forms.

The police made her feel as though they were trying to find a way to blame her for the violence. Some of the questions they kept asking were really hard to deal with. They almost made her believe that she was at fault by simply being present in the apartment. "Why did you go up to the apartment alone with him?" they asked, insinuating she was responsible for the attack. "If you were worried about your safety, why did you stay? Did you at any time tell him no?"

Finally Ellen became upset and called a friend of hers who was an excellent lawyer and advocate for women's rights. Ten minutes later the lawyer arrived at the police department and began chastising the officers. "Amy is not the criminal in this case," she voiced loudly, her dark green eyes flashing like lightening in a wild storm, "and you had better stop treating her like she is, or you may find yourself facing some lawsuit of your own."

Then Amy and Ellen were quickly spirited from the station.

+++++

The next few months turned out to be an extension of that terrible experience in the apartment, but Amy refused to drop the charges against Billy. She didn't want him to feel he could just go out and attack someone else and get away with it.

During the trial three other women found the nerve to come forward and tell their stories. She hadn't been Billy's first assault, but the other women had been too frightened to say anything. He had threatened to kill them if they did, and they had believed him. Yet somehow they found the strength and courage to come forward at the trial and finally put an end to their silent pain. When it was all over with, Billy was sentenced to three years in prison for attempted rape.

+++++

After that traumatic experience with Billy, she had no desire to date again. The price of dating was simply too high. She no longer had faith in her own judgment. She had thought Billy was someone that could be trusted, and look how wrong she had been on that account.

To her, men were experts in deception. They could disguise evil so easily behind their innocent smiles. What socializing she did now was always done in groups. The very thought of Ted coming over to her house when no one else was going to be around was more than a bit frightening. It was actually starting to scare her.

However, after thinking about it for a while, she decided to take a chance with Ted. She couldn't imagine someone who had raised and trained Raphael could possibly be a threat. Besides, he appeared to be a close friend of Edward's, and her brother wouldn't socialize with someone who wasn't honorable.

Maybe it wouldn't hurt to give Ted a chance to prove himself, she thought as she sat at her desk trying to concentrate on her work. Anyway, for some strange reason she just couldn't bring herself to pick up the phone and cancel their meeting.

Besides, she really did like Chinese food, and she was very hungry.

Chapter 26

Ted felt very confused after talking with Amy. The feelings that were taking over his mind...and his heart...were very strong, and he wasn't sure exactly how to cope with them. It had been a long time since he'd had a need to be in a certain woman's presence, and it wasn't because he'd been living like a monk the past few years. There had been a few times he had sought the warmth of a woman's touch, but there never had been anything permanent in any of the relationships on either his part or the women's. The joinings had simply been for comfort and companionship, two lonely people reaching out to share an intimate moment in a time of mutual need. No uncontrolled burning desires had ever heated the sheets covering him and his lovers, at least not since his ex-wife, Kathy, had left him. Instead there had only been a quiet need for a warm gentle touch that had drawn them together to share a moment or two of their lives. The women he had been involved with had made no great impact on him, or he on them. In fact, all of the ladies had already moved on to different lives in distant places, and he didn't even know where they were or what they were doing.

Ted frowned and thought about the conversation that had just occurred between him and Amy. She had been about ready to withdraw the invitation to her house tonight. He had sensed that by the change in the tone of her voice. That's why he had ended their conversation so abruptly. He hadn't wanted to give her the chance to cancel. More than anything he really wanted to see her again. Their short meeting at Edward's house had brought out feelings he thought didn't exist anymore, and he didn't want them to disappear again. The need to be with and to belong to someone had been gone too long from his life already, and he wanted it back. For the first time in years there existed something more on his mind than just work. It felt good to know Kathy hadn't totally shattered his heart. Some of the pieces must be mending back together; otherwise, why would he be so strongly attracted to Amy?

A burning desire started stirring deep down in his soul. Simply the act of bringing up an image of Amy in his mind sent him off on a wave of heartfelt emotions. He wanted to touch her...to pull her body into his...to feel the warmth of her skin against his...to smell the perfumed fragrance of her hair...to feel the silky touch of her lips...to see a look of wanton desire simmering in her beautiful hazel eyes.

A rush of heat suddenly flashed through Ted's body causing him to reach up and wipe sweat from his forehead. He grinned at the strange reaction. He was going to have to find a way to convince

Amy to go out with him. If he didn't...well, he would be in big trouble. They would have to lock him up and hose him down with cold water every hour.

Ted leaned back in his chair and let his mind go where it wanted to go. He closed his eyes and felt himself being swept into a world of long forgotten erotic sensations. The other night, when Amy had accidentally brushed her breasts against his chest, he had instantly thought about carrying her away to a secluded room and covering her body with kisses. He had wanted to touch every part of her, to devour her with his senses, to become one with her. He had needed to hear the heated sigh of passion in her voice and feel the warmth of her breath upon his skin. And now that he was alone and far away from her, all he wanted to do was to get next to her again.

How could someone he had just met become so important so fast? Why did he suddenly feel as though he were only half of a whole without her?

A sweltering fire burned within him; he wanted to do more than to just kiss Amy. He wanted everything. He wanted to give to her all he had and take all she had to give.

Unable to concentrate on his work, he started pacing the floor trying to think of a way to get near her without scaring her off. He moved restlessly from one side of the office to the other without even being aware of what he was doing. He had realized right away that Amy was a person who wouldn't be easy to get close to. There was just something about her that let him know that he had better stand clear and keep his distance. For some reason, if he got within a couple of feet of her, she tensed up. Her actions reminded him of how a deer reacts when it hears a strange sound in the bushes. At the first sign of danger, the deer will freeze and listen intently for changes in the woods surrounding her. The animal's muscles become taut as it makes ready to take flight. Its eyes automatically scan everything looking for a route of escape. Its heart begins to race as it prepares to run. And that's exactly how Amy acted.

At Edward's party, every time he managed to get close to her, he had seen those flight mechanisms kick in. Once he had even wanted to reach over and take her pulse just to see how fast her heart was beating. He had instinctively known that if he had tried to kiss her she would have fled like a frightened deer. So it had been a great surprise when she had unexpectedly looked up with those fantastic eyes of hers and then kissed him goodbye at the end of the party. Even though it had only been a quick peck on the cheek, he had felt more emotions at that moment than with any other kiss he had ever received.

If Amy had just waited one tiny second I'd have returned that kiss, Ted thought, standing quietly by his desk, his mind full of her image. *But instead, she fled before I had the opportunity to even try.*

Maybe I'll never get the chance, Ted thought pessimistically as he paced in his office. *Why would Amy even want to get to know me? What do I have that she would possibly want? Someone like Amy doesn't have to settle for anyone other than the best of the best, and I certainly don't fit into that category.*

Aware that he wouldn't get any work done pacing through his office like a caged animal, Ted finally forced himself to return to the pile of papers on his desk. He had a deadline to met, and he knew if he didn't get busy, he'd be the one canceling the meeting with Amy. And that was something he definitely didn't want to do.

The very thought that he might miss out on an opportunity to be alone with the most beautiful woman in the world quickly brought him back to reality. So with a sigh of resignation he reluctantly picked up his pen and started writing.

+++++

While Ted was slaving over his paperwork, Amy was putting hers away. She couldn't concentrate and had finally decided to call it a day. *Everything will still be here tomorrow*, she thought as she surrendered to the urgent need to escape. *For once I'm going to leave the office on time. Tonight I actually have something more important to do than paperwork.*

As she locked her office door, Amy noticed that Gary's beady snake-eyes were watching every movement she made, and she strongly considered talking to her boss concerning the possibility of getting a new consultant to take Gary's place. But since she was unsure if the problems with Gary were real or if they were the result of personal conflicts, she changed her mind.

+++++

While she was driving home, Amy's thoughts weren't about work or Gary. Instead, she was trying to decide what to wear when Ted came over. She systematically went through her entire wardrobe

231

trying to decide what would be appropriate. It never dawned on her to wonder why she was worrying so much about her appearance.

When she finally arrived home, she found Raphael waiting expectantly at the front door. As soon as she opened it, he bounded out and streaked across the yard. "Raphael, get back here," she yelled when he ran out on the road. "You can't go over there. It's too dangerous. You have to remember that you're not out on the ranch anymore and there are some places you just can't go."

Raphael turned and trotted back into the yard, but he refused to come toward the house. Instead he started running back and forth across the yard barking wildly.

"Oh, all right. I get the message," Amy finally said. "You're not ready to go back inside."

Amy sat on the porch steps and wrapped her coat snuggly around her shoulders to keep warm. She watched Raphael leap around like a puppy as he explored everything, but this time she didn't join him. She simply wasn't in the mood. At that particular moment, it wasn't Raphael that was occupying her thoughts…it was Ted. For some reason she couldn't stop thinking about him.

He was so intriguing. The very first time she had looked into his eyes she had seen a fire blazing deep within them. She knew if she were to stare into those eyes long enough, she would melt from the heat of the flames. And she remembered how his smile had been sweet and gentle, but at the same time, wild and unrestrained…something almost sexy.

Once at Edward's…when she had to squeeze past Ted in the crowded hallway…they had stood face to face for a few moments, and she had noticed an unbridled look of passion cross his face. The kind of look that she'd seen in the old romantic movies where the hero gazes at his heroine with love. Not like in the modern movies where it's only lust that entices the actors and actresses to shed their clothes and make love on television for everyone to watch.

Amy pulled her coat tighter around her body, but she really didn't feel chilled. In the midst of the freezing cold, a gentle warmth had started pulsating from the very center of her heart. It was almost as if someone had lit a tiny fire deep inside. For the first time in years, she didn't feel totally stone-cold dead inside. She closed her eyes and relaxed letting the sensation flow freely. There came to her mind the image of Ted softly whispering how much he needed her as he pulled her into his arms to place passionate kisses upon her neck, her shoulders, her lips.

And she smiled.

And at the very moment that the smile touched her lips, there suddenly arose a voice in the air.

"NO!" a child screamed.

Amy's mind froze at the sound and for one small moment in time she was unable to react. Her heart seemed to stop beating and her lungs ceased to draw in air.

"NO! PLEASE, NO!" the child's voice screamed out again.

Amy's eyes flew open, and they immediately locked onto a nightmare scene. Only twenty feet in front of her lay Raphael

233

hideously butchered with blood spurting from a huge gapping wound in his neck. She saw a massive pool of red liquid spreading out on the frozen ground in front of him, and next to his head was an enormous butcher knife that was slowly being covered by the steady flow of blood pouring out onto the ground.

And kneeling in the middle of the terrible carnage was the ghost child who was weeping inconsolably into her blood-covered hands!

Amy couldn't believe the condition of the girl. She was literally saturated from head to toe with Raphael's blood. It ran in red streams down her hair and across her face. The blood was so thick it had soaked her nightgown, making it stick to her skin.

Amy was unable to turn away and watched with unblinking eyes as the girl raised her head. The horror she saw at that moment on the girl's blood-covered face could never be duplicated on any movie film.

Amy's heart started pounding so fast and furiously that a sharp pain shot down her left arm. For a second she thought she might be having a heart attack, but the abhorrent scene playing out in front of her eyes quickly took all thoughts away from herself.

The little girl opened her mouth to scream, but the blood that was running down her face began to pour into her mouth, and she gagged instead. In a desperate attempt to clear her throat, the girl coughed and spit frothy crimson liquid onto the pile of dirt next to Raphael's body. Then like a wounded animal she began crawling on her hands and feet trying desperately to escape the bloody carnage spread out in front of her.

Amy couldn't turn away. She couldn't run. She couldn't scream. All she could do was sit frozen by fear on the porch steps.

Finally, the emotional turmoil that was being forced upon her mind became so strong and oppressive that she started to slip into unconsciousness.

But just before she blacked out, she saw something else; something that made her skin crawl as though a thousand fire ants were marching defiantly up her back.

The child wasn't alone!

Standing off to the side of Raphael was a man dressed in dirty jeans and a torn white T-shirt. He was holding a shovel and seemed to be watching the ghost child as she struggled to stand. Amy couldn't see his face, but somehow she knew a cruel smile was turning up the corners of his mouth. She also knew that he was something born from the devil because the evil that was surrounding him actually saturated the air, and each breath she drew in seemed contaminated with the stench of his foul odor. It somehow reminded her of the awful smell of her father's favorite cologne.

As the girl's weeping escalated, Amy expected the man to go to the child, but he turned away and totally ignored her. Instead, he effortlessly bent over Raphael's body and picked the dog up, lifting him in his arms as though the animal was nothing but air.

A terrible pain ripped through Amy's heart when Raphael's head rolled to the side, widening the gaping wound in his neck and sending another spurt of blood to the ground.

Amy wanted to shout at the man to keep away from Raphael, but she couldn't make a sound. Terror overrode all of her other senses. It prevented her from speaking or even moving as she watched the man carelessly toss Raphael's limp body into a deep pit that had been dug out in the yard.

Then, very purposefully, very carefully the man picked up a shovel and begun to toss dirt into what was now Raphael's grave.

When the first shovel-full of dirt landed upon Raphael's body, Amy slumped over in a faint as a welcoming blackness brought her relief from the nightmare scene being played out in front of her.

+++++

A few minutes later Amy awoke and found herself lying across the porch steps exactly where she had fainted. And covering her face with wet, slobbery kisses was a very alive Raphael. Shocked to find him standing there in perfect health, her eyes shot immediately over to where she had seen him lying dead only minutes ago. There was nothing…no knife…no blood…no man…and no weeping child. There was nothing around her except scattered piles of frozen ground and patches of dead brown grass.

Suffering from the shock of the experience and from a chilling coldness generated deep inside, Amy couldn't think straight. Somehow she managed to get safely into the house. And once she was inside she turned the furnace up past eighty. Then she fixed a cup of hot tea and wrapped herself tightly up in a blanket at the kitchen table. She sat wondering if she might be losing her mind after all. The terrible thought that she might be going insane kept playing over and over again in her mind.

It was bad enough that she was having nightmares when she was asleep, but to start having them while she was awake was even worse. Maybe she was only deluding herself by believing the sightings of the girl were anything but the delusional fantasies of a crazy person. What else could ghosts and werewolves really be except fragments of an insane imagination? They weren't really real, were they?

Maybe I really should go see a psychiatrist. Maybe I am going crazy. Bitterly, Amy thought about asking Ted if he knew the name of a good psychiatrist, thinking that would be one way to get rid of him. Then she considered asking if he knew of a ghost hunter. She could just imagine his reaction to the news there was a very active ghost haunting her house. He would probably take Raphael and run.

Finally, not sure what to do, she did what she had always done when things started getting to be too much. She chose not to think about it. By doing this, she took away any power something could have over her. If she didn't think about it, it couldn't hurt her.

When her father beat her, she had escaped the pain by not thinking about it. In her mind, she had sent herself off to a place far away where his angry words and violent temper hadn't been able to reach her. It hadn't been possible to stop all the pain, but it had been possible to escape at least part of it.

Because of her ability to mentally escape there were several huge blank spots in her childhood memories that just couldn't be filled up. Somehow she knew those were the times she had sent herself off to another place, but exactly where it had been or how she had done it, she couldn't remember that part. But in truth, she really didn't try too hard to remember. She was simply grateful it had happened.

In fact, there was even one whole year of her life she could hardly recall at all...the year she turned eleven. It seemed the only thing she could remember of that time period is that it was the year Thomas disappeared. Without any problems at all she could remember how much she had missed him and how it had broken her heart.

But Thomas' disappearance is about all she can recall of her eleventh year. She couldn't remember what she learned at school or what Edward had done or even if her father had beaten her. A whole year of her life somehow no longer existed, and she couldn't reconstruct it, even though she had tried several times.

+++++

Amy glanced at the clock and realized that unless she got moving Ted would show up and find her looking as crazy as she felt. After a quick shower, she searched for something to wear that didn't appear to be too elaborate. She didn't want to give him the idea she had gone out of her way just because he was coming over.

She chose a new pair of jeans and a nice blue blouse and quickly dressed. When she stood back and looked in the mirror to view the results she decided that the jeans were just too casual. She immediately stripped them off and tried her favorite, gray pantsuit, but for some reason that outfit seemed so dull and lifeless.

Not wanting to look like an old-maid schoolteacher, she went searching through the closet for the third time. She finally emerged with black slacks and a red sweater. Even though she was less critical over this choice, she still wasn't completely satisfied. The black pants were a perfect fit, making her look taller and more slender, but the sweater was far too baggy. It was more like something she would wear to keep warm at a football game, not for a quiet evening at home. Knowing red was a good color for her because it blended well with her skin tone, she finally settled on another red sweater. However, this one fit a lot more snugly. Pleased with the choices, she stood in front of the mirror admiring the final outcome.

Not bad, she thought, turning to assess how the sweater and slacks accented the natural curves of her body. *Not exactly a ten but close enough to a seven to be acceptable.*

During all the changes of clothing, not once did she ever stop to question why it even mattered what she was wearing. Not one single thought was given to why it seemed important to have the "perfect" outfit on, especially since she had already convinced herself she didn't care. And a few minutes later, when Ted showed up, she didn't try to guess why her pulse suddenly seemed to speed up, or why her face flushed so profusely. She was too busy trying to tell herself what Ted thought didn't really matter at all.

Toni Auberry

Chapter 27

After Ted pulled into Amy's driveway he sat in his car a full minute nervously anticipating seeing her again. He wanted to jump out and run to the door, but at the same time he was afraid of Amy's reaction. What if she didn't want him there? Just because he found her absolutely intriguing didn't mean she would think the same thing about him. She might not want him hanging around her house. Then what would he do? Get up and leave right after they got through discussing Raphael?

He prayed with all of his heart that wouldn't happen.

Laden with several containers filled with his favorite Chinese dishes, he walked up to the front door and anxiously rang the doorbell. As he waited, each passing second seemed like hours. More than anything he wanted to spend time getting to know Amy. He was smart enough to know packages didn't always contain what was expected. Over the years he had discovered that a fantastic packaging job could cover an exceptionally terrible product. His ex-wife had been proof of that. Kathy had been exquisite looking, always wrapped up like an expensive Christmas present, but inside she had been just a plain, empty cardboard box.

As he stood at the door waiting for Amy, Ted started thinking how badly he wanted to uncover what lay underneath Amy's fantastic wrappings. He bet she wouldn't be a cardboard box like Kathy. Somehow he just knew she would be as wonderful on the inside as she looked on the outside.

When Amy finally opened the door and he saw her standing in front of him in her snugly-fitted, red sweater the only thing he could think of was how badly he wanted to start unwrapping.

"Wow! You look great!" Ted's eyes traveled over Amy's body and lingered for a second on her sweater, but then they quickly moved back to her shining eyes that seemed to be a door to her soul.

Amy was feeling very uncomfortable with the way Ted was looking at her and couldn't make herself thank him for the compliment. For a second she seriously considered slamming the door in his face and locking it tight, but that urge quickly passed when he smiled and she felt a fiery spark flaming in her heart that sent her pale cheeks blushing. She hesitantly stepped backward and opened the door wider so he could enter.

Ted immediately clued in to her uncomfortable stance and hurried inside. He didn't want to give Amy the opportunity to change her mind. "I brought dinner like I promised, so I hope you're hungry. I wasn't sure what you liked, so I got a little bit of everything." He headed for Amy's kitchen carrying the food without waiting for a reply from her. From the expression on her face he was very afraid she was going to tell him to leave.

Ted placed the containers of food on the table and looked up. When he saw her standing behind him, he smiled what he hoped was a very charming smile, because more than anything in the world he wanted to charm her…charm her right into his arms and into his life.

Amy smiled back tentatively. "Thanks for bringing dinner. I was so busy at work I didn't get the chance to eat lunch today, and I'm absolutely starved." Her hands shook slightly as she set a place for both of them at the table. She just couldn't get rid of the uncomfortable feeling that was overshadowing her every thought and gnawing at her nerves like a hungry lion crunching on the bones of its kill.

Could Ted be trusted?

As they sat at the table spooning out the delicious steaming food that Ted had brought, neither one talked. Amy was feeling too unsure of herself to start a conversation, and Ted was worrying too much about saying the wrong thing.

The silence was finally broken, not by either one of them, but by Raphael, who had gotten tired of being ignored. The dog approached Ted and nudged him with his nose as if to say, "Hey, what about me?"

"I'm sorry, Raphael, did you think I forgot about you?" Ted reached down and affectionately patted the dog. He suddenly remembered that the reason he was supposed to be there was to discuss Raphael. So he immediately launched into a discussion on the important aspects of Raphael's care and was glad to have finally discovered some common ground to establish a connection with Amy.

+++++

Once they were focused on practical matters, Amy forgot the emotional undertones that had been unconsciously playing between them. Over the years, she had discovered when she was practical she didn't have to deal with the irrational components involved with emotions. Not focusing on emotions had proven to be an effective way to survive in a world where it had been much safer not to be able to feel or need such things as love, joy, or happiness.

Being practical had helped her survive life with her father. Growing up with him had left her emotionally empty inside. He never gave love, understanding, or affection…he only took until she had no more left inside to give. The deprivation of those basic feelings had left a great void in her life—a void she had filled by thinking rationally, sensibly, and intelligently. She had learned early not to view the world from an emotional standpoint but instead, to look at it systematically. By studying the mechanics of everything around her, she had been able to close off those feelings of wanting and needing that other people had to deal with. It had made her life so much easier to survive.

If someone would have told her at that very moment she was falling in love with Ted, she would have laughed and said there wasn't such a thing as love. Love was only a biological chemical reaction that occurred between two people…in other words, love was only lust. And she had no time for such foolishness in her life.

+++++

Two hours later as she sat on the couch staring into Ted's gentle, blue eyes and listening to him talk about his father's tragic death, she wasn't thinking of rational or sensible things, nor was she trying to dissect or analyze her feelings. She simply sat next to him, letting a strange overwhelming sensation flow through her body and her soul. Ted's voice, saddened by the memories of his father, reached deep inside of her, and she felt as though his loss had been hers. She knew what it meant to grow up without the love of a father to lean on when life kicked you from behind, and she wanted to wrap her arms around him to offer comfort and peace of heart. Without realizing what she was doing, she reached over and intimately placed a hand over one of his. The need within her to touch him had become greater than her fear of being touched.

The gentle contact of Amy's hand resting upon his as he spoke of his father's death reminded Ted of how his mother had also placed her hand on his as she had told him of the fatal accident. A single tear started to trickle down his face…a tear cried by the little boy inside that still desperately missed his father.

Embarrassed by the emotional display, Ted started to turn his face away, but Amy stopped him. She reached up and gently wiped the tear away. Then she softly caressed his cheek as she continued to gaze into his troubled eyes. No words were spoken between them, but the silence in the room went unnoticed. Both were hearing the beating of their own hearts as a powerful force drew them together.

245

The tormented look in Ted's eyes faded as the passion between them began to flare higher and higher. The caress of Amy's hand upon his face had quickly vanquished the sad images of his past. All he could think about was holding her, touching her, kissing her.

As Ted's lips found hers, Amy let herself be carried off on a cloud of sensations. The feel of Ted's hands upon her body burned her skin; every nerve in her body tingled from the heat. The craving for his touch quickly surpassed the fears that had kept her locked in an emotionless prison for so many years, and a moan of desire escaped her lips. She pulled away from Ted for a moment, her eyes smoldering from the fire he had flamed.

"Oh, Amy, I have wanted to kiss you from the very first moment I saw you," Ted whispered, his voice deepened by the passion sweeping through him. Then he brushed his lips along the side of her neck in soft, feathery kisses and lingered for a moment at the curve of her throat.

The light touch of Ted's breath on Amy's skin felt like a thousand tiny caresses, and she felt the longing for him encase her in its powerful grasp.

"Do you know how much I need you?" Ted said, as desire sent his lips searching for hers again.

Amy's hands moved downward seeking to feel more of him. She wanted to know what the touch of his skin would feel like under her fingertips. Her hands slipped under his shirt and rested on the taut muscles of his abdomen. The heat from his body warmed her hand, and she could think of nothing else at that moment but the wonderful sensations running uncontrolled through her body. Rational thoughts were swept away and there only existed a deep, driving hunger in her soul that made her want to seek him out.

"Whore! That's what you are! You are the reason this keeps happening." Amy's father's angry voice suddenly screamed in her ears. It was the same loathsome voice she had heard when he had thrown the boy off their front porch when he had caught them kissing, the same voice that had followed her in her dreams all these years after his death, taunting her, ridiculing her, making her feel tainted and unclean.

"You're nothing but a bitch in heat, driving men to do the devil's work."

Her father's words sent her into a panic that roared through her mind like a flash fire. She forcefully pushed Ted away and jumped up from the couch. As she tried to flee from the unseen entity that was shouting obscenities at her, she paid no heed to her surroundings. She covered her ears and backed away from Ted, stumbling over the coffee table and then almost tripping over Raphael. Her eyes darted frantically around the room in a crazed attempt to find her father even though she knew he couldn't be found.

Dad is dead! He can't be here, she thought as the terror in her mind fought to drive her crazy. *It isn't possible; it just isn't possible!*

"Slut!" her father's voice bellowed loudly in her ear. **"Look what you did to me!"**

"No! No! I didn't do anything to you!" Amy shouted loudly in a futile attempt to drown out the voice. "It wasn't my fault! God

247

knows it wasn't my fault!" She spun in a tight circle desperately scanning every corner of the room searching for that monster from her past.

Where is he? Why can't I see him?

"Amy! What's wrong?" Ted said, rushing toward her, fearful that she might turn and bolt from the room, and he didn't want her to do that. If she started running from him she might not stop, and he was afraid that he'd never be able to be with her again.

"Please, tell me what's happening," he begged. "Maybe I can help if you'll only tell me what's wrong." He grabbed Amy, pulling her into the circle of his arms and offering himself up as a shield from whatever it was that had upset her so much. He wanted to protect her, to guard her, to save her…even if she didn't want him to.

The moment Ted's arms protectively surrounded Amy, the terror fled from her mind leaving her emotionally limp. She felt like a rag doll with useless, cotton-stuffed legs. If Ted hadn't been supporting her, she would have just dropped into a heap on the floor right were she stood.

"Please…I…I…just need to sit down for a minute," she stammered. "My head is spinning, and I'm afraid I'm going to pass out."

Ted didn't know what to do. The blush of passion that had painted her cheeks pink only minutes before was gone, leaving her face drained of color, and the light that had been shining in her eyes had dimmed and entirely disappeared. He watched with alarm as a cold sweat broke out on her forehead, her hands started trembling, and her breathing changed to short gasping breaths.

Ted swept Amy up in his arms and carried her to the bedroom, gently lying her down on the bed. "I think you need to see a doctor."

"No! I don't!" Amy protested strongly, the mention of a doctor giving her the strength to adamantly voice her objection to Ted's suggestion. "I only need to rest for a minute. I just remembered something from a long time ago…that's all. It's nothing I can't handle. These same memories have been haunting me for years, and I've learned how to cope when this happens."

"Well, it seems to me you're not doing a very good job of coping. The look on your face a few minutes ago showed you aren't handling things very well at all. You looked like a Vietnam vet who has gone ballistic because he thinks he's seeing Viet Cong shooting at him. What in the world happened? Did you have some kind of flashback? You were acting like you were really scared…almost like you were seeing a ghost or something as equally terrifying."

At the word "ghost," Amy paled even more. The chilling coldness that she'd felt all of her life settled itself even deeper in her soul. It was as if all her life-sustaining blood had suddenly drained from her body. She felt totally helpless…just like she had years ago when her father had came for her and there had been no way for her to escape.

"It's nothing, nothing at all," Amy finally replied.

Ted looked at her thoughtfully. There was much more to the incident that had just happened than what she was telling. This was no little thing. It had been real fear he had seen flashing so strongly in her eyes. She had definitely been scared…but by what? And why was she trying to hide it?

"Come on Amy, talk to me. Tell me what's going on." Ted pleaded, sitting down on the bed next to her and taking one of her hands in his. "Remember when I told you it helps if you can talk about the bad things that have happened to you? Well, talking really does help. I promise you it will."

"Something happened to me a long time ago, something I really would rather forget. Every once in awhile it sneaks back and surprises me when I least expect it. Talking about it wouldn't help at all. I want to forget it…not discuss it. Let it drop."

"I don't think you should do that," Ted said with concern. "I don't know what happened to you to frighten you so much, but if it happened that long ago and you're still this scared, the problem isn't going to go away by itself."

Ted looked at Amy thoughtfully and wondered if she could have been raped when she was younger. In college, a close friend of his had acted just like Amy, and that's what had happened to her. His friend had gone out on a date and had been forced to perform oral sex. The guy had thought since the sexual contact had only been oral it didn't constitute being classified as rape. But it had been, and it had taken his friend more than five years to get over her fears of being alone with a man. The rape had traumatized her so much that she had been left with the feeling she was worthless and somehow contaminated, and her whole personality changed overnight because of that one terrible experience.

Ted kept staring at Amy's face searching for answers. Maybe he was way off base, but for some reason he felt positive that something like that had happened to Amy. He had read articles about how women sometimes reacted after being raped. Sometimes the psychological damage from the experience could continue for years, especially if the woman tried to bury the memories of her trauma instead of working through them.

"Have you ever heard of something called Post Traumatic Stress Disorder?" Ted asked, as he reached up and gently touched Amy's check and tilted her face toward his.

"No." Amy said, refusing to meet Ted's eyes. The knowing expression crossing his face made her feel ashamed. It felt as though he was looking into her soul, and she didn't want that. She didn't want to know what lay buried deep inside her mind, and she certainly didn't want him to know either.

"Post Traumatic Stress Disorder happens to people after an exposure to some traumatic event that causes extremely high levels of stress. Like war, muggings, child abuse, or—" he paused, "rape. Any psychological event that is outside of the range of normal human experience can trigger the syndrome. In Vietnam combat veterans it has been estimated that over twenty-four percent of them have symptoms of the disorder because of the awful experiences they had to endure."

"I don't think that's my problem; I wasn't over in Vietnam," Amy replied angrily. She wanted Ted to stop asking questions.

"But something else has happened to you that might have been just as bad. You don't have to go to war to be put in the middle of a battle."

"I don't know what you're talking about. Can't you understand…I don't want to discuss this subject any more tonight."

"Have you had a lot of flashbacks? What about nightmares or insomnia or—"

"What happened to me occurred years ago," Amy interrupted Ted. "It shouldn't be bothering me now."

"Post Traumatic Stress Disorder can affect people for decades after the initial experience."

"Can we discuss this some other time? I said I don't feel like talking about it right now." Amy turned away from Ted and lay on the bed with her back to him. She wanted him to leave her alone.

"Will you at least think about talking to someone about what happened to you?"

"I can't think right now. My head hurts too bad." Amy curled into a fetal position and almost started crying. The pain of a migraine was steadily building pressure inside her head. "Could you please just get me a couple of pain pills out of the medicine cabinet in the bathroom?" she pleaded.

"I'll get them right now," Ted said, hurrying to the bathroom. After a couple of minutes he returned with the pills in his hand and a glass of water.

"Thanks," Amy said, sitting up and taking the pills. "I think maybe it's best if you go home. I really don't feel like company right now."

"I'll leave in a few minutes. I just want to be sure you're going to be all right. I couldn't sleep tonight not knowing if you were still hurting this bad."

"I'll be fine. This is nothing new to me; I've had migraines since I was ten."

"I think this is more than just a migraine; you're so pale."

"Please just go. I won't be able to rest if you're here," Amy insisted, as she rubbed at her temples trying to ease down the pressure building within her head.

"I guess I really don't have much of a choice, do I?" Ted reluctantly commented.

"No, not really."

"Well, how about I just stick around till you fall asleep. I promise to sneak out very quietly and not disturb you." Ted tenderly covered Amy with a blanket and then lay beside her with one arm wrapped protectively around her. After she drifted off into a drug-induced sleep, he quietly got up to leave. As he left the room he glanced back at her lying in the bed looking so defenseless against whatever demons were chasing her in the deep recesses of her mind. His heart cried out for him to stay and protect her, but he didn't know how. So he reluctantly gathered up his coat and went home, even though he really didn't want to leave.

Chapter 28

The pain pills quickly lulled Amy into a deep sleep, and in the timelessness of dreams, she became a child again. She was hiding in her bedroom closet, burrowed deep under a mountain of stuffed animals. In a desperate attempt at making herself invisible, she was sitting on the floor scrunched up in a ball with her knees pulled tightly against her chest. She believed that she would be safe if she couldn't be seen. So she waited silently in the dark buried under a pile of fluffy teddy bears, rabbits, and dogs. She felt like a frightened mouse hiding from a hungry cat...except she was hiding from something much bigger and much more dangerous than a mere cat.

She was hiding from the beast that came for her in the night.

Suddenly the silence surrounding her was broken by the noise of her bedroom door slowly being opened. Terror filled her heart as she heard heavy footsteps crossing the room heading toward her secret hiding place. She was afraid to look so she pinched her eyes so tightly closed that she saw little stars swirling in the blackness, and she kept repeating silently to herself, *If I can't see it, it can't see me. If I can't see it, it can't see me.*

The closet door squeaked as it swung open telling Amy that the beast was almost upon her. A burst of overwhelming fear shot straight through her heart, almost stopping its frantic beating. She didn't want to breathe; breathing made noise, and the beast might hear it. She remembered precisely what happened the last time it had found her, and she didn't want that to happen again.

Weighted silence hung heavy on the air as Amy tightly held her breath. For a moment she thought she had fooled it. A dim hope crossed the boundary of her mind, *Maybe it doesn't know where I am.* She clung to that belief even though she knew that it couldn't possible be true. The beast always found her no matter where she hid.

She tried to keep her eyes closed, but the suspense became too great. She had to know what it was doing. Cautiously she attempted to peek through the mountain of stuffed animals piled on top of her. When she couldn't see anything, she tried to shift a pink bunny just enough to make a tiny hole to look through. Unfortunately, the movement sent the bunny tumbling down the mountain of toys. Even though it hit the floor with only a soft thud, the sound echoed loudly in her ears. Her mind cried out in terror, *Oh no! Now it will find me for sure!*

She peered through the opening left by the displaced bunny and saw the beast framed in the doorway. Its huge body filled up the entire opening like a gigantic grizzly standing at the entrance to its cave. She saw how thick and muscular its legs were, and she knew that it could run faster than any animal alive. She had tried to escape it more than once, but it had always caught her no matter how quick her legs had carried her.

Fear sent adrenaline pumping wildly through her small body and her heart raced faster and faster. It began pounding so furiously she thought it would jump out of her chest.

Go away! Amy screamed in her mind, even though no words came from her mouth. She knew better than to speak. Speaking only made the beast angrier and more dangerous.

No don't! She wordlessly screamed again as the beast reached in with its hairy arms pulling her from her hiding place. The teddy bear she had been holding onto for comfort was ripped from her hands and tossed to the floor. She had been clutching it so tightly that one of the bear's small, brown arms remained grasped within her tight fists.

She sealed her eyes shut, choosing not to look at the beast. Feeling its hands on her body was nightmare enough; to actually look upon its face would be more than she could bear.

Forced down on her knees in front of the hideous creature, she recoiled as one of its powerful hands threaded its fingers through her long hair. Gripping her hair tightly in its fist, the beast held her head firmly so she couldn't pull away. Then it reached down with its other hand prying at her mouth trying to force it open. She wanted to resist, but its fingernails raked the side of her face leaving long bloody scratches. She couldn't stop it from doing whatever it wanted to do.

Then she couldn't breathe. It had filled her mouth with its foulness.

Holding her head tightly within its hands so she couldn't escape, the beast began moving in a rhythmic motion, rocking back and forth. With each thrust of its hips the monster forced her head to move with it. She could only breathe in desperate gulps whenever the creature would pull back for an instance from her face. And when she could breathe, a musky, pungent odor filled her nostrils making her gag. Bile rose up in the back of her throat. It took all of her concentration not to throw up.

But she had let that happen once before, and she vividly remembers what the punishment had been. There was no way she could forget; she had long, red scars upon her legs that reminded her every day. So she concentrated very hard on not thinking about what was happening. She tried to force her mind to go somewhere else, just like she had done many times in the past, someplace where the beast couldn't follow her.

Except this time she couldn't escape. Her mind wouldn't let her leave. She was trapped in that room with her nightmare.

Just when she thought she could not bear it for one more instant, the beast groaned as a shiver traveled down the length of its body. The death grip on her hair was released, and it pulled away.

Unable to prevent it, she gagged, and filth spewed from her mouth. The beast cast her aside with a single violent shove, then it turned and left the room without even looking back. Too afraid to remain out in the open, she crawled like an injured animal back into the closet and buried herself among the stuffed animals again. Tears streamed down her face, and she lay in a dejected heap on the floor crying silently until her world faded into nothingness.

+++++

Aroused from her drug-induced sleep by the shrillness of the alarm clock, Amy groggily tried to open her eyes. Her thoughts were slow to come, and as the alarm buzzed continuously in her ear, she wondered why it sounded so far away.

With her eyes still half-closed she reached over to shut off the clock's irritating noise, but instead of the bedside dresser, her hand hit a wall.

She wasn't even in her bed!

Through heavy, swollen eyelids Amy tried to focus more clearly on her surroundings. After a few confusing moments of uncertainty, she finally realized where she really was. Some time during the night she had crawled into her closet and burrowed beneath a pile of discarded clothes that had been left on the closet floor.

Struggling to sit up, Amy gasped in surprise as the walls began spinning in tight circles.

What is happening to me? Why am I so dizzy, and how did I get from my bed to the closet floor?

Her confusion only intensified with each passing second when she could find no real answer.

She was so lightheaded any movement sent the room twisting and turning wildly. Afraid to budge even an inch, she sat as still as possible. She forced her mind to try to think clearly.

The last thing she remembered doing was taking a couple of pain pills and then lying down in bed. Of course, she usually only took one pain pill instead of two, but there was no way taking two of them would have made her feel this groggy.

As Amy's eyes adjusted to the closet's dusky interior, she noticed a faint image forming over in the corner by the door. At first it was only a blurry shadow…like tiny dust particles amassing together in the air. Then it began to take shape and suddenly where there had been nothing but emptiness, the girl from the painting stood looking straight at her through tearful, tragic eyes.

Amy felt her heart instantly become heavy from the weight of all the pain and sadness resting in those eyes. An oppressive sorrow that seemed to come from nowhere settled heavily on the air, and she felt an overpowering need to reach out to comfort the child. Opening her arms, Amy beckoned for the girl to come forward. A feeling of relief washed over her when the child started moving slowly toward her.

But that feeling quickly disappeared when Amy noticed with horror the terrible state the child was in. The poor little thing had been very badly beaten.

"Mommy, help me," the child whimpered pathetically from busted swollen lips. *"Please, Mommy, I hurt so badly."* The girl reached out to Amy with bruised arms. *"Why don't you love me?"* the child whispered sadly, pitifully. *"Why do you hate me so much? Why Mommy, why?"*

Amy looked with shock at the thin outstretched arms. And when she saw a set of long bloody scratches running down one side of the girl's battered face, she almost fainted from the anguish that arose from deep within her own heart. Dark images of a monstrous werewolf burst upon her mind immediately sending the room spinning and swirling again.

A piteous moan escaped from Amy's lips, bringing Raphael bounding into the closet. As he pranced in through the door with his tail wagging excitedly, he simply walked straight through the girl's image, scattering it into the air. The weeping, broken child vanished instantly, leaving Amy alone with Raphael in the closet.

Too nauseated and dizzy to walk, Amy began crawling toward the bathroom. She definitely didn't want to remain in the closet for one more second.

Vomiting into the commode, she felt so weak she could hardly hold her head up. When she leaned against the bathtub to rest before trying to stand up, she spied a prescription bottle lying empty on the bathroom floor next to the commode. Picking up the bottle, she studied it and was surprised at what she saw.

"Raphael, what's going on here?" Amy's voice was full of disbelief. "There should be at least twelve pain pills left in this bottle. Where are they?"

She crawled across the bathroom floor franticly searching for any of the pills that might have spilled out, and as she searched, she grew more and more confused. *What had happened to the rest of the pills?* She had only taken two last night…that was all. She definitely remembered Ted giving her only two pills before she fell asleep, and even if he had offered her more, she wouldn't have taken them. The medicine always made her head feel funny, and she was afraid of getting addicted.

Maybe she'd had some kind of weird reaction to the drug. She had heard of such things happening to other people. Was it possible that the medicine could have messed with her mind so she hadn't realized what she was doing? But even if that were the case, she really didn't think she would have purposely taken a whole bottle of pills. She had worked too hard on surviving to give it all up...even if she weren't in her right mind.

So why are all those pills missing?

Clutching the prescription bottle tightly in her hand, Amy tried to force her mind to reveal what had transpired during the past few hours when she should have been sleeping. But a thick, black cloud of nothingness hid the night's images from her, and she could remember nothing after Ted gave her the pain pills.

She couldn't understand what had happened. Why would she have taken the pills, and why had she buried herself in the closet under a pile of old clothes? And why did she now feel overcome with such sadness and pain so deep in her soul?

She struggled to stand on shaky legs to look into the mirror over the sink. Her eyes were red and puffy and felt as though sand had been poured into them. She looked as though she had cried all night long. Her hands automatically went up to her cheeks. The skin was unblemished, but for some strange reason she had expected to find long, bloody scratches trailing down her jaw.

Splashing cold water on her face to help clear her thoughts, she wondered why her mind was such a blank. *Maybe I accidentally took the pills*, she thought uneasily. *I surely wouldn't have done it on purpose! Would I?*

But then, she thought warily, as she glanced at her pitiful reflection in the mirror, *this wouldn't have been the first time I've supposedly tried to kill myself and didn't remember.*

Once before, when she was twelve, she had emerged from one of those blank periods of her life and had found herself in the hospital with two broken legs and pain exploding through her entire body.

Her neighbor had told everyone in town she had purposely walked out in front of a car and had tried to kill herself.

But she didn't remember doing it.

Her mother had said she had only tripped while walking along the side of the road, but truthfully, she never did think that was what had really happened.

Amy put more faith in the neighbor's account of the incident than her mother's. In fact, she remembers trying to tell the doctor that her mother had been wrong, but he hadn't listened to one single word she had said, just like all the other times.

When her father had heard her trying to talk with the doctor, he had made sure no one else got the chance to question her again about that little accident. He spirited her out of the hospital quicker than a blink of an eye, broken legs and all, and no one ever had the opportunity to ask again what had happened to her that day. Somewhere in her medical records it is recorded that she accidentally tripped in front of a moving car while walking along the side of the road...and that's all. But in her own heart, even though she didn't remember, she knew that the neighbor had told the real truth and that her mother had lied.

Amy frowned as she stared at her image in the mirror. Thoughts about that accident were making her stomach hurt.

How I hate not being able to remember things, she thought as a cramping pain sliced at her belly.

The doctor had told her mother that her memory loss had been the result of trauma from the accident. No sinister cause was ever attributed to that particular memory lapse...or to any of the others. In fact, nowhere in her hospital records, or in any of her medical files, had it ever been recorded that there were whole pieces of her childhood gone...vanished as though parts of her had never really existed at all.

And now I've lost another piece of my life again and have no idea where it went, she thought as she climbed back into bed, pulling her covers tightly around her to ward off the chill that was slowly seeping deep into her bones.

She thought about calling and making an appointment to see a doctor, but old habits are hard to break. She really didn't trust doctors. Not one doctor had recognized that all those injuries she had as a child were the result of abuse. Or if they did, they didn't do anything about it. If only one of them had opened his eyes to the many signs that had been there, maybe she could have been saved from the life of hell she had been forced to live. But they hadn't been able to see beyond her father's position in the community. It had been far easier for them to believe she was a clumsy, accident-prone child than to believe that Randy Tedrow could have possibly been a child abuser. Child abusers don't go to church every Sunday, don't have high positions on the town council, and don't own and successfully run their own companies...do they?

+++++

After resting for an hour, Amy finally felt well enough to get up without collapsing. She fixed some very strong coffee and drank several cups of it to help flush the pain medication out of her system, but she still didn't feel up to going to work yet. Picking up the phone, she called the office. She knew Susan would have arrived already and would be wondering where she was.

"Susan," Amy said with a slight tremor in her voice, "I'm not going to be in to work till after one o'clock. Do me a favor and watch over things for me. I promise to get in there as soon as I can."

"Hey, what's going on? You never miss work."

"I'm just not feeling very well right now. I'll make it in as soon as I can. Promise to keep an eye on Gary. If he doesn't keep those roaming hands of his to himself, I need to know."

"I really do have to talk to you about him." Susan hesitated for a second before continuing. "I think he's bothering that new girl you hired last week. You know, the one who just graduated from high school and is helping out for the summer to earn money for college."

265

"Mr. Smith's niece, Carrie Himsell? The one that looks like she's still twelve years old?"

"That's the one. I don't like carrying tales, but every time Gary gets near her she acts very apprehensive. I don't quite understand what the problem is. When I ask if Gary is bothering her, she looks at me with this scared look in her eyes and shakes her head no. But I don't believe her. Something is very wrong, and I just know it involves Gary."

A little tight ball of anxiety formed in the pit of Amy's stomach. She had a good idea what the problem might be, and she didn't look forward to dealing with it. "Well, just keep an eye on the two of them this morning until I get there. Send Carrie out of the office to run errands if possible. I'll talk with her when I get there this afternoon."

"Are you sure you even want to come in today? You sound awful! Maybe you should take the whole day off. I can handle things around here for one day. I promise not to mess it up too bad."

"For now I plan to be in after lunch sometime. If you need me before that just page me."

Amy hung up the phone and headed for the bathroom. Filling up the tub with steaming hot water, she started to climb in. But just before stepping in, she turned and hurriedly placed a huge beach towel over the bathroom mirror on the back of the door. She didn't want to see any more dripping pools of blood in its reflective surface.

As she relaxed and allowed the soothing heat to take the edge off her jagged nerves, she tried to make sense of the mysterious happenings that had been going on the last couple of days. She couldn't decide if she was going crazy or if there really was a restless spirit calling out for someone...anyone...to help.

Sinking deeper into the steamy water, the thought crossed her mind that if she wasn't already crazy, she might be before it was all over with.

Chapter 29

Dr. James Perry looked over the last page of Tommy William's file while he was waiting for his young patient to speak. Tommy needed to acknowledge what his brother had done to him three years ago when he had been only eight years old. If Tommy couldn't say it, he wasn't ready to accept the full impact of the abuse his older half-brother had put him through. And until he could talk about it, he would probably never get any better.

James knew that people often thought it was cruel of him to make children talk about the painful things that have happened to them. But he also knew that it would be more painful for them to keep it hidden inside where it would eat at them until all their strength was devoured by the constant struggle to keep their tormented secrets concealed.

James was purposely avoiding looking at his patient because Tommy couldn't tolerate someone watching him. He didn't want to make the boy feel any more uncomfortable than he was already feeling. Instead, he kept his eyes on the paperwork in front of him. He wanted Tommy to think about what he had just said. Tommy had been under his care for over six months now, and he still hadn't gotten the boy to speak the truth about what was really bothering him.

But James already knew what Tommy's problem was, just like he knew with most of the other troubled children he saw at his clinic. He had been born with the ability to understand what other people were feeling and sometimes even thinking. It had been a gift he had inherited from his grandmother, and was one of the main reasons why he was considered to be an excellent child psychiatrist. The kids didn't have to come right out and tell him what was wrong. Most of the time he had a general idea before they even got through their first session.

He supposed some people would say he was psychic, but he never looked at it that way. Actually, he hardly ever looked at it in any particular way. Whatever it was that happened between him and other people, it happened without any call for assistance from him. He accepted it without even thinking, as if it were an every day occurrence, which in reality it was for him.

+++++

"Dr. Perry, what did you mean when you said I needed to talk about what Steven did to me? Why do you think he did anything? Just because I hate him doesn't mean he did anything." Tommy sat fidgeting in his chair, his eyes focused on a single spot on the floor, while his hands constantly moved from one spot to another.

"Are you saying your brother never did anything that upset you or hurt you?"

"Steven wasn't my brother," Tommy's voice flooded with anger. "He was just my half-brother. We only shared the same mom, that's all. That sure in hell didn't make us brothers."

"Doesn't having the same mother make you brothers?"

"Brothers stand up for each other. They don't—" Tommy closed his eyes and grabbed the arms of the chair as though he had to hold himself down to keep from exploding. "That jerk wasn't my brother! I don't care what he said. It wasn't my fault!"

"Tommy, look at me." James said gently, then waited until Tommy's eyes focused on his. "Just because someone hurts you and makes you do things you don't want to do, doesn't mean what happened was your fault. Steven was wrong to do what he did to you. You don't need to keep carrying all that guilt around. It wasn't your fault. You can let that feeling go...here...now...by finally telling someone about it."

"I didn't do nothing to feel guilty about."

"That's right. You didn't. Steven made you do those things with him. You didn't have a choice."

"How do you know what he made me do? I never told a single person. Not one. How come you know?" Tommy looked at James through milky-blue eyes. He quit the constant fidgeting in his chair, and his face paled.

"Because sometimes...I just know things. Like now. I know what Steven did to you. I can see it in the way you move and in the

271

way you talk. Body language can tell a person a lot." *Plus my grandmother's gift helped.*

"How long have you known?" Tommy bowed his head in shame, avoiding James' gaze again. "I didn't want anyone to ever find out."

"I've suspected it from the beginning, but I've been waiting for you to tell me about it."

"But, I don't want to talk about it. I want to forget any of it ever happened."

"To heal, you need to let loose of those feelings you have locked up inside of yourself. What you tell me doesn't go beyond these doors. You can talk about anything you want and I'll listen. I want to help you work though your pain. It's possible to start feeling better about yourself and your life; it really is. Please, let me help you find a way to do that."

"I…I don't know." Tommy paused, picking some unseen lint off of his sweater. Then his eyes searched through the room as if he were looking for an escape route. He looked everywhere but at James.

"Your panic disorder isn't going to get any better unless you can get to the root of your problems. Don't you want to be able to leave you house without feeling like the whole world is crushing down on you?"

"If you know so damn much, tell me why he did it," Tommy angrily lashed out. "Why did he have to make me do those terrible things? I didn't want to do them, but…but he made me. He was so much bigger than me. He told me if I didn't do what he said he would cut my...my...you know, my thing off. He had the knife to do it too. He carried it around with him all the time. I saw him use it once on this girl out by the school. He cut up her face real bad for telling the cops where he had hid his dope. He said he'd do the same thing to me if I told. I begged him to leave me alone, but that only made it worse. I don't understand. Why did he have to do it? I was his brother, he shouldn't have done it."

"Abuse frequently happens because one person feels the need to have power and control over another. Your brother probably didn't have much control over very many things in his life, so he may have used his power over you to make himself feel good. But I can't tell you for sure if that's the reason why Steven acted like he did. At least not without talking to him."

"You can't talk to him. He's dead. He got shot during that drug deal. You know, the one where he knifed that cop."

"I know. We've talked about that before. This time we're discussing something different." James laid Tommy's file down on the desk and sat back in his chair. "Tell me, does what Steven did make it harder for you to face people?"

"I don't like to go out in crowds. I keep thinking someone will figure out what I am and then tell everyone else. I can't face that, so I just stay home. It's safer."

"Just what do you think you are?"

"Steven said I was…was gay, you know, a faggot. That's why he did all those things to me. He said since I was gay I had to learn what that meant. Then he pushed me down on the bed and…and—"

James saw the fear flashing across Tommy's face as the young man allowed himself to go back in time. "And now you think you're gay because of what your brother did?"

"That's what makes you gay, having sex with other guys."

"Not if you're forced into it."

"That's not what Steven said. He said I was gay because I got a…a… hard-on when he was doing it to me. He said I…I enjoyed it. But I didn't, honest to God, I didn't."

"Tommy, everyone's body has a way of reacting to stressful situations with normal reflexes, and most of the time you can't control those reflexes. That doesn't mean you enjoyed it. It doesn't mean anything at all. You need to—"

"I don't want to talk about this anymore," Tommy rose from his chair so fast he tripped over his own feet.

"That's fine." James realized Tommy had closed himself off again. "Your Mother will be here in a few minutes anyway. We'll talk more at your next visit."

"You're not going to tell Mom are you? I don't want her to know. She'd tell that bastard she's married to, and he'd throw me out of the house. He hates fags. I got no place else to go."

"The law requires that I report certain things. But I will help you get through this, and your life will get better."

+++++

At the sound of the door closing behind Tommy, James sighed. The price of his job was high. The amount of emotional torment his patients had experienced in their young lives could devastate the heartiest of men. There were some days he thought he would crack under the weight of so many hidden secrets. It seemed like every new day brought with it a new burden for him to help some poor child carry. Why did it have to happen? Children should be protected and loved, not beaten, burned, or brutalized.

He glanced up at the clock on the wall. It was noon already and he needed to get going or he wouldn't make it to the Outcast by twelve-thirty to meet with Amy Tedrow, the young woman who had his grandmother's painting. Grabbing his jacket off the back of his chair, he headed out the door.

In his car, he started thinking about Tommy's question. How did he know what had happened without being told?

Visions of his grandmother's smiling face crossed his mind. She was a grand lady. Even if some people did think she was a witch.

Smiling, he thought about her. She might not be a witch, but she sure could cast a spell on you. Just a touch of her hand could calm the wildest of spirits. He could see where some people could get the impression that she had extraordinary powers. The truth being told...she did have. She had been born with the ability to see into people's minds and tell what they were thinking. There were even a few times she had actually predicted the future. Unfortunately all the predictions had been unfavorable ones and that had scared people. They didn't want to know what lay ahead if it was going to be bad.

It had been through her bloodline that he had received his gift of insight, though his wasn't as strong as hers. And he was glad for that.

When Grammy was young, before she was married, she had lived in the country in a small, dilapidated farmhouse with her mother. The pregnant women in town used to go to her to find out what sex their babies were going to be, but that had stopped immediately after she had gotten married. Once his grandfather had entered the picture, his grandmother had to stop using her gift. His grandfather had said that he was afraid that she might get into trouble or get hurt if "she kept messing with what shouldn't be messed with."

But James had suspected that his grandfather had probably been more afraid of something else. He guessed that his grandfather didn't like the thought that his wife had the power to read his mind.

+++++

Maneuvering expertly through the noon traffic, James arrived at the Outcast with plenty of time to spare. *Good, I'm here a few minutes early,* James thought, looking at the clock on his dashboard as he parked.

Once inside the restaurant he glanced quickly around the room. *No red pantsuit yet,* he thought as he headed toward the bar. *That means I can have a beer, and I sorely need one today after that session with Tommy.*

Though he usually didn't approve of drinking this early in the day, the session with his young patient had left him feeling emotionally drained. He quickly decided that a little artificial lift to his spirit wouldn't hurt anything. He didn't have any other patients to see the rest of the day; only a ton of paperwork waited for his attention back at the office.

He took a seat at the furthest corner of the bar and placed his order.

Ms. Tedrow's phone conversation had been very intriguing; he couldn't wait to meet her. But he wanted a couple of minutes to watch her unobserved before they got together. It was important for him to get a general impression about the woman before they actually met face to face, especially if he was going to tell her the story behind his grandmother's painting. He didn't talk to just anyone about Grammy.

He wondered why she was so interested in the history of the painting anyway. It seemed a little strange to him, but then strange things were always happening every day. That was the main reason people kept seeking him out, to help explain the strange happenings in their lives.

As he diligently watched the entrance, he found he was filled with a strange sense of anticipation. There was nothing better then a good mystery, and the phone call yesterday morning with its unusual undertones definitely fit that category.

Maybe this meeting with Ms. Tedrow will add something interesting to my life, he thought as his thoughts started to drift back to his patients. *God knows I need it!*

Toni Auberry

Chapter 30

James sat at the bar and sipped on his beer while he watched for the appearance of a young woman dressed in a red pantsuit. In his mind he had already formed an image of what Ms. Tedrow would look like—a shy, reserved person, who would spook easily at the first sign of trouble. There had been something in the tone of her voice that had given him impression she was subdued. So he was totally unprepared for the impact she made when she entered the restaurant, and for once he was thankful his intuition had turned out to be totally wrong.

Amy strolled into the restaurant like a model walking onto a runway, catching the attention of every man in the place. She was an exceptionally beautiful woman, and while her outfit looked very professional, it couldn't mask the graceful curves of her body. She walked with a natural ease as she made her way to a table near the front of the establishment. The sexy movement of her hips brought hungry looks to the eyes of more than a couple of the men sitting in the room.

Smiling, James watched as a young waiter almost tripped over his own feet in his hurried attempt to reach her table. Amy definitely didn't look like the type that would spook easily. She seemed more like a woman who could kick ass if she had to. There was an inner strength that showed in the way she moved. He bet that if one of the men in the restaurant were to approach her she would put him in his place without even blinking an eye.

James sat back in his chair observing the reaction of the men in the room as Amy began to scan the area looking for him. You could actually see the disappointment on some of their faces as her eyes glanced over them without stopping. When her gaze finally fell upon him, he nodded and pointed to the white carnation in his lapel. As Amy smiled tentatively, he rose from the barstool and walked over to join her at the table.

"Hello, you must be Ms. Tedrow. I'm James." James cordially extended his hand, and the moment their hands touched he felt a sudden surge of energy travel straight up his arm, almost as if an electrical current had passed between them. Surprised at the intensity of the emotional turmoil flowing out from her, he held on to her hand a little longer then necessary.

My God, he thought, *she is so close to losing control!*

He never would have guessed by her outward actions how badly she was suffering inside. When she had walked into the room, she had done so with such an air of self-assurance he hadn't been able to perceive how insecure she really felt.

As the energy flow between them grew stronger, James felt as if he was being sucked into a whirlwind of confusion, and he knew that her mind was in chaos. He could tell by the way her energy moved around her that its rhythm was totally out of synch.

Holding tightly to her hand, he knew without a doubt she had been severely abused as a child. In his mind he heard the swish of the belt as it sped through the air just before it struck. His body felt the impact of the strap as it landed upon his back, and then he felt something more—

+++++

Amy was checking James over as he walked toward her and was pleased with what she saw. He had the appearance of someone who might be reasonable. She guessed his age to be about fifty-five. He didn't have that little potbelly a lot of middle-aged men acquired as they grew older. His silver-streaked, brown hair had receded a little, but that didn't detract from his appearance. He was six feet tall and walked with a touch of confidence in his step. He had a definite air of stability about him. His smile conveyed warmth that reached even into his eyes...just like Ted's. And somehow she knew there wasn't anything fake about him.

Accepting James' offered handshake, Amy took an instant liking to him. "And I'm Amy," she said as their hands touched. A few seconds later she didn't even realize that the handshake was lasting longer than it should have. There seemed to be an unusual strength, an aura of power, surrounding James, and that strength was comforting. Her hand in his didn't make her feel the least bit intimidated.

Amy looked up at James and automatically returned his smile. "I'm glad you could make it," she said, feeling drawn to him, not as a woman is drawn to a man, but as a child is instinctively toward a new friend. "You have no idea how imperative it is that I find out some information about the painting."

"Are you sure you wouldn't consider letting me buy back the painting from you?" James asked, reluctantly letting go of Amy's hand before he sat down across the table from her. "It really is very important to me."

"If that's true, why was it sold?"

"The painting belonged to my grandmother. I have been abroad in England the last couple of years and only got back in the States six months ago. While I was gone, my grandmother had a stroke and had to move into a nursing home. Before I got back, her house had been put up for sale and a lot of her belongings were auctioned off. I had never told anyone I wanted the painting, so, unfortunately, it was sold with the other things. Somehow all the paperwork from the auction got jumbled up, and it took me this long to locate it. I had just about given up hope when I discovered where it was; only I was a few days too late."

"Why is it so important to you?" Amy carefully watched his reaction to her question. "Is there something special about it? You have to have a reason for wanting it badly enough to spend all that time tracking it down." She halfway hoped he had also had an experience like hers. *Maybe he had seen the ghost child too.*

"Like I said, the painting belonged to my grandmother. She is very special to me, and the painting is a part of what she and I have shared over the years. I assure you it's not valuable to anyone but me. Have an art appraiser look at it and give you an estimate. I will pay anything reasonable." James could tell she was waiting for him to say something else, but he couldn't figure out what it was.

"I might consider selling it to you, but not right away," Amy replied cautiously. "There is something I have to do first before I can let it go. And to do that I need to find some things out about the girl who is in the painting."

"Why? What could that possibly have to do with whether you'll sell it to me?"

"I can't really explain. You would think I was crazy." Looking at James thoughtfully, Amy decided to continue. For some reason, she suddenly wasn't afraid of what he might think. She almost felt as if some unseen force was drawing her words out of her. "Actually, I'm not so sure I'm not going crazy. Some really strange things have been happening since that painting showed up in my life, and I am really wondering if I should see a doctor, or better yet, a psychiatrist. I can't tell if the things that have been happening to me lately are real or if they are something I've made up in my mind. But whichever it is, that painting is directly linked to all of it."

James didn't say anything for a few seconds. He knew she had the right to be told what type of work he did. "Before you go any further you need to know I am a psychiatrist." Worried over her startled expression he tried to undo some of the damage. "I work with troubled kids. It's a very rewarding job, and I love it. There's just something special about helping them discover how to set things straight. Life can really give kids some big knocks, and I like to think somehow I am able to make life a little easier for them. Some of my patients have been through hell, and it's my job to help them find a way to understand and survive."

Amy sat in silence wondering how much to say to James. She didn't want him to think she needed to be one of his patients. And for a second, the thought crossed her mind that it was too bad there hadn't been someone like him to show her the way from hell when she was a child. It would have been nice to have had someone who understood and could have helped her survive. Then she wouldn't have had to do it alone.

"Do you believe in ghosts?" she finally asked.

"Ghosts?" Wondering where the conversation was heading, James thoughtfully considered his answer. "I'm not sure I really believe there are ghosts like we see in the horror movies, but there are so many dimensions to what we know as life that anything could really be possible."

"So you think there could be such things as ghosts?"

"Why is important to know if I believe in ghosts? What has that got to do with the painting? There's definitely an essential ingredient lacking in this conversation. I have a feeling there is something that you need to say but are too afraid to say it. Please understand, anything you reveal to me will go no further than this table, so don't be scared to talk with me. There isn't anything you could tell me I probably haven't heard before."

"The girl in the painting...she's a ghost." Amy spoke in a voice that was only a whisper. "Ever since I received the painting, she has been haunting me, begging me to help her. That's why it's so important for me to find out everything I can about her. You see, I can't help her if I can't figure out what she wants me to do." Amy looked pleadingly into James' brown eyes. "You have to tell me what you know about her."

James realized how wrong he had been. Amy had said something he had never heard before! He had never been told by any of his patients that ghosts were haunting them. Not sure how to react, he was very careful not to respond in a manner that might frighten her away. He wanted to hear more.

"The girl from the painting is haunting you?" he asked.

"I've only had the painting for a few days, but right after I got it, I started hearing a little girl calling out for help. And then the crying started...the sound is enough to break anyone's heart, and I've even seen her a few times. Once she had bruises all over her face and blood dripping from her hands."

"Blood on her hands?"

"Yes! And once I saw her standing over the body of her dog. Or at least I think it was her dog. Someone had taken a butcher knife to it, and she saw the whole thing. It was terrible. Just thinking about it makes my blood run cold."

"Did you have a dog when you were little?" James asked.

"What has that got to do with all of this?" Amy responded, shivering despite the warmth in the room. "Listen...can't you understand why this is so important to me? I'm not crazy. I have to help her. She is in so much pain. But, I can't do anything until I find out something about her, and you're my only link. I promise if you will help me with this, I will give you back the painting as soon as that poor child is able to rest in peace."

+++++

As James listened to Amy's story, he became very concerned for her. Not because he thought she was crazy, but because he recognized what was really happening. Or at least he thought he did. She was seeing a ghost, but not the kind she imagined it to be. There was much more to the drama that was being played out in her head than she could even begin to realize. Knowing that, he wanted to find a way to help.

"Amy, the painting belonged to my grandmother. She's the one you need to talk to. She lives at a nursing home about ten minutes from here, and I think we should go there right now and talk to her." James waited anxiously for Amy's reply. He really wanted her to speak with his grandmother, not because of the painting, but because of his grandmother's gift. She could help Amy more than he could right now.

Amy needed something more than the information she wanted to learn about the child in the painting. He could tell her about the painting, he knew everything about it. His grandmother had told him the story several times, but the story wouldn't be what Amy was expecting to hear. When she found out the truth, she wouldn't understand. She would need a lot of guidance and support. If he were to tell her right here, right now, it could be devastating. He might lose the chance to help her. He needed to get her to a private place where she would be free to express her feelings. Here in the restaurant she would probably get up and walk out, and he might never see her again.

Suddenly it occurred to James that all he had learned in his lifetime had been to prepare him to help this particular woman at this particular time. She was special, someone who had survived her own private hell and kept going. If somehow Amy could find the real answers she was seeking, not those she thought she needed to find, then she would be able to find peace somewhere within herself. And he had to find a way to help her do just that.

Toni Auberry

Chapter 31

James' grandmother, Elizabeth Rinehart, resided at Windsong Manor, an exclusive nursing home located fifteen minutes from the Outcast.

Amy chose to ride with James, but she didn't even seem to be aware that he was in the car with her. Her thoughts were on only one thing—soon she would know more about the little girl in the painting and she would be able to find some way to help her. And at that particular moment, nothing else mattered; all else took second place.

While James drove, he kept trying to figure out a way to approach Amy over an important matter he really needed to discuss with her before they arrived at the nursing home—how much should he tell her about his grandmother?

"Amy, there is something you need to know about my grandmother before you meet her." James paused, glancing over at Amy to see if she was paying attention. "She's special, and not just because she means so much to me, but because she has this ability to see things or to feel things about other people. Things normal people can't see or feel."

"Has she seen the girl, too?" Amy's eyes suddenly glowed with excitement as hope danced wildly in them. "You said it was her painting. Does that mean I'm not the only one the child has shown herself to?"

"No, that's not what I mean. She hasn't seen your ghost. What makes her special is she can see and feel things about the people she touches. Sometimes, she can even predict the future for them. When you meet her, she will ask you to take her hand the minute you walk into the room. It's her way of getting to know who you are. I have to warn you she's going to know things about you that you might not want known. And now that she's older, she isn't quite as discreet about it as she used to be. She might say some upsetting things without realizing it."

"I don't have anything to hide, so that won't be a problem. Maybe it will help her understand how important it is to me that she tells me everything she possibly can about the girl in the painting."

"There's something else." James reluctantly added.

"Oh?" Amy responded questioningly.

"I have the ability to do the same thing, although it isn't nearly as strong as hers." James hesitated for a moment before deciding to continue. "Amy, I know without a doubt that some terrible things happened to you when you were a child. I'm not exactly sure what they were, although I have a general idea." Glancing at her face, he became worried he had said the wrong thing. He saw a look of panic sparking in her eyes, and her lower lip had started trembling as she nervously licked her lips.

Not knowing what to expect next, he pulled the car over to the side of the road. "Amy, listen to me...I am not trying to hurt you. You have this pain, this unhappiness, bottled up inside of you. You're like a powder keg ready to explode. I don't think you've ever had the chance to deal with whatever it was that hurt you so badly. Actually, I really believe you have never even told anyone about it. It's something you have pushed deep down inside and have tried to pretend didn't happen. But you can't go on pretending forever. The pressure could destroy you if you're not careful."

Shocked by James' revelation, Amy couldn't meet his eyes. She turned her face away and sat staring out the window at the passing traffic. She couldn't speak; not a single word managed to force its way from her mouth...just like at her father's funeral. A vise seemed to be clamping down on her throat preventing her from even swallowing. It reminded her of the time her father's hands had encircled her neck and squeezed so tightly that the smallest of breaths couldn't enter her lungs. Her throat throbbed from a forgotten pain and somewhere in the back of her mind her father's voice echoed hard and cruel, "You are nothing but a slut...a good for nothing whore. No one would believe a word you say. So don't you dare say anything. Not if you know what's good for you."

So, Amy said nothing to James. She suddenly felt very lightheaded and had trouble thinking because her thoughts had unexpectedly jumbled into chaotic disarray. The tightness around her throat intensified, and one of her hands automatically went up to her neck.

Of course my father's hands aren't there, she thought as she gingerly rubbed her neck. *He's dead. He can't be here.*

So why can I still feel his hands on my throat? she wondered warily as she felt a heavy darkness descend upon her, a darkness that stole her thoughts and took away the pain that had appeared from out of nowhere and clutched at her heart.

Troubled over Amy's lack of responsiveness, James continued, "I didn't say this to upset you. You don't have to talk about what happened to you if you don't want to. Just remember though, if at any time you need to talk with someone, please call me. If you don't want it to be me, I know several good therapists that could help. You don't have to face things alone."

"Alone? Face things alone? I…I…don't…know—"

Amy sounded really strange. James couldn't tell what was going on in her mind, but whatever it was, he didn't think it was anything good. Her face had suddenly become expressionless, and her eyes looked empty as though she was no longer looking through them.

"Don't you think you had better get going?" Amy finally responded in a flat monotone voice. "I need to get back to work as soon as possible." Then she looked down at the floorboard without saying another word.

"Just remember if you need to talk, please call me." James' eyes sought hers again, but she wouldn't look at him. Sadly, he shook his head. Unless she wanted to talk, he couldn't force a conversation. Pulling his car back out into the flow of traffic, James headed for Windsong.

Amy continued to stare down at her feet. *What did James mean when he said to call him if I needed to talk? Talk about what? The last thing I remember is James saying his grandmother was a little strange. After that...nothing. Why were we pulled off to the side of the road? Why can't I remember the last few minutes? It's not like something bad had happened. We were only driving down the road. Why are those last few minutes of my life instantly gone from my mind? And why do I suddenly feel so overwhelmingly sad?*

+++++

When they finally arrived at Windsong, Amy was surprised by its grandiose appearance. The facility looked more like a summer resort for senior citizens than a nursing home. There was plenty of yard space surrounding the building, and she noticed a miniature garden complete with a walkway and yard swings off to the side of the building. When the spring flowers were in bloom, she knew the garden would be beautiful. Windsong was definitely a place only someone with a strong financial standing could afford.

When Amy stepped into Elizabeth Rinehart's room she got another surprise. A strange brightness seemed to be radiating from the very walls of the room, and almost everything in the room seemed to be a brilliant white. Amy felt like she had just walked onto a bright, snow-covered field. Over in front of an immense light-filled window, sat a petite, elderly woman in a wheelchair. With her snowy-white hair and white, lacy smock, she looked like the snow queen from one of Amy's favorite childhood novels.

Chuckling at Amy's facial expression, Elizabeth motioned her forward. "White is such an energizing color, don't you think? This room literally seems to soak up energy from the sun and then passes it along to me." She held out a hand for Amy to take and smiled warmly. "Come closer so I can see you better. My eyes aren't very good anymore. I don't get many visitors, and I at least like to be able to see what they look like."

Amy stooped down by the side of Elizabeth's wheelchair and gently grasped the elderly woman's outstretched hand. "Mrs. Rinehart, I'm Amy Tedrow, an acquaintance of your grandson, James. I wonder if I could possibly ask you a couple of questions."

"Oh heavens Child, just call me Elizabeth, Mrs. Rinehart makes me sound like I'm an old lady." Cupping Amy's hand between hers, Elizabeth smiled at James, acknowledging his presence in the room. However, the smile quickly faded as Amy's energy flowed into her.

Elizabeth held Amy's hand tightly between hers as she searched the young woman's face for a sign that would verify what she was feeling. But there were no outward expressions of the amount of grief and loneliness brewing in the girl's heart. Elizabeth shivered from a strange chill as Amy's deep sorrow passed to her and worked its way into her heart.

The look upon the old woman's face made Amy feel very uncomfortable, and she wanted to withdraw her hand. Yet, she couldn't seem to find the strength to do it. It was as if her willpower were flowing out through her hands into James' grandmother, somehow bonding her to Elizabeth.

"Goodness, Child, what terrible things someone has done to you! It was only by the force of your own inner strength that you survived. Such evil...such vileness for one so small to have faced alone." Stopping for a moment, Elizabeth took a deep breath before continuing in a voice that seemed to be too strong and deep for such a small woman. "The demon that violated you is dead, but he planted his seed deep in your heart. You keep that seed alive by feeding it the fear it needs to remain alive. The creature that the seed produced grows stronger each day because it has a steady supply of food. It stalks you in the night, haunts your dreams, and is slowly stealing your soul. What you don't know is that you can kill this evil thing by confronting it. It needs your fears to keep growing. Without this fear it will not have anything to feed upon, and it will die. You alone keep this creature alive, and you alone must be the one to destroy it. All you have to do is face it and then the healing will start."

Elizabeth faltered slightly as the intense emotions coming from Amy made themselves known. James watched his grandmother's face grow ashen, and when her eyes started to glaze over and her breathing became slightly labored, he decided that it was time to break the energy flow that was bonding her and Amy. Amy's negative force was very powerful right now, and his grandmother wasn't as strong as she used to be. He didn't want anything to happen to her. He bent over the two women and unclasped their hands, gently breaking the link between them.

"Grammy, Amy wanted to ask you a couple of questions about something special she needs to know."

After the connection between her and Elizabeth had been broken, Amy felt despair ebb through her body, and she wanted to cry but the tears were locked inside. She heard her father's voice whispering in her ear. "Don't you cry. Don't you dare start that awful wailing. You know what will happen if you do."

"Amy," James called gently to her, "it's all right. We're here with you. Don't be afraid."

"I'm fine, there's nothing for you to be concerned about," Amy finally responded. Rising from the side of Elizabeth's wheelchair, she crossed the room to the white recliner by the door and sat down.

James moved Elizabeth's wheelchair next to Amy so the two women could talk. Then he sat down on the edge of the bed and waited for Amy to make the next move.

After a disquieting moment of empty silence, Amy asked the question she had come seeking an answer for. "Elizabeth, do you remember a painting that belonged to you before you moved here, a painting of a little girl with her arms wrapped around a collie? James told me it used to hang over his bed when he was a child."

"I know which one you are talking about. James got very upset when he discovered it had been sold at the auction. He's been looking for it ever since he got back into town. I really hope he finds it. If I had known how important it was to him I never would have allowed it to be sold."

"By a strange twist of fate, I'm the one who has the painting now, and there are a couple of questions I need to ask you about it."

"As bad as my memory is, I can still recall when my father had that portrait painted."

"So you really know who the child in the painting is?" Amy felt her heart fluttering with excitement. *Am I really going to find out this easily?*

"Why, of course! It's me," Elizabeth said with a smile on her face as she thought about the painting. "My father wanted it as a gift for my mother's twenty-fifth birthday. I can still remember how angry I got because he had made me sit and pose for it. I wanted to go outside and play with my cousins and he wouldn't let me."

Amy sat on the edge of the white chair with her hands clasped so tightly together that her fingers were almost blue, and she couldn't believe what she had just heard. *The child in the painting can't be James' grandmother! She's still very much alive, and you can't be a ghost if you're still alive. That isn't possible. Heaven help me, if the ghost isn't real, then what am I seeing?"*

Caught up in the memories of her childhood, Elizabeth wasn't paying attention to the change in Amy, and she kept talking. "That's why there's such a pouty look on my face. I refused to smile the whole time the man was painting it. My father got so upset with me, but it didn't matter. I was such a spoiled little thing back in those days. My mother and father usually gave me whatever I wanted, so I didn't know how to act when I didn't get my way."

Amy turned her accusing eyes toward James; a silent question hung on the air between them. *Why didn't you tell me it was your grandmother…you knew*!

+++++

James had known what his grandmother's response to Amy's question would be, so he had watched Amy intently for any signs of distress. Knowing that the next few minutes would be a critical time for her, he kept his eyes locked on her face. It was entirely possible that Amy might not be mentally or emotionally strong enough to handle what her mind was trying to tell her. But James was fairly sure that she would be because she wouldn't be trying to seek out the answers if she weren't in some way preparing herself for the knowledge that would come with the questions she was asking.

He hoped bringing her to meet his grandmother had been the right decision. He really thought if he had told her that the child in the painting had been his grandmother, who was still very much alive, she wouldn't have believed him. Amy was so sure she was seeing a ghost that it wouldn't have mattered what he told her. She would have thought he was lying.

James stood up and walked across the room to Amy, who was still seated on the edge of her chair. He gently placed one of his hands on her shoulder and the other one under her chin, tilting her head up so she could look directly into his face. "Amy, there are answers to the questions that are haunting you; only they aren't the ones you are expecting. It is much more complicated than you could possibly imagine. Those answers are deep inside your mind; you just haven't realized it yet. You can discover what they are, but you will need help. Trying to do it alone is too dangerous. You need someone to guide you safely."

Amy didn't respond. She didn't know what to feel or believe anymore. Nothing made any sense at all.

Elizabeth didn't understand the sudden tension in the room. "I'm sorry I was rambling on," she said worriedly. "Please forgive me. I didn't mean to take up your time with my old stories."

"You didn't Grammy," James said, "but I think you have had enough excitement for today. Let me help you back into bed; you look tired."

Elizabeth agreed, feeling the heavy weight of exhaustion resting upon her shoulders. "I am really tired right now," she said wearily. Turning to Amy, she looked at her with great concern. "Remember what I said. Your healing can only start after you face the fears within yourself."

James picked Elizabeth up from the wheelchair as if she were weightless and carried her to bed. "We have to get going now Grammy, but I think we will be back soon." He kissed her on the forehead and turned to leave, but he stopped when she grabbed his hand.

"James," Elizabeth said in odd voice.

"What Grammy?"

"I want you to always remember that I love you. If I don't get the chance to see you again for a long time, know you will always be in my thoughts. No matter where I am."

"You talk like I won't be seeing you soon. I promise to be back in a couple of days." James smiled at his grandmother as he placed a loving kiss on her forehead. "I love you, too."

Amy didn't say a word. She just stood up and headed toward Edward's car without even saying goodbye to Elizabeth. She couldn't think. Nothing made any sense; her mind was exploding in a kaleidoscope of thoughts and feelings. When James joined her in the car, she didn't even acknowledge his presence.

Worried, but not wanting to intrude into Amy's thoughts, James kept silent. Amy would have to take the next step on her own. Unless she asked for help, there wasn't really anything he could do. Each person has to choose his own path to walk. His calling in life was to offer what support he could while allowing those individuals he was assisting to make their own choices. He knew he couldn't force someone to see what that person didn't want to see.

Amy didn't speak a single word during the drive back to her car.

James kept glancing over to make sure she was all right. When they were crossing over Hollow Bridge, he had this funny feeling in the pit of his stomach that she was seriously thinking about opening the car door and jumping out. He reached over and hit the automatic door lock, and the sound of the locking doors echoed through the car.

But Amy didn't appear to hear them. Her facial expression seemed cast in stone. She wasn't even blinking. Instead, her eyes were following the river below. It looked so peaceful, and she wanted to be with it, to become part of it. Maybe out there in the water she could find an end to the pain throbbing through her head. How easy it would be to walk out and let it accept her. So very easy—

+++++

When James dropped Amy off by her car, he took a business card from his billfold and wrote his home phone number on the back. "Remember to call if you need me at any time, no matter what. You have my work and home phone number. I promise I will do my best to get to you as soon as possible. It is very important at this time to realize that you're not going crazy. There is a reason for what is happening to you. When you are ready to understand, the answers will come."

Amy reluctantly accepted James' business card, staring at it for a few seconds before finally acknowledging he had even said anything. "Thanks for the offer. I'll remember to call if I need to. Right now I just have to think about a few things. I'm not sure about anything in my life. I feel so foolish, so very foolish. A ghost, for goodness sakes, I really thought I saw a ghost."

"Maybe, in a way you did." James placed a hand upon Amy's shoulder hoping to offer her a little touch of comfort. "Come talk with me, and I'll help you find out exactly what you did see."

Amy pulled back from James without saying a word. Her eyes, blank and expressionless, told him to leave.

301

+++++

Amy sat in her car watching as James pulled into the flow of the afternoon traffic. She tried to escape from the overpowering pain threatening to consume her, only she couldn't do it. Her tears poured out for over an hour before she managed to force them to stop. Her calm exterior had been shattered into a thousand pieces, and she didn't know how to put it back together again. Finally, while still immersed in a state of confusion, she started her car.

What am I going to do now? Go home and go crazier?

No, she decided, *it would be better to go to work where there were a million things that needed to be done.*

Chapter 32

As Amy pulled her car into Comtec's parking lot, she glanced into the rearview mirror and was shocked by her appearance. Her eyes, swollen and red from crying, made her look as though she had been weeping for days. She rummaged through her purse until she found a rumpled Kleenex and quickly wiped away the tears that were staining her face.

After carefully applying a heavy layer of makeup, she felt somewhat better, although a profound bitterness weighted down her heart. *A new coat of paint can do wonders in covering up damaged goods,* she thought as she inspected her face in the mirror. *Look how well Mom was able to hide all the bruises I had as a child. No one ever suspected a thing.*

+++++

Before Amy went into her office, she first stopped at Susan's desk to pick up her mail. James' business card fell unnoticed from her purse when she laid it down on the desk so she could shuffle through the stack of letters waiting for her.

"I'm really glad you're here," Susan said, thankful Amy had finally showed up. "Things with Gary have started to get a little out of hand, and I wasn't sure how to handle it." Susan looked up from her computer and noticed Amy's puffy, red eyes. She realized immediately something was very wrong because Amy never cried. "Hey, what's wrong? You were so late I've been thinking about paging you. I was really starting to get worried." Susan looked at Amy with concern. "It's not like you to miss work."

"I've just had a really rough morning, that's all." Amy purposefully avoided the questioning look in Susan's eyes.

"Well, maybe this will cheer you up a little. While you were gone, this gorgeous man came in asking for you. When he found out you weren't here, he said to tell you that he'd be back later today. He sounded like he really wanted to see you." Susan grinned at Amy. "Have you got a secret I don't know about? I haven't seen this guy around before, and I would have remembered him. He said his name was Ted."

"I wonder what he wanted." Amy replied, perking up at the mention of Ted's name.

"Oh, he said something about being concerned about you." Susan looked at Amy with the spark of a mischievous twinkle glinting brightly in her eyes. "It seems you weren't feeling very well when he helped you to bed last night. No wonder you were late getting here today. If a man like that had helped me to bed, I sure wouldn't be up early the next morning either!"

"Oh Susan, I just had one of my migraines, and he kind of tucked me in bed. That's all." Amy blushed as she thought about what her friend had insinuated.

"I'll just bet that's all that happened. Well, he could tuck me in any time. The next time he comes in here I'm going to tell him I have a headache and need help getting home and into bed."

A tiny smile crossed Amy's face at Susan's teasing. Her friend had a way of making things seem a little less tense. However, she didn't want to answer the questions she knew were forming in Susan's mind so she quickly changed the subject. "I really do need to get to work. Give me a few minutes to get organized, then fill me in on what's happening."

Amy headed for her office and closed the door behind her. She needed some privacy. She wanted a few minutes to get herself together before tackling any big problems, especially ones that involved Gary.

Susan returned to working on the proposal she had been typing, but out of the corner of her eye she noticed a slip of paper that didn't belong on her desk. It hadn't been there a few minutes ago, and curiosity got the best of her. She reached over and picked it up. *A business card? Where had that come from?*

Then she remembered Amy had just picked up her mail, and she figured her friend must have dropped it. Susan checked out the name on the card—Dr. James Perry. And she suddenly became very concerned. *What was going on with Amy? Was she sick? Maybe that might explain why she'd been crying this morning.*

The more Susan thought about it, the more worried she became. Amy had been having a lot of migraines the past couple of months, and each week they had seemed to grow in intensity. She had been encouraging Amy to have a check-up. Maybe she had followed the advice, and maybe the doctor had found something seriously wrong.

Susan knocked on Amy's office door. She felt she needed to say something to Amy but she wasn't sure what.

"Come on in." Amy looked up from letter she had been reading.

"I wanted to see if this was yours," Susan said, handing Amy the business card. "I found it on my desk, and I thought it might be something important." "Yes, that's mine. I must have dropped it when I picked up my mail. Thanks for bringing it to me." Amy put the card in her purse without giving Susan a single clue as to why she had the doctor's business card.

Susan started to ask about Dr. Perry, but then her phone rang in the other room, and she reluctantly left to answer it. As she went back to her desk, she decided that she would try again later to find out what was going on with Amy. If something was really wrong, she didn't want her friend to face it alone.

When Susan picked up the receiver she heard Edward's voice come across the line.

"Hi Susan. Is Amy available? I've been trying to get in touch with her all morning."

"Yes, she finally showed up a couple of minutes ago. If you'll hold for a second, I'll ring you into her office."

"Wait. I want to talk with you first. Has Amy said anything to you about those headaches of hers? I think they've been getting worse, and I'm really worried about her."

Susan knew Edward well enough to realize that he was truly concerned about his sister, so she didn't feel too bad about mentioning Amy's problem. In fact, she was actually a little bit relieved to be able to talk to someone about it. "You're right about the headaches. They have been getting worse lately, especially over the last two weeks. It seems like she has been having one every day, and today she didn't come to work until after two. I really think she spent the morning crying."

"Crying! I haven't seen her cry for years. Maybe I had better come over to the office and talk with her today. I need to find out what's going on."

"There's something else, too. I'm not sure I should be saying anything, but I think she might be seeing a doctor. She had a business card from a Dr. James Perry in her purse."

"James Perry! He's a child psychiatrist. Why would she be seeing him?"

"Well, maybe I've jumped to a conclusion about that. It could be she is seeing him for personal reasons. Maybe she's making up for lost time. You should have seen this one guy that came in here today looking for her. He looked like a Greek god. Said his name was Ted. If he hadn't been asking for Amy, I might have tried moving in on him myself."

"Ted was there! Hey, that's the best news you could have given me. It would be so fantastic if the two of them connected. He's really a great guy. I've wanted them to meet for a long time, and I finally pulled it off at her birthday party."

"Sorry I had to miss it, but I had other plans that couldn't be canceled. But, the next time you have a party and arrange to have guys like Ted there, I'll be sure to make it. I don't suppose you have any more friends like him hanging around? I'm available, you know."

"I'll see what I can do. I do have a friend or two that might be interested."

"Thanks. But don't keep me waiting too long. I'm in big demand, you know. I would hate for your friends to get upset with you because they had the chance to meet me, and you blew it for them. They might not forgive you."

"I'll keep that in mind. I certainly don't want to make any new enemies." Pausing, Edward's thoughts went back to Amy. "I don't believe Dr. Perry would be someone Amy would be dating. I wonder what is going on? I have this funny feeling inside that there is something very wrong happening, but I can't place my finger on what it is. I guess I really need to sit down and talk with Amy. Is she going to be in the office the rest of the afternoon?"

"From the looks of her schedule she should be here until five or six."

"I'll try to make it over to Comtec to see her sometime in the next couple of hours. If she's been crying, I need to find out why."

"That might not be a bad idea. She doesn't know it yet, but things are going to get a little complicated around here the rest of the afternoon. I have to tell her about a problem here at the office that she isn't going to like to hear, and it's only going to add to her stress level. It'll be good for her to have you to talk to."

"I'll be over in an hour or so. Don't bother to tell her I called. I'll just surprise her."

"She might not be in the mood for surprises."

"That's true, but this way she might not have time to put up those defensive walls she always uses when people start to get too personal."

"If I wasn't so worried about her, I wouldn't be doing this. It's probably going to make her mad that I talked to you."

"I promise not to tell her where the information came from."

"It really doesn't matter as long as Amy is all right. I'm glad she's got you to help. Not everyone is lucky enough to have a brother who really cares."

"I wouldn't really say Amy is lucky to have me as a brother, but she's kind of stuck with me whether she wants it that way or not. So, guess I'll be seeing you soon. Maybe by the time I get there, I'll even have a list of potential dates lined up for you. I don't think it would take very long to get a list started. All I have to do is tell them how beautiful you are."

"You never change. You've always been the perfect charmer. If Ellen didn't already have you all wrapped up, I would let you charm me into a date. Oh well, guess I'll have to learn to live with my disappointment. See you soon."

Chapter 33

"Gary was at it again today," Susan announced to Amy when they were alone in Amy's office. "I caught him backing Carrie up against the copy machine this morning. She told him to leave her alone, but he just laughed like it was all a big joke."

"Well, it certainly isn't a joke," Amy replied, angry that Gary hadn't taken her warning seriously.

"I heard him tell her if she didn't want his attention then she shouldn't dress like a little slut and that she was inviting men to come on to her by wearing such short skirts."

"It doesn't matter what she's wearing. That's not the issue." Amy felt her anger growing with each passing minute. "I will not tolerate sexual harassment in this office. It's wrong no matter what the circumstances."

"Guys like Gary don't have enough common sense to realize what they're doing is wrong. They think it's their right to treat women any way they choose. After I caught him with Carrie, the

311

arrogant jerk actually smiled at me. Then he walked out of the room like he owned the whole building and could do whatever he wanted. I wanted to trip him as he walked by, but I didn't want to give him anything to complain to you about. Still, the urge was very hard to suppress."

"Where is Carrie now?" Amy knew she needed to talk with the girl to verify exactly what had occurred between her and Gary and get her to fill out a written complaint. "When I take the matter up with Mr. Kessler I have to have substantial proof that Gary is harassing her or he will simply brush the whole matter aside without doing a thing about it."

"After that last encounter with Gary, I found her crying in the bathroom. I told her to take a long lunch break."

"Where's Gary?"

"He left for lunch right before Carrie, and he's been gone for over two hours. He doesn't seem to care if he gets his work done. In my opinion he's useless, and it would be in Comtec's best interest if they got rid of him. The company that sent him here surely has someone a little more professional to handle its training."

"If they want to keep our business, they had better." Amy could feel resentment growing because the company had sent Gary in the first place. "From the way he is acting this type of conduct isn't something new for him. The behavior patterns are too well set in place. I don't understand why someone hasn't reported him before now or why he hasn't been fired. I wouldn't keep any employee on my staff that behaves the way he does."

"You know how it is," Susan said with disgust, "there's a good chance no one ever reported him. Even today women are still being taught that they are supposed to be subservient to men, which of course, includes putting up with their sexist remarks and unsolicited advances. Some men really believe women enjoy that type of absurd behavior, and to make things worse, women aren't taught how to fight back. They are trained to keep their mouths shut to avoid making a scene. That's what Carrie is worried about…making a scene. Can you believe that! Gary is pawing all over her, and she is worried about something as idiotic as that. If it'd been me, I would've put my knee right into his precious little—"

"Susan! I don't think that would be an efficient way to handle the problem…at least here at work. We can't let ourselves sink down to his level. I have worked too hard to get where I am to allow someone like him to bring me down. Once I talk with Carrie and get the proper paperwork ready, then I'll deal with Gary. If you could find her and send her in, I will see what can be done to fix things."

"All right, but sometimes you take away all my fun." Susan paused at the door and turned to face Amy. "I know you're right, but my way would have been much more enjoyable…at least for me."

+++++

Susan found Carrie by the copier next to the break room. "Amy wants to see you in her office right away."

"Do you know what for?" Fear flashed in Carrie's pretty emerald-green eyes.

313

"She needs to talk with you concerning Gary's behavior this morning." Susan noticed Carrie's hands were trembling and her face had paled at the mention of Gary's name.

"Is she going to fire me?" Carrie's voice wavered and she avoided Susan's eyes as she handed over the papers. "I really need this job. I don't know what I'll do if she fires me."

"Why would you even think such a thing? She only wants to talk with you."

"I sure hope that's all she wants," Carrie said, fear showing in her eyes. "I promise I won't cause any more problems if she'll just let me stay."

Susan watched as Carrie walked dejectedly toward Amy's office, and she shook her head in disgust. Gary had the poor child scared to death. The girl's personality had changed dramatically in only one week. She was acting as if she were about to receive a death sentence.

+++++

Amy looked up from her paperwork when she heard a timid knock on her door. At first, the sound was so faint she thought she had imagined it. Then she heard it again. Through the tinted glass on her door she could make out the shape of a woman, and she knew it had to be Carrie.

"Come on in Carrie. I've been expecting you. Pull up a chair and sit down."

"Susan said you wanted to talk to me. Have I done something wrong?"

"No! Whatever gave you that idea?"

Carrie's pallor grew worse under Amy's questioning gaze. Stammering she tried to explain. "Well…it's just…it's just that Gary said…he said—"

Amy's ire at Gary grew as tears started flowing down Carrie's cheeks. "Calm down Carrie. You're not in any trouble. I simply need for you to explain to me what has been happening in the office that is making you so upset." Amy tried not to seem overbearing as she questioned the girl. She had suspicions that Carrie could be easily intimidated, which may be one of the main reasons Gary had chosen her to hit on. Guys like Gary prey on women like Carrie. It makes them feel more powerful when they can intimidate and control other people.

"I just don't know if I should say anything. I really need this job," Carrie finally responded, her eyes looking pleadingly at Amy. "I don't want to get fired for causing any problems. My uncle told me to just do my work and keep my mouth shut. He said the other employees wouldn't want to work with someone who whined to the boss."

"There's a big difference between whining and reporting inappropriate behavior," Amy gently explained. "I believe something is happening here in the office that is really bothering you. Now, it's my job to handle problems, but I can't do that unless you cooperate. If you're having a problem that should be addressed, I need to know."

Unable to force her eyes to meet Amy's, Carrie sat in her chair staring at her hands and twisting a handkerchief into a tight knot. "I don't want to cause any trouble. I only want to do my job."

"You're doing a fine job. I have no complaints with your work. That's not what I called you in here for. I need for you to tell me if there is anything happening in this office that could account for this sudden change in your behavior."

"What do you mean?"

"I think you have an idea what I am talking about, but you have to be the one to tell me. I can't do your talking for you."

Carrie finally lifted her head forcing her gaze to meet Amy's. "It's Gary. He keeps bothering me. Every time I turn around he is right there; I can't get away from him, and he is always touching me. I keep begging him to leave me alone, but he just laughs. He told me if I caused any problems for him he would get me fired. I can't afford to get fired. I need the money for college this fall."

"Where is he touching you? You need to be specific." Amy gently coaxed Carrie to continue.

"He keeps putting his arm around my shoulders, and a couple of times he's touched my breasts," Carries said, a small blush coloring her pale cheeks. "Once he came up behind me at the copy machine and pressed his whole body against mine. Then he whispered he could make me feel really good if I'd just let him. He said that the only thing I needed was a good…uh…oh, I can't even say the word." Blushing even more, she continued with a little less restraint. "Once he came into the break room when I was there alone, and he grabbed my hand and placed it on…on his…thing, and that really scared me. I didn't know what he was going to do next. I tried to jerk my hand away, but he's so strong. He just laughed at me, and I hurt my arm."

"Why haven't you told someone? This type of behavior in the work place is illegal." Amy's anger showed in her voice. She was very frustrated that such things were happening in her office.

"I told my uncle what Gary did, but he told me to just ignore him. He said that kind of stuff happens all the time, and that I had might as well get used to it. He said that was simply the way men were, always trying to sniff out some action. Then he told me to just stay away from Gary and not to do anything to entice him. He said I only had to hang on for a little while because Gary would be gone in a couple of weeks. My uncle didn't want me causing any problems that might reflect back on him, and he'll be really angry at me if I caused any trouble here."

"Your uncle couldn't be more wrong. You don't have to put up with such behavior at work, or any other place for that matter. Maybe twenty years ago women couldn't do anything about sexual harassment, but they can now." It really infuriated Amy that a man could still believe it was acceptable for a woman to be touched without her consent.

"Gary said if I told anyone he would deny it. I've only been working here a little while, and he has so much more experience than I do. He said you would take his side because it would be much easier to replace me than him, and that I was only a little peon and you wouldn't think twice about getting rid of me if I caused any trouble."

"Well Carrie, his actions were way out of line. He's the one who is going to have to go. His behavior is not acceptable here in this office or in any other office for that matter." Amy reached into the file cabinet by her desk. "What you have to do is file a written complaint. I want complete details of everything he said or did that made you feel uncomfortable. When you get finished bring it into me, and I will do the rest."

"You mean I'm not fired?" Carrie looked at Amy with astonishment. "I can't believe it. I was scared to death to talk to you." Carrie picked up the forms Amy had placed in front of her, and she actually smiled. "I promise I'll get this report written up for you right away."

As Carrie left the office, Amy could already see a difference in the young woman's attitude. Maybe the next time Carrie would be able to stand up for herself a little better. But who knows for sure? A lifetime of learning how to be submissive is very hard to undo. She knew all about that in great detail. To learn how to stand up for yourself was hard, especially when someone kept trying to knock you back down when you tried.

Chapter 34

Gary leaned against the wall by the coffeemaker slowly sipping on a cup of steaming hot coffee and silently watching Carrie as she left Amy's office. He intuitively knew Carrie had been blabbing her mouth off to Amy. He could tell by the way she refused to let her eyes meet his; she was acting just like a child who had gotten caught telling her best friend's secret.

"Stupid slut," he mumbled as Carrie attempted to pass him on the way to her desk. He had purposely positioned himself so she had to practically push him out of the way to get past. He could tell she didn't want to touch him, but there wasn't any way she could avoid it. When she tried to squeeze past he grabbed her wrist.

"What's the matter, Carrie?" Gary growled in a low, threatening voice. "Why the big hurry? Are you afraid the big boss lady is going to say something if you stay and talk with me for a while?"

"Leave me alone." Carrie made a weak effort to pull away from Gary's hold, but all she managed to do was hurt her arm as Gary tightened his powerful grasp. Huge tears formed in her eyes, and fear stole her voice so she couldn't speak.

Pleased with Carrie's reaction, Gary felt the omnipotent feeling of power surge through his whole body as she cringed at his touch. Sudden warmth heated his groin and the pulsating pleasure stirred his blood. He smiled at Carry with a wicked grin before he finally released his hold. As he watched her scurry past, he allowed an underlying anger to rise from within his heart. Her rejection of his advances made him want to smack her right in the mouth.

Run away, you stupid mouse; I'll still catch you later. His angry glare followed Carrie as she crossed the room heading toward her desk. He knew she was aware that he was still watching and she wouldn't be able to resist the urge to glance back. And he was right. After she sat down, she did just that. Smirking, he waved. When she jerked her head around to stare at the wall in front of her desk, he laughed just loud enough for her to hear. He wanted her to know he wasn't afraid of anything she might say about him to Amy.

There wasn't any doubt in his mind whatsoever that Carrie had complained to Amy about him, but he wasn't the least bit worried. Nothing she could possibly say would affect him in any way. He hadn't done anything wrong, except maybe pick the wrong girl to go after. He had only been trying to have a little fun to ease the boredom of his godforsaken job. He should have known Carrie would run to her boss about it. She looked like the whimpering kind.

God, how he hated stupid, whimpering women! They weren't good for anything at all. They weren't even any good in bed; they expected men to be nice and treat them like delicate porcelain dolls. To make things worse, they usually wanted you to talk them, too. Hell, if he wanted to talk to someone he would go out with his friends to a bar and have a few beers. What he wanted when he was with a woman was someone who would keep her mouth shut and take care of important matters, which of course, meant taking care of him.

When he had picked Carrie to go after, he didn't think she would be one of the stupid ones. She had simply seemed very shy and reserved. And that was precisely the kind of women he liked to bed because once he managed to work his way around their barriers, they were usually hell raisers in the heat of the night. The hardest part was getting them past saying no all the time. He had learned that shy women always say no at first, but what they really meant was yes, only they just didn't know it. It was his pleasure to show them the truth behind their own desires. Although it sometimes took him a little bit of time to get them to understand that they really did want it. Of course, he had to use a little force once in a while, but then women do have fantasies about being dominated by a sexy man, and who was he to deprive them of their fantasies! He was always ready to oblige a woman on that account. Nothing turned him on more than to have some woman begging and pleading with him to stop. It was all part of the game. They would be begging for him to leave them alone, while at the same time their bodies would be so wet and moist just waiting for him to take them. He knew "no" meant "yes." Their bodies would give it away every time.

Too bad Carrie turned out to be such a fool. We could have had such fun. Oh well, it's her loss, he thought, heading outside to take a cigarette break. Lighting the cigarette, Gary started thinking about Amy. *Now there was one ball-breaking woman. The looks she gives me are so hard they could drive nails into a coffin. I'll bet she's never had a good night of sex in her entire life. Maybe her problem is that she doesn't like men. Boy, would that be a loss. She has a body that was built to please a man, especially this man. It would be a shame if it were being wasted on another dumb woman.*

What fun I could have with that bitch if I could just get her alone for a couple of hours, although I usually don't like to mess with women with big attitude problems. But in her case I could definitely make an exception. Man would I love to get my hands on her breasts. They're so full and firm looking, and I'll bet if I squeezed them just right, it would knock some of the cockiness out of her. A little pain went a long way sometimes. Boy, wouldn't she look fantastic groveling at my feet wearing nothing but a face full of tears. I bet I could have her begging and pleading for a piece of me in no time at all. I would probably have to get a little more rough with her than some of the others, but that would only make the whole thing much more interesting.

Lost in his fantasy, he didn't hear one of the secretaries, Amanda, calling his name. Her tap on the shoulder startled him, and he burnt his finger on the last bit of his cigarette. "What do you want?" he growled.

"Sorry about that." Amanda apologized, although her eyes didn't convey that message. "I need some help. I can't get the correct program to come up, and Amy said to get you to show me what I was doing wrong."

Reluctantly, he headed back into the office. Why had he been so foolish as to take a job where he had to work with so many ignorant women? They all reminded him of his mother, and he hated to be reminded of her. If that old bag had only been a little smarter, maybe his life wouldn't have been such hell when he had been growing up. If the woman had just once been strong enough to stand up to his father, life would've been so different. It might have been a little tough, but it wouldn't have been nearly as bad as it had been living with that bastard.

If...if...if...He was so tired of thinking about all the ifs that could have changed his life. It didn't really matter now anyway. He had finally escaped his parents when he turned eighteen and was doing just fine without either one of them. He hadn't seen them in five years and had no intention of ever seeing them again. He didn't even know if they were still alive and didn't really care.

+++++

As Gary worked with Amanda, visions of his mother kept popping into his mind. He could see her crawling on the floor trying to escape from his father, her mouth cut and bleeding from the fist that had just slammed into it, a big bruise showing itself around one of her eyes as she squinted trying to see through the rapidly swelling tissue. She had been so pathetic with all that crying and begging she did, but her tears never did her any good. His father never stopped until he had been good and ready to stop. If he got tired of beating up on her, he had no difficulties finding another victim to choose from.

Gary felt his anger flaming higher and higher as he remembered the days and nights of hiding in closets, under beds, in the basement. How he had hated the old bastard for doing that to him. He had hated him enough to even think about killing him.

In the beginning he had cried and pleaded with his father to stop the beatings, to leave Mom alone, to leave him alone. He had honestly believed the son of a bitch had wanted to kill both of them. He had begged his mother to leave, to run away. But she never did. She had spent all her time trying to please his father that there had never been any time left over for him. "I've no choice," she had said time and time again. "A boy needs his father, and besides I can't support us with what money I could make. We don't have no friends or family to help us. Your father has seen to that. There is nothing I can do. We have to stay."

So they had stayed.

After a time he had learned to just keep out of his father's way. When the old man had been on a rampage, he had discovered it was safer to hide than to stay and try to help his mother. Besides, it had been her own fault she had gotten smacked around like she did. She could have left if she had really wanted to. The simple fact was she was too stupid to do anything about it. After a few years he finally wised up and decided it wasn't worth the pain of getting punched around simply because of her stupidity. After all, it had been her choice, not his.

Now that he was older, he realized being dumb was just part of being a woman. Too bad it had taken him so many years to grasp that one simple little fact. He might have gotten along better with his father if he had only known how really stupid women were. Unfortunately, he had started to understand only after he had gotten out in the real world and had been able to see how his mother was like all the other women in the world. Now he knew his father had been right all along. Man was meant to be the aggressor over women. Why else would all that testosterone be flowing through their bodies? No women-libbers could change that fact, no matter how much they bellyached about women's rights. Man was born to be in power. It's in the species, and who was he to fight Mother Nature?

+++++

As Gary stood over Amanda while she sat at her desk entering codes into the computer, he felt the urgent call of nature stirring his blood again. When he placed an arm across her shoulders, he felt her muscles tense under his touch. The feeling of power that swept over him at that moment heightened all of his senses. He could almost smell the fear that was coming from her.

"Here…this is what you need to do to get this to work right," he said, innocently working the keyboard with his free hand, while he let the other hand softly caress the back of Amanda's neck. He smiled as he felt a small tremor go through her body.

325

A new game begins, he thought as he leaned suggestively up against her. Forgetting all about his problems with Carrie, he felt a surge of energy go straight through him. *Amanda wants me, I can tell. I only need to persuade her of that fact, and I'm an expert on persuasion.*

Chapter 35

Good news sure travels fast, Amy thought as she thumbed through the pile of complaint forms lying in front of her. *It took less than an hour for the news about Carrie to travel through the office.* Reading the four additional, newly filed complaints against Gary she had in her hands, she was amazed how one man had managed to create so much chaos in such a short time. He was a feminist's nightmare and had acted like Comtec was his own personal hunting ground for fresh meat.

Amy picked up a pen and started writing. She wanted to turn in the complaints to her administrator before the office closed today. As her fingers hurriedly completed the supervisory follow-up forms that needed to accompany the complaint write-ups, she mentally listed everything that had to be done to properly process the complaints. She wanted to follow up with the grievance process in a legitimate manner. Gary wasn't going to be left with a way out of the corner he had painted himself into. Everything needed to be done exactly by the book.

Gary didn't seem like the type to take kindly to criticism in any form, and though she would never admit it, she was a little afraid of him. With minimum effort, she could visualize him stalking her through the hallways with a gun or a knife.

Laying down her pen, she took a long, deep breath. Maybe she was being a bit paranoid, but she didn't really think so. Gary's eyes had a dangerous aura shining in them. She had seen that look in her father's eyes and knew exactly what it meant.

Armed with the appropriate paperwork, Amy headed toward the administrator's office. She didn't have an appointment to meet with Mr. Kessler, so she hoped he would be free to talk with her. This late in the day he was usually busy trying to complete his own work, and she didn't know if he would even see her.

When she walked though the doors to Mr. Kessler's reception area, the first thing she saw was his secretary, Mrs. Arms, sitting at her desk absorbed in a romantic novel. Amy saw the brightly colored book cover that portrayed two vibrant lovers closely entwined in each other's arms and wondered why women would believe the garbage printed in those things. *Love is so vastly overrated in romance novels, and I don't understand why women can't see that.*

When Mrs. Arms heard the door close she almost jumped straight up out of her chair. She had been so absorbed in the romantic interlude going on between the two lovers in the book, she hadn't heard Amy's approach. Quickly shoving the novel into a drawer, she blushed and attempted to put on a professional face.

"Good afternoon, Ms. Tedrow. What can I do to help you?" Mrs. Arms asked.

"Do you think I could have a minute or two with Mr. Kessler? I have an important issue that needs his immediate attention."

"He just returned from a meeting and doesn't have anything on his agenda. He might be able to see you right now." Mrs. Arms quickly punched a couple of buttons on her intercom system. "Give me a minute while I check with him." After a few seconds she motioned for Amy to go on in.

Amy immediately felt dwarfed by Mr. Kessler's huge office. Everything in the place seemed twice the normal size it should be. Even his desk was a mammoth production. It made her desk look like a miniature replica in a dollhouse. Of course Mr. Kessler did need a big desk to fit his big frame. In his younger days he had been a professional football player, and he still looked the part with a thick neck, muscular arms, and enormous hands.

When Amy entered the office, Mr. Kessler stood up and offered a welcoming handshake. For a second, when his big hand engulfed hers, she felt panicky. When she was a child her father's hand used to cover hers the same way, but she refused to let that feeling take control. She had more important things to worry about right now than her father's haunting memories.

"Good Afternoon, Ms. Tedrow. Mrs. Arms said you needed to talk with me. Is there a problem?"

"Mr. Kessler, I have had several complaints concerning Gary Stevenson, the computer specialist who is assisting with the installation of the new computer programming system."

"Gary Stevenson?" Raising one eyebrow in a questioning look, Mr. Kessler wondered why Amy had such a grave look on her face. "I met him yesterday, and he seemed to be a nice enough guy. What kind of complaints are you talking about?"

"Sexual harassment," Amy replied.

"The last sexual harassment complaint I had turned out to be nothing more than some woman being mad at her boyfriend," Mr. Kessler said, suddenly looking annoyed. "I don't have time to waste on childish motives, and I certainly hope you're not going to take me down that road again."

Wordlessly, Amy handed him the written complaint forms and sat quietly waiting while he read them. Her face showed an expression of absolute determination. She wasn't going to let this case be smoothed over.

"These are fairly common complaints," Mr. Kessler said, glancing over the forms. "I've dealt with this type of behavior before. From your report I see you recommend that the gentleman be replaced immediately, and I'm not sure that's the right thing to do. It could place us in the middle of a huge lawsuit if Mr. Stevenson fights his removal. Plus, it would be a blemish on his work record, and I hate to do that to any man unless it is necessary. I believe if I talk to him in private it will solve the problem." Handing Amy back the complaint forms, Mr. Kessler appeared to be dismissing her.

Furious at Mr. Kessler's lack of concern over what she considered a very serious matter, Amy didn't take his hint to leave. "Gary has already been talked to privately. I warned him what would happen if he continued with his unprofessional behavior, and he has chosen to ignore the warnings. I think you had better worry more over a lawsuit from the women if you don't take these complaints seriously. These women have definite grounds for pressing a sexual harassment suit if you don't follow through and find a way to protect them from further unwanted advances from that man. Simply talking to him didn't solve the problem before, and it won't solve it now. In my opinion, if you don't handle this situation immediately by tomorrow you may have even bigger problems facing you."

Amy practically shoved the forms back in his face and stood her ground. She refused to leave the office until she felt that the complaints were going to be properly addressed. The women in her office were depending on her to make sure they would be safe, and she would do just that.

"You seem to be awfully upset over this. Is there some kind of personal problem between you and Mr. Stevenson?" Mr. Kessler condescendingly replied, ignoring the forms in Amy's hands. "If that's the case, I don't think it would be fair to ruin a man's career because you aren't happy over something. I still think it's best to handle it my way. I'll talk with him about it. Maybe he simply didn't take you seriously."

Amy felt her anger grow with each word that came out of Mr. Kessler's mouth. She gritted her teeth, shook her head in disbelief, and then continued. "Are you saying it's not important that he didn't take me seriously? I wasn't hired by Comtec to be ignored by an employee simply because he chooses to ignore me. I am not just a piece of decoration in this office. The man was instructed in very plain language what to expect if he continued with his inappropriate behavior, and not only did he continue with it, he got worse."

Finally, in a patronizing manner, Mr. Kessler accepted the complaints from Amy, but laid them down on his desk without even glancing at them. "This is starting to sound more and more like a problem between you and him. It appears you're upset because he didn't treat you seriously. Now, that may not have been good judgment on his account, but it still isn't a reason to get so carried away. We're talking about a man's future here."

"I think you had better read those complaints again. If you had checked over them thoroughly the first time, you would know this is not about me. For heaven's sake, the man has groped his way from one end of the office building to the other." Furious over his lack of concern, she pointed at the papers laid on his desk. "Do you see my name on those complaint forms? No, you do not! The only place you'll see that is on the documents showing I am following up on legitimate complaints from the employees working under me."

"I still think you are getting a little carried away over a trivial matter, but I will read everything again and decide what to do from there. Will that satisfy you?"

"What will satisfy me is for you to do the right thing. My name may not be on one of the complaint forms right now, however, if you do not handle this situation immediately, then it definitely will be. I will hand-deliver to the president of this company a written complaint from me concerning the inappropriate way you handled a very serious matter." Turning abruptly, Amy marched out of Mr. Kessler's office with an air of dignity that would have been hard to match.

Toni Auberry

Chapter 36

Who does that woman think she is? Mr. Kessler thought, tossing the complaint forms that Amy had handed him into his top desk drawer without even glancing at them. *She has a lot of nerve trying to tell me how to do my job!*

But Amy's last words kept repeating themselves in his mind. He didn't want her running to the company president and causing him trouble. He had enough to do without something like that messing up his day.

Maybe it would be in my best interest to be sure that I'm right, he decided. Pulling out the complaints, he began reading them in greater detail. As he finished reading the last one, he thoughtfully laid them on his desk. Maybe he had been a little hasty in dismissing the whole issue so lightly. If the women wanted to push it, they did have solid grounds to press sexual harassment charges against Mr. Stevenson.

That is if they were telling the truth.

The trouble with problems like this one is deciphering the real truth from the supposed truth. It did appear Gary had gotten a little carried away with his actions, but it was entirely possible the women initiated the contact. He had similar situations happen to him. Women were always sending out subtle invitations. That was just part of the benefit package of being in management. Being in management meant being in power, and women have this thing for men in power, which is one of the reasons extramarital affairs were more than common in the business world...they were the norm. It would be a shame to prosecute a man for doing the same thing everyone else seemed to be doing.

He had even taken advantage of a couple of invitations himself. The trick was to know how to do it without getting caught. Getting entangled in a web with a business associate had destroyed more than one man's career...and marriage. The number one rule was to always be discreet.

Unfortunately, as he read the complaint forms Amy had shoved at him a few minutes earlier, Mr. Kessler realized Gary had definitely not followed that particular rule. Even if the man had only been responding to the women's signals, he was guilty of being too indiscreet, too evident, in his actions. And since the women were choosing to make an issue of Gary's behavior, the breaking of that one rule could turn out to be the man's downfall.

Mr. Kessler shook his head in disgust. *I'm not putting my job on the line because of someone else's stupid mistakes.* Deciding it would be in his best interests to immediately follow up on the complaints as Amy had suggested, he had Mrs. Arms call Gary into his office for a little man-to-man talk.

+++++

Thirty minutes later, Gary nonchalantly strolled toward Mr. Kessler's office acting like he didn't have a care in the world. He knew there wasn't anything to be worried about. He had been called to the big boss's office before and nothing had ever come of it. It seemed that the women he worked with were always complaining about him, and he couldn't understand why they didn't just leave him alone.

Women should learn to keep their mouths shut and do their jobs, he thought bitterly. *No one wants to listen to them whine all the time. Especially me. I don't understand why I always end up working with so many of those crybabies.*

A small smirk crossed Gary's face. *Fortunately I'm lucky in other ways.* Since all of his bosses have been men, he had never really gotten into trouble over the incessant carping those boring, insipid women directed at him, and that was because men understand men. There is this routine speech the big boss men are required to give him about treating women with respect while at work, but he can see the little twinkle in their eyes while they are spouting it off.

Men know other men have certain needs that have to be met and that there are certain liberties allowable at work. All through history it has been the same. Women have been, and always will be, there to meet men's needs, and that is all there is to it. It's no big mystery. Unfortunately, some dumb cunt always seemed to be trying

337

to change things, especially at work. Women have managed to fix it so it looks like they are special or something. Can't even talk to one of them or give a friendly hug without getting into trouble. For instance, take that bitch, Amy. If she somehow manages to kiss her way up the business ladder, she'll make it hell on the men working under her. She's not the type that would cut any man a little slack. She would probably fire a guy just for trying to get a little action. What was the world coming to when a man can't do what comes naturally? Might as well just kill off all the men and let the women take over everything. I can certainly see where my father was right about one thing. Women like Amy, who try and control everything, need to be put in their place before they can do any damage. Men were born to be in control. Why couldn't women quit trying to act like men? It would make life so much easier on everyone.

+++++

Mrs. Arms wasn't at her desk when Gary arrived to see Mr. Kessler, but that didn't stop him. He didn't think he needed anyone to announce his entrance. After all, hadn't the big man himself summoned him? Why should he have to stand out there and wait to be told when to come in? What was he? Some kind of little peon like that insipid Carrie.

Without even bothering to knock, Gary arrogantly strolled in through the main doors into Mr. Kessler's office. He was so full of himself and of his self-importance that he didn't even recognize the angry look his unannounced entrance caused.

"Someone told me you wanted to talk to me right away." Gary pulled a chair over from the side of the room and plopping down in it like an insolent high school student reporting to his principal. "Well, here I am. What's so important anyway?"

"I usually don't have people walk into my office unannounced," Mr. Kessler spoke sharply, irked by Gary's behavior. "You should have waited until Mrs. Arms checked to see if I was ready for you yet."

"You mean that old bat that is always out there guarding the front gate? She wasn't there, so I just came on in. I don't see what the problem is. After all, you're the one who sent for me. What's your beef anyway?"

"My "beef" is the uncalled for behavior you've demonstrated over the past few days. Don't you have any common sense at all in that arrogant head of yours? Hasn't anyone ever explained to you that you can't go around making suggestive remarks or touching co-workers?"

"Those women are making a big thing out of nothing. Just because I'm an affectionate guy and give people a hug once in a while doesn't mean I'm doing one single thing wrong."

"I don't think giving a woman a hug involves placing your hands on her breasts."

"That's just someone's imagination working overtime. The woman who said I did that must have been doing a little wishful thinking."

"Then there must have been a lot of women daydreaming about you while they were supposed to be working. I have five written complaints right here on my desk by women who say you have been making inappropriate advances toward them."

"If anyone complained about me, it's that Amy's doing. She wants me out of here because I won't kiss her ass like a nice little boy. Well, let me tell you, there isn't one woman in the world I'd bow down to and do that, and I'm sure not going to start with her. She has no right to tell me what I can or can not do."

"Ms. Tedrow has the right to expect a certain degree of cooperation from you while you are working here. She may not be your immediate supervisor, but she has the right to request you stop harassing the employees who work under her."

"I haven't been harassing anyone! You should see those short skirts one of the girls wears to work every day. If she didn't want the attention, she shouldn't dress that way. She only got what she was asking for. You can't condemn a man for that."

Mr. Kessler watched Gary's face turn beet red from anger. He could understand now why the women were afraid of him. There was definitely a dangerous look to the man's appearance.

"Mr. Stevenson, I think it would be in the best interest of this company if we terminate our relationship with you. We are no longer in need of your services. You don't need to come to work in the morning. Your termination is effective immediately."

"This is all that bitch Amy's fault!" Gary protested loudly. "She doesn't like me, so she talked those other women into writing all this crap to get me into trouble."

"Are you trying to tell me these five women made up all of this just because Ms. Tedrow doesn't like you? They must be very good friends to get their stories to match so perfectly." Mr. Kessler picked up the complaint forms on his desk. He looked at Gary with contempt showing in his eyes. "From the way you're acting right now, there's no doubt in my mind you did exactly what these papers say you did."

"Hey listen, maybe I did get a little carried away, but those women aren't telling it like it really was. They're the ones that started it all. I only followed their lead. You should have seen the outfits Carrie wore to work. She was begging for attention. All I did was give her what she was asking for. You can't dismiss me for that!" Jumping out of his chair, Gary took a step toward Mr. Kessler, his hands clutched in tight fists and a bright rage burning in his eyes.

Seeing Gary's advancement as a threat, Mr. Kessler immediately stood up preparing to defend himself if necessary. "Listen, I can do anything I want if I can back up my decisions. There is enough proof here in my hand right now to warrant having you removed from this office until an investigation can be completed. I am calling your company as soon as you leave here and informing them of my actions in this matter. You are not to come back here or contact any of the women who filed these complaints, or I will take this matter up with the police. I hope I'm making myself clear."

"Fine! This place sucked anyway. I'm out of here. You can take this damn job of yours and shove it right up your ass!" Spinning on his heels, Gary stormed out of the office, slamming the door as he left. As he passed Mrs. Arm's desk he stuck out his arm and swept off a of pile folders that were lying within his reach. The force of his anger scattered the papers several feet across the floor.

Mrs. Arms stared at him with her mouth wide open. She was so shocked by his behavior that she didn't even say a word as she stared at the mess he had made. She had never seen anyone so mad, and she wondered what in the world had happened behind the closed doors of Mr. Kessler's office.

+++++

The moment he was alone, Mr. Kessler placed a call to Gary's company. He needed to inform Gary's supervisor what had just happened and to request an immediate replacement. After three phone routing transfers and just as many holds, he was finally connected to someone from the company's personal office...a not too bright someone.

"This is Mr. Kessler from Comtec. I'm calling to inform you that the employee you sent down here, a Mr. Gary Stevenson, has been asked to leave. I need a replacement for him as soon as possible, preferably by tomorrow morning."

"What has he done this time?" the man on the other end of the line replied in disgust.

"What do you mean *this time?*" Have you had other problems with this man before?" Mr. Kessler didn't like what he had just heard.

342

"Now don't get all uptight. It wasn't anything major. For heaven's sake, don't go blowing a gasket."

"We have just spent a fortune with your company, and I would think you would have sent your best man down here to handle our business, not some trouble-making playboy!"

"He is our best man. When it comes to understanding our system, there isn't another person that can match him. That's why we have overlooked a couple of his minor flaws. None of us are perfect, you know."

"I don't suppose those flaws of his involve inappropriate behavior toward women employees." Enraged over the recent events, Mr. Kessler wanted to go through the telephone line and strangle the guy at the other end.

"I don't think that is any of your business," the voice replied in a nasty tone. "Besides, as long as he does his work, I don't care what he does on the side."

"Well, you had better start caring if you are going to continue to want our business. Because of your lack of concern over your employee's attitude, my company has been put at risk for a major lawsuit. And you can be damn sure if we have to pay a price for your mistakes, you are going to have to carry some of the burden. I am faxing you copies of the five complaints filed against Mr. Stevenson. What you do with them is your business, but I don't want to see his face in this office again. Is that clear? Plus I want a replacement down here by tomorrow afternoon. If not, I am going to have to seriously consider making other arrangements with your competitors."

Without waiting for a reply, Mr. Kessler slammed the phone down.

Chapter 37

Furious over the confrontation with Mr. Kessler, Gary punched at the elevator button to the first floor, hitting it several times. *Damn it, hurry up…I don't have all day! I need to get out of this building and away from all those ignorant people I've had to work with at this hellhole.*

Once the elevator doors closed behind him, Gary exploded. He kicked the metal walls surrounding him and managed to vent some of his anger, but by the time he reached the first floor he was still seething. *This is all that little bitch's fault. If that idiotic woman had just minded her own business none of this would have happened. Who does Amy Tedrow think she is anyway…Hillary Clinton?*

God, how I hate women with attitude problems! They should all be driven out of the country…not trying to run it. The whole world would be better off if they knew their place, which was in some man's bed, not behind a desk bossing people around.

By the time Gary reached the first floor he was seething with a hatred that burned at his soul. When the elevator doors opened to a crowd of Comtec employees, he wanted to take a gun and blow their faces off.

"Out of my way, you stupid jerks!" Gary shouted, forcefully pushing his way through the group, but he stopped abruptly when he noticed one of them was Carrie.

+++++

Carrie stood near the back of the crowd holding an armful of files. As soon as she saw Gary, she unconsciously took a couple of quick steps backwards. Gary was the last person she wanted to run into right now. He was going to be very angry at her, maybe even dangerously so, for reporting him. He had threatened to get even if she ever told anyone about what he was doing.

In her hurried attempt to avoid Gary, she accidentally bumped into the gentleman standing directly behind her. The unexpected collision knocked her off balance, and the man reached out grabbing her arm to offer her support. A little gasp of alarm escaped her lips when she saw Gary had noticed her, and the next thing she knew, he was in her face.

"I told you to keep your big mouth shut!" Gary shouted, practically spitting his words at her.

"Keep away from me," Carrie warned, fighting to control the tears forming in her eyes. "Ms. Tedrow said you're not supposed to bother me anymore."

"Fuck what Ms. Tedrow says! I'm no longer working here, so I can damn well do whatever I please." With a violent push he knocked all of Carrie's files from her hands.

The noise the files made when they hit the floor was the only sound present. Everybody seemed to be holding their breath, waiting to see what would happen next. Gallantly the man behind Carrie stepped forward, placing himself as a shield between her and her assailant.

"Since you are no longer employed here," the man firmly stated, "I suggest you leave right now before someone calls security to escort you out."

Enraged, Gary charged at Carrie's defender, but a couple of the men standing nearby quickly grabbed his arms and held him tight. After struggling for a few seconds he cooled down enough to realize he wasn't going to get anywhere. "Just let go of me and I'll get out of here," he said, cursing the men under his breath. When they released their hold, he took off down the hall. Looking over his shoulder he saw the men helping Carrie pick up her files. While they were busy, he took a quick cut to the right, heading unnoticed toward the stairs. He knew Amy's office was located on the next floor.

"Little Miss Prissy Pants is going to pay dearly for this," he said to himself, taking the steps two at a time. "She's going to get exactly what's coming to her. No one messes with me and gets off scot-free. Dad taught me the importance of standing up for myself, and no damn woman is going to screw me over and get away with it."

As he mounted the steps, he realized that his anger had taken control of his thinking, but he didn't care, anger gave him power, and power was what he craved.

When he reached Amy's office, he quickly noted no one was around. Even Amy's guard dog, Susan, wasn't stationed at her desk.

It couldn't be a more perfect setup, he thought as adrenaline pumped through his body, heightening his senses, and preparing him for battle. *I'm going to teach that conniving witch a thing or two.*

+++++

It was only a coincidence that Amy was in her office at that particular moment. Everyone was supposed to be at a staff meeting on the fourth floor, but unfortunately she had been running late all afternoon.

Grabbing the stack of papers she needed for the meeting, Amy sighed. She had wasted her entire morning on foolishness, and it had been all for nothing.

Not only had she discovered there was no possible way that the child in the painting could be her ghost, she had also begun to seriously doubt her own sanity. With all that had happened the last couple of days she could no longer think straight. She should have been the first one at the meeting instead of the last, but she just couldn't seem to get organized.

As she stepped away from her desk, she noticed the knob turning on her office door. Before she had time to wonder who was on the other side, the door flew open and slammed full force into the wall. Shocked, she stood unmoving as she watched the door's glass windowpane shattered into a thousand pieces. She didn't even flinch as tiny little slivers of glass shot toward her like deadly shrapnel.

Dazed and confused by Gary's explosive entrance, Amy let the papers she was holding slip from her fingers, and they fell from her grasp, scattering across the floor in four different directions.

Fear swept over her in one great tidal wave, and she felt as though she was drowning under its tremendous weight. There was something about Gary that absolutely terrified her.

"W…W…What…What do you want?" she stammered, as Gary's dramatic entrance brought forth images of her father barging into her bedroom screaming and yelling in one of his wild rampages. She almost doubled over as a sick feeling twisted her gut, sending a terrible pain knifing though her abdomen.

"Don't act innocent with me!" Gary mouthed hatefully. "You know perfectly well what I'm doing here, you bitch. You reported that bullshit to Mr. Kessler just to get me into trouble. Well, no one messes with me and gets away with it." Before Amy could react, Gary moved in and shoved her hard with both of his hands.

The next thing Amy knew she was flung backward, and her head smacked into the floor like a falling bowling ball. She heard the thud as it struck, the sound echoing through her mind like the vibrations of a gunshot. Bright flashes of multicolored lights flickered in an explosion of color as pain ricocheted through her head, and then she felt herself falling into an empty black void.

But fear quickly pulled her back.

"If you want to press harassment charges against me, you might as well have something real to report," Gary said, kicking her hard in the ribs.

The force of the blow sent her rolling to one side. She almost blacked out again from the pain, but somehow she managed to rise up on her hands and knees. When she saw Gary moving toward her again, she jumped up on her feet. Without even thinking, she automatically pivoted around and kicked, hitting him square in the groin.

Doubled over in pain, Gary still somehow managed to glare at her through hate-filled eyes. A crazed rage drove him forward, and he charged at her again.

Amy managed to artfully dodge his advance. Then with a forceful, well-placed kick she connected with his left knee.

Gary buckled under the impact, landing with all of his weight on his right wrist. A loud snap resounded through the room, and he cried out in agony.

Amy raced the few steps to the phone and called security. "This is Amy Tedrow. I need immediate assistance in my office. An intruder has just attacked me. Please hurry, I need help right now."

Before she could hang up, a sound from behind caused her to spin around. Gary had risen and was standing only five feet away hugging his arm tightly into his body. Madness radiated from his face, as he stared at the phone in her hand. Abruptly he turned away, running toward the door. At the entrance he paused looking back at her through cold gray eyes…eyes that pierced straight to the center of her heart.

"You little bitch!" he bellowed, his voice full of malice. "This is all your fault! You will pay for doing this to me!"

Then with a violent slam of the door, Gary left Amy alone in her office.

Toni Auberry

Chapter 38

Amy never heard the loud banging of the door as Gary slammed it behind him. Suddenly, instantly, when their eyes had locked just before he stormed from the room, she felt herself being transported to another time…another place. Those cold gray eyes she was staring into weren't Gary's, but someone else's…someone who was standing in front of her bedroom door, glaring hatefully down at her. She was seven years old, lying naked and curled up in bed, hugging her knees to her chest, trying very hard to disappear. Angry words were ringing loudly in her tiny ears. **"You little bitch! This is all your fault! You will pay for doing this to me!"**

Terror filled her soul as she stared into the gray eyes that were stripping her of her humanity. Those eyes…those evil, depraved eyes belonged to the beast…the nightmare creature that had stalked her dreams for years. But this time the beast wasn't faceless. This time Amy saw the loathsome thing for what it really was…***her father***!

Shock filled her veins with ice water, chilling her to the bone as the realization of the beast's identity hit her consciousness. Those ugly, hairy arms that had pulled her so forcefully from the closet weren't the figments of an overactive imagination. The terrifying creature that had crawled upon her bed in the dark of the night hadn't been the product of insanity. If would have been far better if it had been that way. The truth was worse…almost unbelievable. The truth was a nightmare in itself!

Now she knew the sad, crying child she had seen hadn't been a ghost. Instead, it was something entirely different from anything she could have ever imagined. She was her own ghost, her own apparition, haunted by the terrifying memories created by her father.

The memories she had tried to kill off years ago had never died, and they were returning to fill her mind with visions of unspeakable fear and degradation. Her childhood had been more horrifying than she had ever thought possible. Somehow she had managed to survive her own private nightmare, a nightmare that had its beginnings in the supposed sanctuary of her own bedroom by a man who should have been her protector…not her molester.

Scene after horrifying scene began flooding her mind as repressed memories fought their way to the surface. There was no way to stop the flow of images, as the pain, the horror, the suffering she had endured year after year cascaded down around her. She stood frozen unable to move, hardly able to even breathe, as her forgotten past made itself known.

Forgotten memories fell into place, adding many of the missing pieces needed to help complete the puzzle her life had been. Some of the blank spots in her memory were no longer blank. They were filled in with pictures of her father as he used her in the night to fulfill some demon need within himself...used her in the darkness, then blamed her for his own sins.

The weight of those hideous memories fell heavily upon her shoulders. In an attempt to escape from the burden, she tried sending herself away to another place, a place where the images couldn't follow. Just like she had sent herself away as a small child when fleeing from her father's touch. But, this time it didn't work. This time she couldn't escape.

She tried to drive the memories back into the dark corner of her mind from which they had sprung, but the sickening knowledge wouldn't recede back into that secret place where she had kept it hidden all those years. The harder she tried to force the memories back, the faster they came.

A migraine so severe it felt like a hatchet had buried itself in the back of her skull hit with such force that she could hardly stand. Lights flashed in front of her eyes, blinding her to the world around her. All she could see were the images of her father's evil deeds. The present disappeared, the past became her reality, and that was too much for her already burdened soul.

"NO!" she screamed, the pain so intense it seemed as if her head were getting ready to explode. "NO...NO...NO!"

She reached out blindly, and with one huge sweeping motion of her arms she knocked everything off of her desk. The enormous clatter of the phone, pens, and files hitting the floor brought the security men running even faster toward her office.

Susan, who had come up from the staff meeting to check on Amy, had just passed the front desk. She had seen Gary running down the hall when she had gotten off the elevator. There had been no doubt in her mind he had been up to no good, and when she saw the glass from Amy's office door had been broken, she instinctively knew something bad had just happened. At the sound of Amy's screaming, she sprinted for the office door just one step in front of security.

"My God, what happened?" Susan asked, shocked by the look of anguish on Amy's face. "Are you all right? Did Gary hurt you?"

Amy didn't respond. Instead, she whirled around and began violently flinging books off the shelf beside her desk.

Susan didn't know what to do. Every time she started toward her friend, a flying book almost hit her.

"How could he have done this to me?" Amy cried out in misery, picking up a glass paperweight and throwing it against the wall. Through tear-filled eyes, she watched it shatter into a million tiny pieces...just as her life had shattered moments before.

"Who did what to you? Was it Gary?" Susan asked, staying Amy's hand from doing any more damage. "Amy, what happened?" Fear for her friend showed in her eyes.

The two security men, who had rushed up to the office at Amy's call, were standing at the door with no idea how to proceed. Three other employees, drawn by the sound of Amy's crying, were crowding in the doorway. Questions were flowing from everyone's lips, but no one made any attempt to help.

"Amy, what happened to your head?" Susan asked, surprised to see blood matting Amy's hair. "You're hurt. Let me look," she said, trying to get Amy to let her see where the blood had come from.

But Amy kept pushing Susan's hands away. She didn't want anyone ever to touch her again.

"Please Amy, let me help you," Susan begged.

Amy didn't respond. Instead, she collapsed down on her knees weeping into her hands as though her heart were breaking.

Susan reached over, gently touching the back of Amy's head. A knot the size of a small egg had blood seeping from a cut right in the center of it. She pressed on the lump and was surprised when Amy said nothing. Kneeling beside her friend, she gently pulled Amy's hands away from her face. "What happened? I saw Gary out in the hall. Did he have anything to do with this?"

Amy's red-rimmed eyes looked into Susan's. "Oh Susan," she sobbed hysterically, "my father, he...he—Oh, I just can't say it!"

"That's all right, you can tell me later. Right now I think you need to see a doctor."

"No!" Amy reached over and grasped her friend's arm tightly, then her tears started again.

Susan heard someone whispering. "Is Amy having a nervous breakdown?" She glanced up and noticed the crowd of people jamming into the room and angrily retorted, "All right everyone, it's time to go back to work, you're not helping a thing by standing there staring."

Prying Amy's hand off of her arm, Susan stood up, and chased everyone out of the room. At the door she saw Carrie standing by the front desk with a shocked expression on her face. She stepped from the office and pulled Carrie aside. "I need you to do something very important. See if you can find a phone number for Dr. James Perry and call him. Tell him you are calling about Amy, and explain there is something very strange going on, and he needs to get over here right away if possible. Then try to get in touch with Amy's brother Edward. His phone number is in the Rolodex on my desk. After that I want you to stand guard at the door, and don't you let anyone into this office till I tell you different."

Susan hurried back into Amy's office and kneeled next to her friend, who had resumed sobbing hysterically. She gently pulled Amy's hands away from her face again and then spoke quietly but forcefully. "Amy, you have to settle down so you can tell me what's wrong. I can't help unless I know what the problem is."

After a minute, Amy's sobbing subsided, but Susan still couldn't get through to her. It was as if her friend were lost in some private realm where no one else could follow. Amy wasn't crying anymore, but she wasn't doing anything else either. She sat on the floor staring, without even blinking, at nothing at all. Her color was ashen and little beads of sweat were popping out all over her forehead.

Scared, Susan grabbed Amy's shoulders. "Come on girl, snap out of it. You're beginning to scare me. Please speak to me."

Amy only responded by blinking a couple of times.

Susan reached over and tried to take Amy's pulse, but it was so weak she had difficulty counting it. *Was Amy dying?* Alarmed, Susan made the decision to call for an ambulance.

Just as she picked up the receiver to start dialing, a man charged into the room. With an air of authority he advanced toward Amy even before Susan had a chance to object. Kneeling down so he was face to face with Amy, he began talking. "Amy, can you hear me?" Waiting for a response and getting none, he glanced over his shoulder at Susan. "Have you called for an ambulance yet?"

Shaking her head no, she asked, "Who are you?"

"Dr. James Perry. Now please place that phone call. I think she may be in shock."

Taking Amy's shoulders, he gently laid her down on the floor. He removed his jacket, rolled it up, and placed it under her head. The white carnation Amy had laughed at earlier fell off and landed unnoticed on the floor by her head.

Susan frantically dialed 911 and sent an ambulance headed their way. She looked at James and couldn't understand how he had gotten there so fast. Carrie had only called him a minute or two ago. "How did you get here so quickly?" she asked, suddenly suspicious. "You haven't even had time to get our message yet."

At that moment his pager went off. Taking a quick glance at the flashing number, he turned to Susan. "555-1212. Is that the phone number for this place?"

"Yes, but—"

"I was with Amy earlier today, and something happened that really upset her. So I decided to check on her to make sure she was doing all right this afternoon." Turning his attention back to Amy, he kept talking to her even though she wasn't responding. "Amy, I want you to blink your eyes if you can hear me."

No blinking eyes followed his request. Amy only lay on the floor staring without really seeing anything.

James looked at the destruction in the room. "What exactly happened here?" He turned expectantly toward Susan.

Susan shook her head. "I don't know. She didn't show up for our staff meeting, so I came down to find out why. I found her hysterical, throwing things across the room, and crying."

"Did she say anything?"

"Not really. She started to say something about her father, but then changed her mind. She said she couldn't tell me."

James didn't need any more information. He had a good idea what had happened…*Amy's past had finally caught up with her.* He really hadn't expected it to happen so soon. Nor had he expected for the results to be so devastating. He only hoped Amy's mind was strong enough to handle the pain she obviously was facing.

+++++

Susan heard Edward's voice in the hall talking to Carrie, and she ran out to meet him. "I'm so glad you are here. Amy's had some kind of spell. I don't even know what's wrong, but Dr. Perry is here and had me call for an ambulance."

Edward rushed to Amy's side and kneeled down beside his sister. "What's wrong? Why is she staring like that?" Taking his sister's hand, he started talking to her, pleading with her to respond. "Amy, talk to me. Please. You have to talk to me." He realized that there was something seriously wrong, and he started shaking inside, just like he had the day his father had died.

Susan placed a hand on Edward's shoulder. "We don't know what happened. She tried to tell me something about your father, but couldn't seem to bring herself to say it."

"Dad!" What could he have to do with any of this? He's been dead for eight years." Worried about Amy's lack of responsiveness Edward tried to reach her again. "Amy, I'm here. Come on, talk to me. Please talk to me."

Chapter 39

Amy felt herself becoming engulfed by vague, dusky, shadows that swirled like turbulent storm clouds. At first she welcomed the darkness. She could hide among the shadows and not be seen. But then the blackness became thick and heavy, as if she were submerged in a sea of black sludge. Her eyes frantically searched for a light but found none. A heavy weight had entrapped her limbs, preventing any movement. She wanted to run to escape the horror she could feel coming up from behind, yet she couldn't. She screamed, but the sound became part of the darkness and no one heard.

With each passing second the terror within her mind grew stronger. Her father was out there in the darkness searching for her. She could feel him. His presence was like a great, malignant force that couldn't be pacified. Soon he would swoop down to take her to hell with him, and she would never be able escape him again. She would be doomed to endure his hands, his touch, his power over her for eternity.

She tried to cry out for help, but her father's hand shot out from the darkness, clamping down hard and firm over her mouth. His huge hand covered half of her face, and he held on so tightly that she could hardly breathe. She could feel his hot breath against the side of her neck as he began whispering in a tight controlled voice.

"Shut up you sniveling little fool. If any one hears you, they will find out what an evil thing you really are and drive a stake straight through your sinful heart. You don't want that to happen, do you?"

He kept whispering in her ear as one of his hands snaked up under her clothes. "You're nothing but a wicked sinner. God punishes those like you who transgress against him. You'll pay for making me do this. Flaunting yourself like a bitch in heat, forcing me to come to you. You are an evil, sinful child."

His hand ripped away her underwear. "See how you are, just like a dog putting its scent out to draw me in here."

His hot breath against her neck became unbearable. It burnt into her skin like a hot poker. She struggled, but his hand clamped down harder over her face, and then she couldn't breathe at all. Just before she passed out, he let go. She pulled in a deep desperate breath, wishing at the same time that she could stop breathing. Death would be better than what he was making her do.

He rolled on top of her, the weight of his body smashing her into the bed. Pinned beneath him, she became nothing but an object for him to use. A terrible pain stabbed sharply between her legs, and it grew to encase her entire being. Every nerve in her body screamed out for him to stop. But he didn't, and the pain continued.

She wanted to die, to cease to exist, to become nothing because that would be the only way to escape, to finally bring an end to her endless torment.

As her father pounded his body into hers again and again, she willed death to come. She begged for it. Death would be her only release. Unless—

Unless Edward could save her. A prayer went out to the very God her father said would condemn her to hell for the sins she had committed by drawing him to her bed.

Please God, send my brother to me.

Edward will protect me. I know he can save me before it's too late. I don't care if he thinks I'm bad if he can only take the pain away!

As she drew in what she felt would be her last breath, thinking she could not bear one more moment of life, she finally gave up. Death had made its presence known. She felt its welcoming touch deep in her heart. It promised peace and safety from the horrors around her.

But then Edward's voice drifted across the blackness. "Amy, I'm here. Come on, talk to me. Please talk to me."

And she knew God had sent Edward after all. He hadn't left her to die all alone.

Her father's weight shifted, and she felt herself drifting out of the darkness. As the world around her grew brighter and brighter, the presence of her father faded away. Suddenly she could see light again, and Edward's face loomed in front of her. She had never been so happy to hear someone calling her name.

+++++

When Edward saw Amy's eyes focusing on his face an immediate feeling of relief washed over him. "Amy! Thank God, you're back with us." He gathered her up in his arms and held her as tightly as he could. He had been sure they were losing her just a few seconds before. He had actually felt her spirit ebbing away.

James had been thinking the same thing. Susan had told him about the head injury, and he worried about a concussion. He had actually been gearing himself up to start resuscitation on Amy if he had to. He had been monitoring her pulse and had felt it ebb down and almost disappear. He realized that there was the real possibility she could be having some type of internal bleeding in her head, but he couldn't tell just by looking at her. He really didn't even know exactly what had happened to her. Without x-rays and lab tests, he couldn't even begin to guess what type of injuries she had. Emergency medicine wasn't exactly his field of expertise.

Susan paced worriedly outside the office door watching impatiently for the paramedics. She had sent Carrie down to the main lobby to direct them up. When she had looked in on Amy a few minutes ago, she had been shocked by her friend's ashen color. Amy had actually looked almost bloodless.

Susan had been sure her friend was dying. When she heard the relief in Edward's voice, her apprehension eased some. *Maybe it would be all right after all,* she thought, *but I still wish the ambulance would hurry and get here.*

+++++

Finding strength within Edward's protective arms, Amy finally spoke the awful truth that had been buried deep within her soul for so many years. In a voice filled with long-endured sadness and pain, she told him one of the secrets she had whispered to Thomas so many years ago. For the first time, she breathed the words that had haunted her day and night since she had been seven years old. Shaking from fear that Edward wouldn't believe her, she let the words slip from her mouth.

"Edward, Dad raped me…when I was seven. Then he came to me again and again in the middle of the night…in my own bedroom. He made me do things I didn't want to do. Oh, Edward, he hurt me so badly." Sobbing, she couldn't continue. She just couldn't bring herself to tell him anymore.

Edward held Amy tightly within the circle of his arms, and he felt the intensity of her grief. But how could he believe such a thing? There was no way their father could have done that. Amy had to be hallucinating. She needed to get to the hospital right away. In desperation he turned to James. "Shouldn't that ambulance be here by now?"

James knew Edward didn't believe what Amy had just told him. He could easily see the disbelief that was showing on the man's face. It was a good thing Amy didn't notice it. Right now, if Edward turned against her, James wasn't sure how well she would be able to handle it. He could tell she trusted her brother, and he suspected there weren't too many other people Amy trusted. Children that have been badly abused have difficulty trusting anyone. She would need a lot of support to heal, and having an understanding family member could make a big difference in her recovery. But having one that didn't understand would only make things worse.

Family was always important. Unfortunately, in cases of incest or other types of child abuse, the family unit was often dysfunctional. For that reason, more times than not, the family turned out to be a bad source to look for support. Often the victim's family would actually blame the victim for the abuse. James didn't think Edward would react that way, but he couldn't be sure.

James felt he needed to get Amy's attention away from Edward. "We've called for an ambulance. If you want, I can arrange for you to be directly admitted to the hospital, bypassing the emergency room. That is, if you want me to be your doctor. If not, let me call your family doctor to tell him you are coming in."

"I don't need to go to the hospital, and I don't want to see a doctor. I only want to go home," Amy replied firmly.

"Amy, I want you to do what Dr. Perry suggested," Edward insisted.

"No, just help me get up off the floor," Amy said, annoyed at both of them. "I'll be all right in a few minutes. I've made it this far without a doctor, and I'll damn well make it the rest of the way without one."

"I don't think getting up is a good idea," James said. "You've had some kind of fall and could have broken something. It's best that you stay right where you are until the paramedics get here."

"I'm fine," Amy said, struggling to sit up. "I'm smart enough to know if I'm hurt. Just help me get up to my chair."

Edward sighed, helping her sit up. "You can be so stubborn some days."

"Well, look who I had as a teacher," Amy reproached him. "You're worse than I could ever be." Rubbing the back of her throbbing head, she felt a huge lump. "Guess I really knocked my head a good one. This hurts almost as much as those horrid migraines."

"What happened here anyway?" Susan asked, coming into the room.

"Oh, Gary paid me a little visit on his way out of the building. I guess Mr. Kessler sent him packing. I don't think he was too happy with me."

"Right after you get settled in at the hospital, I'm calling the police about this," Edward said, looking at the destruction done to the room. "He could have killed you."

"Or rape me like my father did," Amy said, looking straight into Edward's eyes.

Edward turned his face away without saying a word. Picking up one of the books Amy had tossed to the floor, he glanced at Amy questioningly. "Susan told us you did this part, not Gary. Why?"

"I don't know," Amy said, shaking her head. "I don't remember doing it."

"I think you need to go into the hospital for a check up," Edward insisted. "And not only because of the fall and that knot on the back of your head. This would be a good time to check out those migraines of yours. They have been getting worse lately. You know, there could be something seriously wrong."

"There is nothing wrong...except I finally remembered what a monster my father was. I shouldn't have to go into the hospital because of that. The man's been dead for years, yet he somehow is still able to reach out from his grave to try to destroy me. If I go into the hospital, everyone will think I am crazy, and I am not crazy!"

"I didn't say you were crazy, but you have to admit you have been acting pretty strange lately, and now you are having hallucinations. You need to have a doctor check you out. I won't take no for an answer. You will go to the hospital...now...with the ambulance when it arrives."

"Since when did you get in the position to tell me what I should or should not do?" Amy snapped back at him, but then the expression on her face changed. *What did he mean hallucinations? He didn't know about the ghost.* Then it dawned on her that Edward didn't believe what she had just told him about their father. "Hallucinations! I am not imagining things! You have no idea at all what happened to me when we were growing up. Edward, that man we called our father beat me and raped me repeatedly. Dad just made damn sure no one else ever learned of it. It was a secret. A horrible, disgusting secret."

The doubt showing on Edward's face tore at Amy's heart. If he didn't believe her, no one would. Her father's words echoed through her mind again. *No one will ever believe you.*

+++++

Susan had been staying out of everyone's way after Amy had made that shocking statement about her father, but now she felt it was very important she step in and say something. What she wanted to do was to talk with Amy...woman to woman.

"Dr. Perry...Edward...would you both step outside of the office for a moment. I want to talk with Amy alone."

As soon as the men had left the room, Susan took Amy's hand. "I believe what you just told Edward. I have always thought that there was some dark secret hidden in your heart that you couldn't tell anyone. When you're around men, you are constantly on guard, like you are expecting them to do something to you. I have often wondered why a beautiful woman like you never dated. Now I understand why. Life must have been hell for you when you were growing up."

"There isn't even a way to put it into words," Amy said.

"You don't have to tell me anything unless you want to. I know this must be extremely painful for you. First, Gary storms in

371

here like a maniac and does who knows what, and now this. I think I would have done something more than toss a few books."

"I don't remember doing that," Amy said, pulling her hand away from Susan's. She didn't like the look of pity on her friend's face. *Would everyone else see me as something to pity?*

"What do you remember? Did Gary give you that knot on the back of your head?"

"He shoved me hard when he first came in, and I fell back hitting my head. I think I might have lost consciousness for a short period. The next thing I know, I'm down on the floor, and he's planting his foot in my ribs." Gently rubbing her side, Amy winced as her hand touched a tender spot. "Dad did the same thing to me. I guess I should be grateful this time there wasn't a staircase to fall down."

"Oh, Amy, I'm sorry," Susan said, realizing what Amy meant. "How old were you when that happened?"

"Which time?"

"You mean he did it more then once?"

"At least two that I can remember. You would have thought Edward would have wondered why his little sister couldn't come down the stairs without tripping." Amy laughed bitingly. "The funny thing is: the first time Dad kicked me so hard I fell down the stairs, he told people I fell off my bike; and when he knocked me off my bike, he told them I fell down the stairs. I think it would have been easier for him to keep his stories straight if he had stuck to the original source of my little accidents."

"Why didn't you tell someone?"

"Because he was my father, and I thought he knew everything. He kept telling me I was being punished for being so bad. He used to describe in detail what God would do to me if I told anyone about what went on between us. He made the fire and brimstone theory of hell sound like heaven. I remember once he told me about how huge birds would eat all my skin off piece by piece if I ever said a word to anyone. I didn't play outside for the longest time after that. For months, every time a bird flew over my head I screamed."

"That sounds terrible," Susan responded, feeling the pain in Amy's words.

"When he would come to me in my bedroom, he kept telling me it was all my fault, like I had somehow invited him there. Because I wasn't allowed to speak without permission, I used to scream in my head for him to go away." Amy turned her eyes to Susan. "How could it have been my fault? I never wanted him to do those things to me. I only wanted him to leave me alone."

"Amy, it never was your fault. He knew what he was doing to you was wrong. That's why he made you keep it secret. The blame falls solely upon his shoulders."

When Amy saw the understanding look in Susan's eyes she started crying. Tears ran in streams down her face as she talked. "I have never forgotten those beatings Dad gave me. How could I? I can't even salt my food without thinking of him. Once when I accidentally knocked over a salt shaker spilling it on the kitchen floor, he took his belt off and beat me till I couldn't stand up. Then he made me lick every bit of that salt off the floor. I remember crawling across the floor with blood oozing off the back of my legs and licking the floor."

"How awful," Susan said, tears forming in her own eyes.

"But as vivid as some of my memories of him are, I honestly didn't remember all that other stuff he did to me until now. I've always had these huge blank spots in my memory I couldn't fill in." Amy paused, her heart aching painfully. "In a way, maybe it would have been better not to have known. Having empty spaces filling up my head was better than having it filled with this trash. At least it didn't seem to hurt this bad not knowing."

"But all those terrible memories were still in there, even if you couldn't remember them. They had to come out sometime, in one way or another. At least this way, you can face them head on and try to work through them, instead of letting them work on you."

"I don't understand how he could have done those things to me. He was my father." Amy looked at Susan like a bewildered child. "Why…why did it happen? I swear I didn't want him to do it. No matter what he said, I didn't want it to happen."

"I don't know the answers to your questions, and right now you need answers…a lot of answers. I don't think you're going to find them at home. You really need professional help. You're not being weak if you have to turn to someone else for a while to help you understand. Haven't you realized yet what happened to you wasn't normal? You don't have to keep it secret anymore. It's time to get it all out in the open and go on with your life."

"But, I'm too ashamed. If I go to the hospital, everyone will know what happened. You know how people talk. How could I face them again?"

"So what if everyone knows! It wasn't your fault. You were the victim, not the perpetrator of this crime...and it was a crime. You shouldn't have to keep paying the price for someone else's sins. Give yourself a chance to live again. Don't let your father control the rest of your life. Will you please do what Dr. Perry asks?"

Nodding her head yes, Amy agreed to go do what everyone was pushing for her to do. Besides, her head hurt so badly she couldn't even think. And for some strange reason she had started to see double. Two images of Susan's face blurred together as she looked up at her friend.

Double trouble, she thought as she watched the blurred, double images of the paramedics as they rolled their gurney into the room. But trouble or not, she let them put her upon the gurney to transport her to the hospital. As she was being rolled out of the office building, she felt like everyone's eyes were upon her. How would she ever be able to set foot in that building again? Her secret wasn't a secret anymore, and the whole world would soon know what a terrible person she had been.

Toni Auberry

Chapter 40

While Susan was talking privately with Amy, Edward was pacing restlessly outside of Amy's office door. Because the window on the door had been shattered, he could hear every word that Amy and Susan were saying, and he just couldn't believe the tales his sister was telling. He knew in his heart that their father couldn't have done those awful things to her because there was no way something that terrible could have been kept hidden. *Surely Amy is imagining it all,* he thought. *After all, isn't she sick now?*

Amy's words ate at Edward's soul, and he had to force his mind to consider the possibility that she was speaking the truth. *Maybe Dad was a little strict with us at times,* he thought, *but that was because he wanted what was best for us. It didn't mean that he was abusive. I do remember being on the wrong end of Dad's belt more times than I care to think about, but I wouldn't say that he actually beat me. At least not the way that Amy is suggesting that he did to her. She has to be confused. Her mind must not be working right. There's a big difference between discipline and abuse. Maybe her anger at Dad is making her mind exaggerate what really happened between them. And rape...there's no way that could have happened. Amy has to be very sick to even be thinking such disturbing thoughts.*

Edward sat down at Susan's desk. Exhausted and bone-weary, the weight of Amy's words made his head feel heavy and burdensome. A pounding headache now blurred his vision, so he closed his eyes to rest them for a few minutes. As the pain in his head steadily throbbed with each beat of his heart, he wondered if Amy's migraines had felt the same way

Edward felt a quiet desperation take control. *What was Mom going to say about all of this? The rift between her and Amy was already bad enough. What will happen once she hears Amy is accusing Dad of molesting her as a child? There would be no way to repair the damage that story would bring. It would irreparably destroy any chance the two of them would ever have of making peace with each other.*

James could read Edward's body language and knew what thoughts were flashing through Amy's brother's mind. *Edward didn't believe his sister.* James walked over and gently placed a hand upon Edward's shoulder. "She is telling you the truth," he said softly but firmly.

"How would you know?" Edward lashed out. "You never met my father and know absolutely nothing about him. How can you pass judgment on him using only Amy's bizarre account of something that probably didn't happen anyway?"

"It's my job to know things like this. I hope you realize that your sister is going to need your support to get through this trauma. If you walk away, it could destroy her."

"I'm not walking away. Just because I have doubts that she knows what she's saying, doesn't mean I'm not going to be around to help her get through this. I realize that she's sick and needs me right now."

"You're going to need each other," James said. "Dealing with this situation won't be easy on either one of you, but it's going to be the hardest on Amy. She has kept her secret this long because it hurt too much to even think about it. And in the beginning it's going to hurt her even more as additional memories return, but if she's lucky, she'll find a way to cope with them."

"But how am I supposed to cope with all of this?" Edward asked, his voice shrill, piercing the air with his question. "She's saying Dad was a monster, a child molester. How am I supposed to come to terms with that?"

"What's going to hurt you more, hiding behind a false memory or accepting the truth?" James bluntly replied.

"The truth! How can you tell what the truth is? I remember Dad as being special, someone who I looked up to and wanted to be like. Am I supposed to simply accept Amy's story as truth, when I remember things being so different?"

"Everyone's memories are colored by different perceptions. Amy's abuse was kept a secret from you, maybe even from your mother, and certainly from the neighbors. Secrecy is one of the prime ingredients in abuse. That's why some professionals have referred to child abuse as being a silent epidemic."

"Wouldn't Dad have done the same thing to me if he were that kind of person?" Edward's voice trembled as the pain in his heart filled his mind with questions. "Why would he have hurt only Amy and not me?" he asked.

"In some instances a certain child is singled out for the abuse and the other children are treated normally, often with no explanation," James replied.

"I don't understand any of this," Edward uttered in desperation. "I don't know what or who to believe."

"Let your memories do some of the thinking for you," James said. "To some extent, you and your sister share the same past. Just like Amy, your past holds clues to what really happened back then."

"My memories certainly don't include my sister getting raped by my father," Edward replied grimly. Feeling the urgent need to be near his sister, he stood up and moved toward Amy's office. He heard Amy telling Susan how she had been pushed down the stairs and how their father had said she had fallen off of her bike. The expression on his face changed to one of astonishment and he turned toward James. "I do remember Dad telling me one time that Amy had broken her ribs falling off her bike. It was a surprise to me because I knew our bikes were locked up in the shed. Mom had taken them away from us that week as a punishment. When I questioned Dad about it he got really upset and sent me to my room for calling him a liar, or at least that's the way he saw it. I sure wasn't stupid enough to call him that. I blamed Amy for messing my whole evening up and didn't even feel sorry about her broken ribs."

"Do you think she's lying about being pushed down the stairs?" James asked.

"Maybe it's not really lying," Edward said, a hint of hope edging his reply. "If you're sick and say the wrong thing, that doesn't mean you're not telling the truth."

James didn't answer Edward's question. Instead he pushed Edward to think more about Amy's past. "Do you remember any more of Amy's injuries?" he asked.

Edward closed his eyes for a couple of seconds as he forced himself to recall any unusual events that might lead him toward the answers he was seeking. "Once when I came home after being gone all week-end to a baseball tournament with Mom, I accidentally walked into the bathroom while Amy was changing her clothes. She had huge bruises all over her legs, and she got really upset when I asked her what had happened. She said it was none of my business, then she pushed me out of the bathroom and locked the door. I could hear her crying on the other side, but she wouldn't talk to me. When I asked Dad about it, he just smirked and told me that Amy was nothing but a clumsy cow and had tripped on the stairs again."

"Didn't you even question him about the fall?"

"I loved Dad dearly, but one thing you didn't do was question him about anything. What he said was law and that was that. If he said she accidentally fell down the stairs, then that's what happened. I wasn't about to argue with him. Besides, Amy wouldn't even talk to me for a couple of weeks after I saw the bruises, so I just assumed there wasn't a problem." Edward looked dejectedly down at the floor. "Maybe if I had only—"

"Maybes don't matter right now," James said. "What really matters is that your sister gets some help so she can start working through her pain. Just because some of her memories have came back, it doesn't mean that she is capable at this time of dealing with the trauma and destruction those repressed memories are going to bring with them. In cases like Amy's, it's like being thrown into a raging river. You might be able to work your way to the water's surface, but it's a sure bet you will be covered over time and time again by turbulent waves as you battle to reach the shore. Even if you are a good swimmer, you might not make it to safety. Amy might be strong, but if she doesn't understand the current of her emotions, she might not be a good enough swimmer to make it to safety. Her memories could pull her under and finally destroy her."

"I know right now they're destroying me," Edward said. "In a way, it doesn't even matter if what she is saying is true or not. Things aren't ever going to be the same in my life." He bent down and picked up a couple pieces of broken glass off the floor. Holding them in his hand, he stared at them for a long time before finally speaking. "If she's not hallucinating or making all of this up, then everything I have ever thought about my father will be shattered into a million pieces…just like this glass. And if she is imagining it, she really is sick, and that would break my heart too. So you see, there's no winning today…not for her or for me."

James didn't reply. Right now he didn't have any answers for Amy or Edward. He was more concerned with getting Amy to the hospital and having her head x-rayed to be sure there wasn't any internal bleeding going on. He would worry about Amy's mental status after he was sure she was physically sound.

A strained silence developed between Edward and James, a silence that was finally broken by the sounds of the elevator doors opening. A feeling of relief came over Edward when he saw that help had finally arrived. As the paramedics advanced toward Amy's office, he stood out of the way, letting them go to his sister.

+++++

James pulled his cell phone from his pocket and dialed the number for Charity Hospital. "This is Dr. Perry, and I've got a patient coming in by ambulance. Her name is Amy Tedrow. She should be there in approximately a half-hour. Diagnosis is a possible concussion. I want a CT scan of her head the moment she arrives. Go ahead and bypass the emergency room and admit her directly to the fourth floor. I'm following her in and will give the rest of my orders then."

After he had hung up, he glanced over at Edward, who was waiting impatiently for the ambulance workers to finish with Amy. James really wanted to go over and lay his hand on Edward's shoulder. Not to offer support, but to see if he could get the feel of Edward's vibes. For some reason, Amy and her brother had become a very important part of his life. He wanted them both to survive the tragedy of Amy's childhood. Even though Amy had been the one that had lived through the hell of her father's sins, Edward was going to have to face the reality of those sins and accept that the man he had worshipped growing up wasn't the golden idol he had pretended to be.

A strong believer in fate, James felt it had been his destiny to be here at this moment to help Amy at a time when she needed it the most. He knew there was some truth in the belief that we are all destined to play out our lives in certain patterns. For as far back as he could remember, he'd had dreams that somehow had turned out to be reality…just like his grandmother had. He believed in fate, for if there was no truth in destiny, how could he have dreamed what was to be before it even was?

James didn't think he had some kind of mystical powers. He wasn't a sorcerer or a shaman. Whatever it was that allowed him to know bits and pieces of the future came from the natural powers of the earth. He had been born this way, as had his grandmother, and according to family stories, his great-grandmother. He never questioned how or why it happened that he could at times glimpse tiny little pieces of the future. To be able to know…to feel…to see…what others could not was just a part of who he was. He never exploited this part of himself; he just accepted it.

He thought of the events that had brought him to this moment, and he saw how the elusive hands of fate had twisted things so he would be here for Amy. It had been fate that had allowed his grandmother's painting to be accidentally auctioned and had sent Edward to Cherished Treasures searching for Amy's birthday present. It had also been fate that had brought him and Amy together at a time when she would need what he had to give.

James felt grateful that this time his destiny had turned out to be good…in the sense he could possibly be a source of guidance for Amy and Edward. Too often fate's touch had brought devastation into his life instead of a chance for renewal of hope and happiness. For instance, if fate had just slowed his father's footsteps by only a second, a bullet meant for someone else wouldn't have found its way into his father's heart.

For years he had angrily blamed himself for his father's death. If only he could have foreseen the shooting, maybe he could have somehow changed the future. He had seen so many other things, why hadn't he been able to see what would happen to his own father?

Afterwards, it had been his grandmother who had finally calmed his anger. She understood life far better than any other person he had ever met. She had explained there were some things that were just meant to be, and no matter how much we want them to be different, we can't change the course that has been set. To spend time being angry at what can not be changed was nothing but a waste of precious emotions and energy. It was more productive to work at altering the unpleasant events in life that could be changed than be angry over those events that could never be altered.

Chapter 41

The short trip in the elevator down to the main lobby sent Amy's head spinning. Her double vision caused the images of the paramedics to move like wavy images on an old black and white TV set, and each jarring movement of the gurney sent excruciating jolts of pain through her head. The pain convinced her that the trip to the hospital wasn't a bad idea after all, even if she did hate having to go out of the building on the gurney in full view of everyone from her office.

She didn't speak to anyone until she had been loaded into the back of the ambulance. The people at Comtec were going to have enough to gossip about without her adding more material to the rumors that were already flying. She knew that by the time the ambulance arrived at the hospital all kinds of stories would be spreading around the office, and she didn't want to make matters worse.

Just as the ambulance doors closed, Amy thought about Raphael. Who would take care of him? She couldn't leave him in the house all alone.

"Wait. I can't leave yet," she shouted frantically at the paramedics. "I have to talk to my brother. I can't go anywhere until I talk with Edward."

The paramedic in the back of the ambulance looked at Amy impatiently. "Lady, we're running an ambulance service, not a clubhouse. We don't have time for you to go visiting with people. We're supposed to be taking you to the hospital."

"I don't care. You're not taking me anywhere until I talk to my brother."

The ambulance driver, who had already taken his place up front, turned in his seat giving his partner a chastening look. "Let her speak with her brother. She has the right to talk to whoever she wants."

"Oh, all right, but I thought we were supposed to be an emergency transport, not a social club." Opening the door the paramedic shouted. "Hey is this woman's brother out there? If so, we need you in here. Your sister ain't going nowhere till she talks to you."

"I'm her brother," Edward said, hurrying over to the ambulance. "What's going on? Why aren't you leaving?"

"Because the lady won't let us. That's why," the paramedic said, peeved at the delay.

"Edward, I need to talk to you." Amy anxiously grabbed Edward's hand as he climbed into the ambulance and kneeled at her side. "What about Raphael? Who will take care of him if I'm in the hospital?"

"Calm down, Sis. Raphael won't be a problem. I still have a key to your house, and I'll go get him right after we get you settled in your room. I promise. I'm sure Ted will agree to take care of him until you get home. If not, then I'll do it myself, so don't let thoughts about that dog bother you." Taking Amy's hand in his, Edward forced a smile hoping it would ease some of her anxiety.

At the mention of Ted's name, Amy saw a picture of him in her mind as he had looked last night just before he kissed her...smiling with a light in his eyes that glowed from a warm fire deep in his soul. How could she ever face him again? Once he learned of what had happened between her and her father, he would never want to see her again. How could he? Who would want to go out with a woman who had done such appalling things with her own father? There would be no way Ted would even want to be in the same room with her now, let alone take her on a date.

Edward immediately noticed the difference in Amy's expression. What had he said that brought such a look of despair to her face? He let go of her hand and wiped away a small tear that was trailing down her cheek. "I have to go now, but I'm going to follow in my car and will meet up with you at the hospital."

As he touched her face, a cold fear started building. Amy wouldn't look at him. She was staring off into space just like she had been doing earlier when he had first gotten to her office. She didn't say a word or look over in his direction as he exited the ambulance.

As Edward watched the ambulance doors close behind him, he felt his fears escalate. What if Amy regressed into that trance again? Would they be able to pull her back to reality a second time? He remembered the time she had seemed lost to the world for a full year, and he wondered if that was what was happening once more.

+++++

After the ambulance pulled away, Edward and James immediately headed toward the parking garage. As they were entering the garage's entrance, they met Ted walking out.

"Ted, I need a very special favor from you," Edward said, surprised at seeing his friend there. "Would you pick up Raphael at Amy's and take care of him for a couple of days?"

"Sure," Ted readily agreed, but he was puzzled over the request. "Is Amy having some kind of problem with him? I was just on my way to her office to talk with her, but there was so much traffic I had difficulty finding a place to park. An ambulance was stationed in the middle of the road blocking traffic, and I had trouble getting around it."

Edward looked over at James with such a strange expression on his face that Ted immediately knew something was wrong. He felt his pulse quicken, and he reached out grabbing Edward's arm.

"Has something happened to Amy?" Ted asked fearfully.

Edward chose his words very carefully. He knew Amy wouldn't want people to know what had happened. "She just had a little medical problem. She's better now, but we still thought it was best she go in to the hospital for a complete check up. I'm sure it's nothing too serious."

"That ambulance was for Amy!" Ted almost shouted. "People don't call for ambulances unless something is seriously wrong."

"I did it just as a precaution. It's really nothing to worry about."

"Nothing to worry about! If she's sick enough to require an ambulance, it's something to be worried about. What hospital is she going to?" Ted wanted to go wherever Amy would be. He had to know if she were going to be all right.

"Ted, I don't think Amy will want visitors for awhile," Edward said. "She just had a big emotional upset, and I'm positive she wouldn't want to see anyone right away. I promise I will call you as soon as I learn how she is doing." Reaching into his pocket and pulling out his set of keys, Edward took off Amy's house key. He didn't think she would mind if Ted went directly to the house and picked up Raphael. In fact, it might help her to know someone was already taking care of the dog. He looked expectantly at Ted. "Do you think you could get Raphael right now? Amy would feel better knowing the dog was safe with you."

"That's not a problem. She doesn't need to worry about him at all." Ted took the key and placed it in his pocket. He stood in shocked silence as he watched Edward and James climb into their cars and leave.

Ted didn't want to get Raphael. He wanted to go to Amy. How could he just sit by and not do anything if she needed him? But since he had been told not to bother her right now, he really didn't feel he had much of a choice. He reluctantly got into his car and headed straight towards Amy's house.

On the drive there, all he could think of was how much he wanted to be with her. Morbid thoughts kept cropping up as he maneuvered the car along the busy streets. What if she is dying, and they just didn't want to tell him? She had been having those bad headaches. Maybe she had a stroke. Or he had heard her talking at the birthday party about some guy at work that had been bothering her. Maybe she had been attacked. Maybe...maybe...maybe...there were too many to even think about! Why hadn't Edward told him what was wrong? The suspense was worse than any truth Edward could have possibly said.

As soon as he arrived at Amy's house, Ted headed toward the phone. He quickly thumbed through the phone book looking for the phone numbers for the two local hospitals. The moment he found them, he started dialing. But it was too early yet. Neither facility had her listed as a patient. In sheer frustration he collapsed on the couch, with the phone book still clasped tightly in his hands.

Raphael, excited to see Ted, jumped on the couch and started covering Ted's face with wet, slobbery, doggy kisses, but Ted wasn't in the mood. Raphael's presence brought images of Amy's face as it had looked when she had first seen the dog the night of her birthday party...a beautiful face lit by some magical force so it had seemed the whole room was illuminated solely by her smile. What if by some strange twist of fate, he lost her now that he had just found her? How could he survive? She had already become so ingrained into his heart that the sheer thought of anything happening to her was more than he could bear.

Unable to stand the suspense one moment more, he started dialing the hospitals again. This time he found out she had been admitted to Charity over on Forty-Sixth Street. After checking to make sure Raphael had plenty of food and water, Ted jumped into his car and headed straight toward the hospital. He didn't know what was wrong with Amy. He wasn't even sure she would want to see him. She might not have the same feelings for him that he had for her. But just in case she did want to see him, he wanted to be waiting for her. It didn't matter what Edward thought...because if Amy needed him, he was going to be there.

+++++

After the ambulance doors closed leaving Amy to the professional care of the paramedics, she couldn't look at them, just as she couldn't look at Edward a few seconds earlier. She was too ashamed. What would they be thinking about her? Seeing the medical workers' gloved hands, she knew the men didn't want to touch her. She felt so contaminated, so unclean. Who would ever want to touch her again?

She thought about how she had felt when Ted had held her last night, and she started crying. Now it would never happen again. There was no way Ted would want to hold her once he found out the type of person she really was. It didn't matter that it had all happened years ago. She would always be tainted by the filth of her father's touch. There could never be anyone for her to love because no one would be able to love her.

She wanted to turn away so no one could watch her cry, but when she tried to move, she found that she was strapped tightly into the gurney. She felt like a prisoner...a prisoner trapped in a world from which there was no escape. Tears poured out, and her breaths came in great gulps between periods of hysterical sobbing. Years of unshed tears flowed out in rivers from eyes that had seen such terrible sadness and pain.

How could she have let her father do those unspeakable things to her? There must have been a way she could have stopped it. Maybe it really was her fault, like her father had said. When he had been on top of her, sweating and grunting like an animal, he had kept repeating how she caused it all. Had he been right? Had she somehow enticed him to the point that he couldn't control his urges? Some men were weaker than others. Had he been too weak to resist?

+++++

In an effort to calm Amy, the paramedic sitting beside her spoke in a firm voice. "Try to relax, Ms. Tedrow. We'll be at the hospital soon, and Dr. Perry and your brother are going to meet you there. You'll be feeling better in no time at all. You'll see, everything will be all right."

Amy didn't dare look at the paramedic. She didn't want to see the contempt she knew would be in his eyes. Her tears continued to fall unabated, and she could hardly talk. "It...can't...get any...better," she sobbed, "and it will...never be...all right. I just want to...die. Please just let me die!"

"You're not going to die. Come on now, calm down."

Closing her eyes, Amy suddenly stopped crying. She didn't want to stay in the ambulance one second longer, so she went to a place deep within herself, a place where she had been before but had forgotten about a long time ago. But now she remembered, and she gladly followed the path her mind drew her down.

It had been here that she had hidden from her father when he came for her and she hadn't been able to escape his touch. In this private world where only she existed, she had been surrounded by gray mists of nothingness and had sought and found her only source of refuge from the living nightmare of her childhood. Now as she allowed herself to drift into this quiet, peaceful world again, thoughts of Ted followed her. She imagined that he was there holding her hand as she moved away from the pain and anguish holding her captive. She pretended he wouldn't ever find out about her sins and would hold on to her forever. Even though she knew deep in her heart that wouldn't really happen once he learned the shameful truth about her.

+++++

The paramedic watching over Amy shook his head in frustration. *First the woman had been sobbing and crying like some kind of nut, and now she was off in never-never land. A person could sure tell she was one of Dr. Perry's patients.* "Hey Chris, how about speeding this thing up a bit. I don't want to be back here if she starts going crazy on me. The last one of Dr. Perry's patients who acted like this tried to take a bite out of my arm."

"Sure, Greg, your wish is my command," Chris replied as he stepped on the accelerator and switched on the siren.

"She's too beautiful to be one of Perry's weirdoes," Greg said, reaching over and taking Amy's pulse. "What a waste. I haven't had a woman this pretty back here for a long time. She sure fills out that red shirt just fine."

"Keep your mind on your job. You're supposed to be taking her pulse, not watching her chest."

"I'm not hurting anything. She can't hear me. She didn't even flinch when I took her blood pressure a couple minutes ago."

"What are her vital signs? I'll call them in to the emergency room."

"She's not going to the ER. She's a direct admission to the floor. They're supposed to be setting up a scan of her head. Good thing too, she's acting like a zombie back here."

"Are you sure she can't hear you? You shouldn't be talking like that in front of her. It could get you, and me, in big trouble."

"She's out of it." Pumping up the blood pressure cuff again, Greg placed the end of his stethoscope at the bend in her arm. Amy's eye's popped open, and he jerked his hand back. "Hi, welcome back," he said, "I'm just getting your blood pressure, nothing to be afraid of."

When Amy didn't answer, Greg shook her arm to see if he would get a response. She only blinked her eyes a couple of times, and then closed them again.

"She's definitely one of Dr. Perry's patients, even if she is a little older than most of them." Greg said.

"The problem could be that bump on her head. I checked it out when we picked her up. She got a pretty good whack to her skull. I'd say there's a good chance she's got a concussion, maybe even some internal bleeding."

"I guess it doesn't really matter what's wrong with her. My job is to pick them up and deliver them. The hospital takes it from there." Greg moved up toward the front of the ambulance. "But I still wouldn't mind doing something more with this one than just delivering her. We don't get to see too many women that look like her in this job. I wouldn't mind it one bit if she just lay there while I did all the work. Hell, that's all my old lady does anymore."

Chris glanced contemptuously over his shoulder at Greg, "You know, some days you really disgust me. Go back there and do your job. That poor woman has enough problems without you drooling over her."

"Oh, get off your high horse. I'm not any different than any other man. Don't go acting so righteous." Greg went back to Amy. Taking her blood pressure and then her pulse again, he wrote the results down on his log.

Chapter 42

Edward didn't go directly to Amy's room when he arrived at the hospital. Unfortunately someone from the Admissions office waylaid him on the way into the facility. Amy hadn't been able to give them the information they needed to complete her admission papers, so he had to stop and answer their questions before he could even see his sister. It seemed no matter how sick a person appeared to be, the paperwork had to be done.

Edward frowned at the woman sitting across the desk from him and wondered where in the world the hospital had found her. She didn't smile or even twitch a single facial muscle as she spouted off questions and shoved papers at him to sign. Apparently the patients at Charity Hospital weren't even allowed to die without filling out the proper paperwork first.

Edward uncomfortably shifted his weight in the hard metal chair as he quickly scribbled his name on several forms. *I didn't have to give out this much information when I took the loan out on my*

399

house, he thought. Irritated by the delay, he voiced his frustration. "Can't we hurry this up a bit? I want to get upstairs and find out how my sister is doing."

"Right now she's down in x-ray getting a scan of her head," the stone-faced woman replied. "It will be a while before she'll be in her room, so try not to worry. The staff here is excellent, and they'll take good care of your sister. Now, what type of insurance does she have?"

+++++

Twenty minutes later Edward found himself in the hospital lobby waiting for Amy to get situated in her room. He really needed to call Ellen. He knew it would help tremendously if he could just talk to her for a few minutes. He stood in the far corner of the lobby with his cell phone clasped tightly in his hand and wondered how much to tell his wife. What was he supposed to say? *Hello Honey, Amy just told me Dad raped and beat her when she was a little girl. No, I didn't know anything about it. I only lived in the same house with them. How was I supposed to know such trivial things like that?*

After five rings he heard the click of the phone being picked up. "Ellen," he said, wanting desperately to hear the sound of her voice

"What's wrong?" Ellen knew immediately something had happened, just by the way he had said her name.

"I'm at Charity Hospital. Amy has just been admitted."

"What happened? Is she all right? Was there an accident?" Ellen didn't even pause between questions long enough to give Edward time to answer. "I'll be right down."

"Hold on, Honey. You don't need to come all the way down here. I don't think it's serious enough for you to rush across town and maybe hurt yourself."

"Are you sure? Amy absolutely hates doctors. She wouldn't be at a hospital unless it was something serious."

"As of right now, everything seems under control. Amy's getting some x-rays taken and then we'll know more."

"X-rays? Of what?" Ellen asked.

"She fell and hit her head," Edward said. "It appears some guy attacked her at work."

"She was attacked! It wasn't that computer guy that was helping with the new systems, was it? She complained about him at her party. I think she said his name was Gary. She said he really made her feel uncomfortable and reminded her of a rattlesnake."

"That's the one. It seems she reported him because of something he did, and he got booted out of the office because of it. I guess he didn't take too kindly to a woman telling him what to do."

"Do you know exactly what happened?"

"Well, as far as I can tell, some pushing and shoving went on, causing her to fall and hit her head. Then I guess he kicked her a couple of times."

"Oh my!" Ellen gasped.

"I think Amy got in a few punches of her own," Edward said. "You know my sister, a fighter to the end. From the way Susan talked, the guy got the worst of it. Apparently his arm might have been broken."

"I guess I shouldn't have laughed at Amy and her karate lessons. It appears they came in handy after all. Maybe after the baby comes I'll check that class out myself."

"I don't know how wise that would be. I might be too scared to kiss you then." Edward chuckled, but without any enthusiasm.

"There's more you're not telling me," Ellen said, hearing the tense undertones in his voice. "Come on, tell me the rest. Is Amy hurt worse than what you want me to believe?"

"No, not physically. At least I don't think so. There's a possibility she might have a concussion, so the doctor is doing some testing. He's also going to see if he can find an explanation for those headaches of hers."

"Good. I've always felt there had to be a reason for them."

"There might be a reason...a very good reason," Edward said very quietly, almost in a whisper.

"What aren't you telling me?" Ellen demanded. "I can tell there's something wrong by the way your voice sounds. You'd better start talking. Otherwise, I'm coming down there right now."

Edward glanced up and down the hall to see if anyone was listening. When he saw the lobby was empty he said, "Amy told me some very disturbing things about Dad, and I'm having a hard time believing her. It's some pretty awful stuff. I really can't talk about it on the phone. I'll tell you all about it when I get home."

"All right. But remember, if Amy needs me, you call me right away. Promise."

"I promise." Edward paused. "Ellen—"

"Yes?"

"I love you."

+++++

Edward hung up the phone. With the baby being due so soon, he didn't want to upset Ellen, but he really needed her advice. She was so levelheaded. She would be able to help him figure out what was real and what was make-believe.

He thought about what Amy had revealed to him, and considering how she had been feeling lately, it was hard to actually decide what he really believed to be true. Either answer he was looking at wasn't very good. If Amy was only hallucinating, she was probably sick…how sick he had no idea. Or, if there was any truth in what she had said about their father, he had no idea at all how he would handle the knowledge that the man he had loved and worshipped had raped and beaten his own daughter.

As sick as it sounded, even to him, part of him wanted there to be a medical reason for Amy's strange behavior. Nothing big…just something that would explain why she would suddenly start imagining things. It had to be something medical…the idea that their father had abused Amy was as hard to believe as a story about Mother Teresa being a terrorist. How could a man, who'd had the whole town trusting him, have been anything less than perfect? That many people couldn't have been wrong, could they?

+++++

By the time James got the chance to check on Amy she was already in her room. The initial x-rays had been done, and he was waiting to see the results before deciding what course to take. If it turned out there was a physical problem he would need to call in another doctor to consult with. Normally he didn't deal with physical health problems. His specialty was mental or behavioral disorders.

Prior to entering Amy's room, James stopped at the nurse's desk. He was concerned about Amy's mental state and wanted to talk with the nurse who had done the initial admission assessment.

"How is Ms. Tedrow?" James asked.

"I couldn't get her to talk to me," the nurse said with concern. "She's not responding verbally. If I pinch her arm, she'll draw it back, but that's about all. She's not actually unconscious; it's more like a fugue state. She periodically opens her eyes and looks around, but I don't believe she's really seeing anything. I think whatever it is she's really seeing is in her mind, not in the room. Her vital signs are a little unusual. Her blood pressure is low, and her pulse is only fifty. Her breath sounds are normal, and I don't see any type of respiratory distress, although her respiratory rate is down." The nurse looked thoughtfully up at James. "It's almost as if she's placed herself into a trance."

"I was hoping she wouldn't fall back into that state again," James replied. "That's how she was acting earlier. It's going to be hard for me to treat her if she's shut her mind off from the world."

"You'll figure out something. You seem to have a gift for reaching the patients no one else can reach."

"This is one patient I really want to help," James said hopefully. "Do me a favor, call down to x-ray and tell them I want her report as soon as it's available."

+++++

James entered Amy's room and placed his hand upon her arm. He could feel very little energy flowing from her. Somehow she had shut herself down, and that was a very bad sign.

As he tried to examine Amy, she totally ignored him. She sat up in bed and swung her legs over the side. Then she got up on her feet and wandered over to the window. Like a lost soul, she stood alone staring up at the evening sky. She placed both of her hands upon the windowpane, then pressed her face up against the glass looking out without really seeing anything.

James went over, took her hand and gently escorted her back to the bed. He explained to her where she was and that he was going to order some more tests to see if he could find out what was wrong with her. Then whispering softly, he talked of other things. "It's safe here, Amy. You don't have to hide anymore. Your father can't hurt you any longer. It's all right to talk about what happened to you. Remember what my grandmother said—your healing will start once you face the fears within yourself. And now that you have finally been able to tell someone the truth about your childhood, you've taken the first step in that direction."

James had no way of knowing whether Amy understood what he had just said, but she did turn toward him and let a tiny smile cross her face before she slipped off into her own private world again. When he saw the empty look that was reflected in her eyes, James had doubts that he would be able to break down the barrier which existed between the real world and the one Amy was in right now.

James took her chart and wrote orders for several tests that he wanted done. He ordered a complete blood workup to rule out any abnormalities in that area. After thinking for a few minutes, he added an antidepressant and ordered suicide precautions to be followed. Finally, he wrote an order for a consult with the hospital's rape counselor, although he did add he wanted to talk directly with the counselor before she went in and started working with Amy.

Chapter 43

Just as James finished writing Amy's new orders in her chart, Edward popped into the room. "How's she doing?" he asked, heading over to Amy's bedside. "It took me forever to get through the admission office. Someone really should find a way to streamline that process. A person could die before he got the paperwork done to get admitted into this place." Edward smiled at Amy hoping it would help disguise the fear he knew would be echoing in his voice. "Hi, Sis. How are you feeling?"

When she looked right past him as if he weren't there, Edward's concern for his sister skyrocketed.

"Damn it, Doc, what's wrong with her? I've never seen anyone act like this except on TV and those people were locked up in an asylum." Frustrated at his inability to do anything for his sister, Edward slumped down in the chair at her bedside. "She's not going crazy, is she?"

James looked at Edward for a moment, trying to decide how much he could tell him. "I don't think she is insane, or crazy, or whatever you might want to call it. I think she endured some very traumatic experiences a long time ago that she has buried deep in her subconscious, and now that the memories are surfacing, she's having difficulty dealing with them. Although to be on the safe side, I am running several other tests to rule out a physical cause for her problems."

"You don't really believe that ridiculous story about Dad raping her, do you? I mean, if such a terrible thing had been going on at home, wouldn't I have known about it? How could Dad have kept a thing like that quiet?"

James didn't want to talk in front of Amy, so he motioned for Edward to follow him out to the lobby. There weren't any other people about, so they were able to talk freely. James chose his words very carefully. He didn't want to make an enemy of Edward. "Incest is almost always kept a secret, otherwise so much of it wouldn't be going on. What happens behind closed doors is seldom spoken aloud in front of witnesses."

"But, I lived in that house with them. Wouldn't I have heard or seen something?"

"I bet you spent a lot of time out of town because of those extra activities you were involved with. Remember…you told me your father pushed you to compete in every sport your school had. Plus, you had several friends, didn't you? If you had a normal childhood, you probably frequently spent time over at those friends' houses. Maybe you weren't home as much as you might have thought you were."

"What about Mom?" Edward's anxiety made him almost shout out his questions. "Wouldn't she have known if something that horrible had been going on between Dad and Amy? And wouldn't she have stopped it?"

"I can't answer those questions. I've never met your mother, so I have no idea what she would have allowed, or not allowed, to happen. But there have been documented incidents where the mother has actually encouraged or even arranged for the sexual contact to occur between the daughter and the father."

"No, not my Mother! She's not like that."

James paused a moment before continuing when he saw the look of anguish that was covering Edward's face. "Truthfully, it's too early for me to tell you exactly what took place. If what Amy is saying is true, there are at least three things that could have happened. Either your mother didn't know what was going on, or she did know and chose not to do anything about it, or she suspected and just denied it."

"I can't believe my mother could have just stood by and let such a hideous thing happen to her own daughter."

"It appears she stood by and let your father beat her."

"You don't know that for sure. Amy might just be talking crazy."

"I really don't think she's talking crazy. I'm going to tell you exactly what I think...your sister is a survivor of physical, emotional, and sexual abuse. And right now she is in a critical period. What happens in the next few days could make a big difference in how the rest of her life is going to go. She can come out of this stronger or she could fall apart. Now, I think she is a fighter, but she has been fighting this alone for so long that she may not be able to keep it up. She will need you, your mother, and her friends to support her as much as they possibly can."

"I can't believe any of this is really happening!" Edward declared in a voice that shook with each word. "Just yesterday, my life was going along smoothly, normally, and now this. I don't understand how the whole world could suddenly turn so topsy-turvy." He felt drained and totally empty inside. He slumped down on one of the lobby chairs and almost started crying. But the moment the wetness seeped from his eyes, he forced it to stop. *If anyone should be crying it should be Amy, not me,* he thought pushing the pain away from his heart.

James pulled up a chair so he was sitting directly across from Edward. "Tell me a little bit about your parents. It will help me understand Amy better. The more I know, the more I can help."

Edward hesitated. The last thing he wanted to do was discuss his parents, especially his father. It made him feel like a traitor. But he kept seeing in his mind the sadness and sorrow that had covered Amy's face, and he realized that right now his sister's health was more important than his own feelings. And he knew he had to do everything that he could to help her.

Edward took a deep breath and began describing his parents. "Dad was a unique person. He had a very dominant personality and always needed to be in control. He worked very hard at being successful at his job and was well respected by everyone in town for the work he did for the community and for his church. You couldn't have found a man who worked any harder. His main drawback was that he expected everyone else to work just as hard. He made all of us toe the line, including Mom. What he said was law, whether you agreed with him or not. I can remember a couple of times when we got into disagreements where Dad's solution to the argument had been a belt to my backside…but nothing like what Amy is describing. Dad felt he had the right to dictate to all of us every aspect of our lives. I learned early how to work it so I stayed out of his way and not get into trouble, but Amy never did figure out how to accomplish that feat. He was always yelling at her about something. I know he scared her when he got mad, so I tried to teach her how to stay on his good side."

"What about your mother?" James asked, giving his full attention to Edward as he talked.

"Mom was, and still is, a very passive person. When Dad was alive, her personality was almost nonexistent. She lived and breathed just to take care of his needs. I can't say she was particularly happy with having things that way, but she had been brought up to believe it was a woman's duty to serve her husband. So that's exactly what she did. Sometimes I got really mad at both of them because Dad would treat her like a servant, but he'd just laugh and say that it was a woman's duty to take care of her man. Right after Dad died, Mom really had a tough time making it on her own. She wasn't used to making decisions or looking after herself. It took her a long time to learn how to be self-reliant, but she does fairly well on her own now."

James sat listening attentively to everything Edward was saying. He wanted Edward to keep on talking. Any details at all that would give him a clue to Amy's state of mind would be beneficial for developing a plan for her treatment. "Some studies show that incest is more prevalent in homes where the mother simply isn't strong enough to protect her children from interfamilial sexual abuse." James paused for a second before continuing. He was worried that his next question would disturb Edward. "Do you think that could have happened within your family?"

"Even with Mom being so passive, I really have a tough time believing she would have allowed my father to molest Amy. She has always been a prude about sex. I can still remember all of those little speeches she used to give me about the sins of premarital sex. According to her, a boy wasn't even supposed to look at a girl, let alone touch her, until he was married. And to tell you the truth, I honestly believe that she thought sex was just sinful in general. I can't even recall one time that I ever saw Dad kiss her. If he came over and put his hands on her, she would push him a way. I think sex may have been the only thing she actually had any control over. If it weren't for Amy and me, I would have serious doubts that they had even had a sexual relationship. As a matter of fact, once I heard her tell a friend that sex was meant to allow women to get pregnant and since she had all the children she wanted, sex wasn't something worth messing with anymore."

Edward paused as a shocked expression crossed his face. "Would that have anything to do with what might have happened? I mean...if Dad wasn't getting any sexual satisfaction from his marriage, could that have driven him to turn to Amy?"

"Well, recent evidence indicates it isn't really sexual dissatisfaction as much as it is the lack of a satisfying emotional relationship between the husband and the wife that is associated with incest by the father. But in my opinion, neither reason is enough to validate sexual misconduct with any minor."

"I was just wondering if that might have been a reason for...I mean, a reason *if* such a thing had happened with Amy."

"Do you believe there is any chance at all Amy is telling you the truth...that your father may have physically and sexually abused her?" James asked, feeling it was very important for Edward to look closely at his parents' relationship to see how it was possible that the impossible could have occurred.

Edward leaned forward in his chair and buried his face in his hands. For a moment he said nothing. Then sitting up, he looked James straight in the face. "I have no idea at all what I truly believe at this moment. Never once has Amy ever lied to me about anything. Why should she lie about something as awful as this? Still, how can I believe those terrible stories about Dad? I don't know how they can possibly be true! I mean, child abuse happens only in the slums or places like that, right? We didn't live that way. Dad owned his own business, worked hard for the community, and he even went to church every Sunday."

"Incest and child abuse occurs all the time, at all levels of society, in all types of households. It's a silent epidemic that no one likes to talk about. That's one of the reasons it keeps happening. No one will talk about it. The victims are too ashamed and the abusers are usually in a position where no one questions them."

"Why wouldn't anyone report abuse if they knew it was happening? If I were being molested or abused, I would tell someone...the preacher...the police...a schoolteacher. Or if I saw a child being treated that way, I would find someone to tell. That's what we have laws for. To protect people so things like that can't happen to them."

"One of the problems is that the abusers are often from households which are very patriarchal. This type of lifestyle centers around the traditional theory that the man is king of the household and has the right to do whatever he wants to do with his own family members. When someone is looked at as being a king by everyone in the family, it's hard for any family member to try to upset that person's rule. How can you fight the king when you're just a little servant? Unfortunately, women are frequently taught to be subservient to men from almost the moment of their birth. Once this role has been instilled into them, it's a hard pattern for them to break."

"Just because Dad believed he had the right to rule over us doesn't mean he would have molested Amy. He was a deacon at church for heaven's sake."

"You might be shocked to know in cases of father-daughter sexual abuse in which the daughter is physically mature, the father is often very devout, moralistic, and fundamentalistic in his religious beliefs."

"How can that be possible? I have trouble believing any god-fearing man would molest his own children. That's one of the main reasons I have such doubts about Dad. He was very active in church, and every Sunday he made sure all of us attended with him, even if we didn't want to go. How could he believe so firmly in the church principles, then go home and do the unspeakable?"

"It happens all the time. Some theorists think a religious man who commits incest may tend do it when he is sexually frustrated in his marriage for whatever reasons, yet is constrained by religious codes from seeking gratification through masturbation, prostitutes, or extramarital affairs. For some men, it appears more preferable behavior to keep sexual contact within the family."

"How could any man think that having sex with one's own daughter, even if she were mature enough for it, would be more acceptable than having sex with another adult?"

"That's something I can't answer. Some older explanations about incest have actually pointed fingers at the children, saying they asked for the sexual contact by their seductive behavior. Can you imagine a grown man being seduced by a six-year-old! Fortunately, that concept isn't viewed as being acceptable any more."

"No matter how hard I try, I just can't picture Dad touching a child in that manner, especially his own daughter. He was the one who chased off all the guys that came around wanting to go out with Amy. He didn't let any of them get near her. He'd preach fanatically about how sinful it would be for her to have sex before marriage. Once he even threw a guy off the front porch for simply trying to get a goodnight kiss. And I remember the night he found her out in the driveway sitting in this guy's car talking. He charged out of the house with a loaded shotgun, pulled the car door open, shoved the gun barrel right into the poor guy's chest, and demanded to know what the hell he was doing out there with Amy. He told the boy that no one was going to touch his daughter and that he'd better get off his property while he still had his legs to do it. Everyone at school had thought it was pretty hilarious at the time, but I don't remember Amy even dating after that incident. Everyone was too scared of Dad."

"Maybe he was protecting what he considered to be his property. A lot of abuse is centered around power and control. Sexual abuse may not even have anything to do at all with sexual gratification. It can simply be a means for the abuser to feel more powerful and in control. An abuser usually has some compelling need to feel that way. Having control over another person's body is one of the ultimate powers anyone can have, and a child is so much easier to manipulate than another adult. With the right threats, a child can be forced into doing a lot of horrible things."

"The right threats! What kind of threats?" Edward sat up straight in his chair so he could hear everything James was saying. *Maybe I can make some kind of sense out of Amy's accusations if I can only understand how it might have happened,* he thought as forced himself to listen.

"There are all kinds of threats that abusers use," James said, thinking of his young patient, Tommy. "It depends on the victim. Everyone has certain fears that push their buttons, and the abuser will try and use the ones that will grant him the most control. For instance, there may be threats to kill the victim if she says anything. Or the threats could be directed at harming other family members or close friends. Maybe the abuser will tell the child that she will be taken away and placed in foster care or be thrown out of the house to live in the streets. You said that you would report it if anyone were molesting you…but, could you do it if the molester told you he would slit your mother's throat if you said anything? Especially if you were only five years old and the molester was a close family member, who could carry out his threat very easily. Or what if you were told if you even said one word, you would be sent away to a place where you would be castrated. Or maybe the abuser would chain you to the bed and threaten to cut your heart out, or would lock you in a closet for days without food or water or even a place to relieve yourself. A few days sitting in your own excrement could change your mind about reporting the abuse."

"I can't believe this kind of stuff really happens." Edward shook his head in disbelief. He was totally shocked by what he was hearing.

"Well, it does happen all the time. The threats some children face every day are very real. Most of them only try to find a way to survive day to day." James looked straight into Edward's eyes. "I know. I deal with such horror every day with my work. I hear the stories first hand, not from some book or movie screen."

"How could I not have known such dreadful things were happening, maybe even in my own house?" Edward said, bowing his head in shame.

"Don't be so hard on yourself. The important thing now is— What are you going to do about your sister? If she's telling you the truth, are you going to support her? If you turn away, she will have a much harder time working through all of the emotional turmoil she is going to have to face. You need to think hard about how you are going to handle this situation. Your sister's future depends a lot on how you react to what she told you today."

Edward didn't know what to say. He stood up without making any further comments to James and headed back to Amy's room. All of a sudden he wasn't so sure of his father's innocence. Long forgotten memories of Amy's many injuries were starting to pop up, and he felt his faith in his father faltering.

Edward recalled how hard he had worked to make sure his father had been proud of him. It seemed everything he had accomplished had been because he had wanted his father to look at him with pride. Unfortunately, he found out how easy it had been for his father to lose that look. If he ever questioned his father about anything, that shining look in his father's eyes would quickly disappear, so he learned how to preserve it. He learned not to interfere with how his mother was treated, and he learned not to question anything that happened to his sister. And now that he was faced with the possibility his lack of questioning could have resulted in a life of hell Amy, Edward felt the overwhelming burden of guilt weighting down his mind, and it was a load he did not want to be carrying.

Toni Auberry

Chapter 44

When Amy opened her eyes she was surprised to find that the paramedics had vanished and that she wasn't even in the ambulance any longer. Instead of being strapped to a gurney listening to a siren screaming in her ears, she stood on a small, grassy knoll surrounded by a thick, heavy, gray mist. The mist was so dense she couldn't even see her feet. The funny thing was, she didn't feel the least bit afraid. What she felt was relief. All of a sudden there existed no pain, no sadness, no grief in her heart.

Then she remembered...*this was her Gray world.* The place she used to send herself whenever the horror of her father climbing on top of her would threaten to destroy her sanity. It was a place only her mind could reach, a refuge from the hell her father had made for her in the real world.

She giggled, recalling there among the surrounding gray mist, she could even fly. Raising her arms, she leaped forward into the air. Like a bird gliding on the wind, she soared through the dusky atmosphere. Then she relaxed, letting a gentle, warm breeze carry her upward. No pain…no evil…no unhappiness could touch her in this place. She was free. *Like an angel,* she thought, *but without wings.*

For what seemed an eternity, she quietly followed the softly flowing air currents that were carrying her steadily upward toward a bright light shining far in the distance. *This time I'm not going back,* she thought. *I'm so tired of fighting that beast in my dreams, and I'm so weary of the emptiness that fills up my soul leaving me with no room to love. I know there is only peace and comfort up there beyond that light. And I know with all of my heart and soul that is where I must go. It is where I now belong.*

Amy's heart was light and carefree. She wasn't thinking or worrying about anything. Tranquility flowed through her, around her, with her. For the first time in years she was at peace with herself, and she knew it would remain that way forever if she could only reach the bright light that was pulling her toward its warm glow. Once she reached it, nothing would ever be able to hurt her again. And she wanted more than anything in the world never to hurt again. Somehow, deep in her heart, she understood that beyond the light ahead would be the love she had never received as she was growing up.

A demanding urgency began to push her forward, and she could feel herself moving faster and faster. *If I can only reach that light all will be well,* she thought hopefully.

Then something strange happened. Another presence suddenly appeared from out of nowhere and took its place beside her.

Fear instantly stabbed at Amy's heart, and she didn't know what to do. She was too afraid to even look over to see who it might be. The frightening thought that it might be her father had seized her mind and she was too terrified to react.

But then her fears were quickly abated when James' grandmother's gentle voice drifted across the gray mist. "Amy, you have to stop," Elizabeth said, halting Amy's flight upward toward the light. "It's not time for you to go up there yet. You have to go back...right now, before it's too late."

In desperation Amy cried out, "I don't want to go back. I have to go on. Please...you can't make me stop now." Despair overwhelmed Amy because the very last thing she wanted to do was to stop her journey toward the light. "Can't you feel what it would be like to be by that light all the time? Can't you feel the joy surrounding it?"

Turning, Amy saw Elizabeth's faint image floating alongside of her. Like two angels suspended in mid-flight, the two figures hovered in the mist next to each other.

"Yes, I can feel it." Elizabeth said. "But Amy, you have to go back. There's someone waiting for you, and he desperately needs you. If you leave him now, it will surely break his heart. His happiness depends on you being by his side."

Amy became aware of the touch of Elizabeth's hand upon hers. It felt like a soft whisper of air as it brushed across her skin. Amy gazed intently into Elizabeth's eyes, searching for a reason not to continue her journey upward, but she could find none. Turning back toward the light, she felt the heat radiating from it gently warming her face. Her life has been so cold and empty for so very long. Why would she ever want to go back to that?

"How could anyone need me?" Amy asked, her heart heavy with the sorrow her father had placed there. "It's not possible. No one will ever want me. Especially now that the whole world knows how my father has contaminated me with his awful filth."

"Have faith in yourself, Amy. Your father's sins are not yours. The one who waits for you has a love that is strong enough to pull both of you through the troubled times ahead. When he offers his heart, don't deny him the chance to show you that you are worth loving."

"Even if someone could bring himself to offer me his heart, what do I have to give in return?" Amy asked in despair. "How can I ever be free to love with all this hate and anger inside? I'm not sure I'll ever be able to stand the touch of a man's hands again. What man would want a woman who couldn't love him back?"

"Child, remember what I told you...your healing will start when you face the fears within yourself. You are strong enough to do that. And now you will no longer have to face those fears alone. Go back and find out what it feels like to truly be loved. And in being loved, you'll discover how to love."

A rush of warmness surrounded Amy as Elizabeth moved forward and placed a feathery kiss upon her check. Then Elizabeth pulled away and headed toward the shining light that loomed just ahead, leaving Amy with a heavy sadness filling up her heart. She knew her friend was leaving and that she couldn't go with her.

"Please tell James not to worry about me and that I'm sorry I couldn't wait for him to say goodbye," Elizabeth said, looking over her shoulder at Amy. "Tell him everything is going to be just fine, and that someday we will see each other again."

Amy continued to watch as Elizabeth moved forward into the gray mist. When James' grandmother got closer to the light, Amy felt the presence of another person, and she somehow knew Elizabeth wasn't alone any more. She peered into the mist trying to see who it was, but she couldn't see anything except swirling gray clouds. But apparently Elizabeth saw someone. Amy heard Elizabeth's gasp of happy surprise and then she heard the name Steve spoken with such sheer joy that she realized Elizabeth must have recognized who the person was. Amy strained her eyes to see, and she caught a glimpse of two shadowy figures coming together, and then she saw them walking hand-in-hand into a brilliance that illuminated the gray mist like a bright neon sun. She gasped in surprise as a flash of lightning unexpectedly lit up the grayness that surrounded her, and then as the light faded Amy realized she was alone again.

+++++

Suddenly Amy didn't feel as happy or content as before. Unsettling thoughts of Ted were going through her mind, and she discovered that she couldn't continue her journey upward any longer. Her flight toward the light halted abruptly, and she felt herself starting to spiral downward. Turning and spinning like a swirling top she fell into the grayness that surrounded her. With each spin the gray mist surrounding her grew darker and darker until she was enveloped by the dark of night. And when the spinning finally stopped, she found herself naked in the middle of her old bed and the beast that had been her father was towering over her like a monstrous ogre.

She saw his hands reaching to unbuckle his belt. Fear…terror…shock consumed her mind and her soul as she watched him remove the belt and hold it doubled in his clutched fists. She curled into a tight little ball and cowered as she heard the whoosh of the belt traveling though the air. Then she felt biting pains exploding upon her back as the belt connected with her skin.

Once…twice…three times the relentless pain rebounded through her tiny body.

Her father's voice, deep and husky from lust, reached her ears. "You little whore," he shouted, "look what you have done to me. I'll beat this wickedness from you. You shouldn't flaunt yourself before me like a bitch in heat."

She clamped her eyes tightly closed so she wouldn't have to see what was coming next. She wanted to run, to scream, to do anything that would stop her father from doing what she knew he would do. But she could do nothing…like every other time when he had come to her secretly in the dead of night.

"You lie there in your nakedness enticing me. A Jezebel, that's what you are, scheming with the devil to destroy my soul." Her father dropped the belt from his hands. The sound of its silver buckle hitting the wooden floor echoed off the walls in the darkened room.

Alone and frightened, Amy began praying for help. When she heard the sound of her father's pants being removed, she begged God not to let him do it to her again.

But God hadn't helped her before, so she didn't expect him to help her now.

When she felt her father's weight fall upon the bed, she prayed for death to come. Death would be her only release, her savior from the hell her life had become.

But then something different happened. A new voice reached her ears. Instead of her father's words, she heard Elizabeth speaking to her. *"You keep this demon alive by feeding it with your fears. Without fear it would have nothing to feed upon, and it would die. You alone keep the beast alive, and you alone must be the one to destroy it. All you have to do is face it."*

Tired of being afraid, weary of running, Amy opened her eyes and looked upon the beast that was crawling upon her bed. And this time…instead of waiting for her nightmare to take control and suck her into the depths of its depravity, she chose not to let fear guide her steps one moment longer. This time she fought back. Kicking and shouting with a fury that she didn't know she possessed, she refused to let the silence that had overshadowed her entire life continue on.

"Edward!" she screamed. "Help me! Please help me! Don't let Dad do this to me anymore!"

Through her terror she heard Edward calling out to her.

"Amy, I'll help you. I promise I'll help you."

427

Instantly her father vanished into the night, as she saw Edward rushing toward her calling out her name.

+++++

After talking with James, Edward sat in the lobby for a long time trying to make up his mind about Amy, but he couldn't decide exactly what he really did believe. When he finally headed back toward Amy's room, he could see his sister through the open door thrashing about in the bed as though she were fighting a demon. Breaking into a run, he heard her screaming his name as he shot through the doorway.

"Edward! Help me! Please help me! Don't let Dad do this to me any more!" Amy cried out, her voice full of years of pain.

"Amy, I'll help you. I promise I'll help you." Edward swore, rushing to her bedside.

Gathering Amy up in his arms like a child, he felt his own tears streaming down his face. "I'm here, Sis. No one will hurt you again. I promise, never again."

As the strength of Edward's touch eased away the horror of her father's memory, Amy slowly settled down. Clinging to her brother like a child awakening from a nightmare, she cried until there were no tears left. Then, exhausted from the emotional outpour of years of pent-up tears, Amy fell back in the bed weak and drained.

Mentally, she was unable to fight the shame that began flooding her senses. She turned her face away from her brother and started to withdraw again. She had wanted him to know what their father had done to her, but now that he did, she felt soiled and tainted.

How could he ever look upon her again and not see the awful, terrible person she had been?

Edward saw the look of withdrawal crossing his sister's face again, and it scared him. "Amy, don't. I need for you to talk with me. I need to know if what you're saying is true. Did Dad really do those things to you?"

"Everything I've said is true," Amy replied in a tiny, whispering voice, her eyes downcast, staring at the floor. "My life has been nothing but a lie up until today, and I didn't even know it." Her voice almost became inaudible. "Dad didn't start hitting me until after that first time he came to my room in the middle of the night. He blamed me for what he did, and the beatings, I think, were my punishment. I was only seven years old when it started. There's still a lot I don't remember, but that part I do remember. It really did happen! I know it with all my heart."

"But, Amy, if all those terrible things did happen, why didn't you remember any of it until today?"

Amy lifted her eyes to meet his and spoke without hesitation. "I have always remembered the beatings. I just never told anyone." Then she turned her face away and whispered, "Secrets aren't supposed to be told."

Afraid to ask...not really wanting to know the answer...Edward asked anyway. "Did Mom know what was going on?"

Carefully choosing her words, Amy thought for a moment before speaking. "She knew about the beatings...maybe not all of them, but some of them. Dad did a lot of the things to me when no one was home but us. I hated it when you went out of town. As soon as you would leave, he would come hunting for me."

"But did Mom know that he raped you?"

"I don't know if Mom ever really knew that he came into my bedroom and did those other things to me, but sometimes I would catch her looking at me as though she were silently accusing me. After it all started, she grew so cold toward me."

"Surely she wouldn't have blamed you for it. Mom loves you."

"She stopped loving me years ago. I lost both my mother and my father all in one sudden swoop. I never wanted to believe that she knew, because how could I live with knowing my own mother didn't love me enough to protect me from such horrible things? It was bad enough she let him beat me. How could I accept the awful truth that she let him rape me night after night?"

"I can't possibly believe Mom knew. There is no way she would have let it happen. I realize Dad was very overbearing and lorded over her just like he did us, but surely, she wouldn't have let him rape you. She would have stood up to him for that. I know it. How could she have lived with the fact such a sinful act was occurring under her own roof?"

"Edward, she stood by one day and let him almost beat me to death simply because I wouldn't undress with him in the bathroom. She didn't raise a hand to help me while he beat me or even afterwards when I lay upon the floor covered in blood. When he told her to just leave me alone, she turned and walked down the stairs without even looking back. I hurt so much after the beating I had to crawl to my bedroom, and she did nothing, absolutely nothing to help me."

"Where was I when that happened? I would have remembered if you had been hurt that badly."

"I don't know. I can't remember everything." Upset with the doubt showing in Edward's voice, she didn't want to talk with him anymore. It was just like her father had said it would be.

No one believes a word I'm saying about him, she thought as her heart emptied of hope. That's why she had always whispered her secrets to Thomas and no one else. If she hadn't had him, she would have given up the first year the abuse had started. Thomas had been her only lifeline to sanity. When he disappeared, she lost more than a pet; she lost her mind. The memories of that whole year after his disappearance was still nothing but a huge blank spot in her mind, and after what she remembered today, she wasn't at all sure she wanted to have that year back. Maybe it was better to leave it alone. Maybe she forgot for a very good reason.

"I don't want to talk anymore tonight," she said, reaching down and pulling the bed covers up over her body. "I'm just too tired to even think about my father right now."

"But I need—" Edward started to plead with Amy.

"I don't care what you need right now," Amy said. "Go home, Edward."

"Amy you have to talk with me," Edward begged. "I have to know if what you are saying is true."

"If what I am saying is true! Do you think I would just make up such terrible, awful lies for no reason? What purpose would that serve? Edward, you have no idea what my life has been like. You've always been wrapped up in your perfect little world where life was always good to you. It blinded you to the truth. Everything that happened to me went on right before your eyes, and you didn't even see it."

"It's not my fault, Amy. Please don't blame me. I didn't know. Honestly, I just didn't know." Edward stood up and walked away from Amy's bed. He had suddenly begun to feel very defensive. *Maybe some of it is my fault,* he thought. *Maybe if I'd only been more attentive to Amy's needs, maybe I could have helped her. That is, if it really did happen. Oh, I'm so confused. One minute I believe her and the next I don't.*

"I don't blame you. Why would you even think that?" But all at once Amy wasn't so sure that she didn't blame him. As much as she loved him, maybe part of her did condemn him for not helping her. Right now, she wanted him to hurt just as much as she was hurting. Why should he have the right to think their father was anything less than that vile beast that had crawled into her bed and had stolen her soul away? It wasn't fair. Their father had destroyed her life, and Edward had no right to believe in him anymore.

+++++

James felt the tension in the room the moment he stepped through the doorway. Sensing Amy had been through enough, he pulled Edward aside. "Your sister needs to rest. I think it would be best if you went home. The nurses will keep a close watch over her tonight."

"Are you sure it would be wise for me to leave? What if she starts acting strange again?" Edward glanced over at Amy then turned his eyes back toward James. "I think she needs me here."

"I'm the physician," James said, "and I deal with problems like this all the time. I know what's best."

Amy spoke up, a little angry over the discussion about her. "Maybe the two of you should ask me what I want."

Both men turned at the sound of her voice. Amy was right. The decision was hers.

"Right now, I simply want to be left alone," she said. "I don't want to think. I don't want to talk. I don't want to do anything. My whole life has suddenly been turned into a tangled mess, and I simply can't concentrate. So why don't both of you just go and leave me alone?"

+++++

Amy turned her back on them and curled up in the bed wishing with all her broken heart that Edward and James would leave. As much as she wanted to tell Edward everything, the lessons she had learned about keeping silent were repeating themselves very loudly in the back of her mind. Years of learning were hard to erase in one single day, and she truly didn't think that Edward had believed a single word she had said.

Chapter 45

When Edward left the hospital he didn't head straight home. He decided that if Amy couldn't answer his questions, maybe his mother could.

Angry and confused he found himself standing on his mother's front porch banging on the door, yelling at her to come down from the bedroom and let him in. He hit the door so hard that his hand started throbbing from the blows.

Damn it, why does Mom have to keep the house locked up like this anyway? Edward rubbed his now aching hand. *At the very least, she ought to give me a set of keys so I can get into the house in an emergency. But no, she wouldn't even do that. No one is allowed to have keys to her house. Sometimes I wonder if she's afraid of me like she seems to be of everyone else.*

A light went on upstairs, so Edward knew his mother had finally heard him. He stood impatiently waiting on the porch as she made the long trek down the stairs to open the door. He was anxious and couldn't stand still. Looking at the tightly locked house, he thought how foolish she was for keeping every door and window in the place closed up twenty-four hours a day. It made the house smell musty and damp. He had tried his best to talk her into at least opening the windows once in awhile to let some fresh air in. The whole building really needed a good breeze to blow through it to drive away the stale odor, but no matter how much he insisted, she still wouldn't do it.

For some strange reason his mother had an unreasonable fear, almost a phobia, of strangers. Whenever she would hear on the news about a woman getting killed, raped, or beaten, she would proudly point out how right she was in keeping the house locked tight. "Better safe than sorry," she had said at least a thousand times.

To him, living as a self-imposed prisoner in your own home was something to be sorry about. Being safe wasn't necessarily better if it meant giving up your freedom to relax and enjoy life.

After waiting five minutes, Edward finally heard his mother fumbling with the locks, then the door started inching open. It was time for his mother's inspection ritual. Even though she knew the sound of his voice, she still refused to open the door until she was absolutely sure it was really him. He often wondered who she was afraid she would see standing on the porch. He had asked her several times, but she never did answer.

Slowly the door opened about three inches, and he could see the shadow of her face peering out at him. A car drove by, and the beam from its headlights reflected off her eyes, giving them a wild crazed look.

The shock of seeing that look upon her face made him wonder if his mother needed to see a doctor more than Amy. *What is happening?* Edward thought anxiously as he stared at the strange reflection in his mother's eyes. *First Amy is suddenly sick and now this. A week ago, my life was perfect. Now I can feel my whole world changing, literally crumbling underneath my feet. What could possibly happen next?*

When his mother finally opened the door all the way, he wasn't surprised by the anxiety etched on her face; it always seemed to be there. She hadn't smiled in years.

"What in the world is going on?" Connie asked, a pinched frown tightening her lips. "It's the middle of the night and decent folks should be in bed, not gallivanting around town." Then she noticed that Edward's hair and clothes were rumpled and his tie was missing. "What in heaven's name happened to you? You look like a horse threw you off and stomped on you."

She paused, waiting for answer, but before he could explain, she switched modes, becoming hysterical. "It's Ellen, isn't it? Something has happened to her and the baby, hasn't it? Oh, I knew it would. She didn't look very good the other night. I told you Amy's party would be too hard on her. It's all your sister's fault. If she hadn't insisted on you having that party—"

"It's not Ellen or the baby. It's Amy. She's in the hospital." Watching his mother's face for some signs of concern for his sister, he felt disappointed when none appeared.

"Thank goodness for that." Connie let a big sigh of relief escape her lips. "For a moment, I was afraid Ellen had gone into labor. It's still far too early for that. All kinds of things could go wrong."

"Aren't you going to bother to even ask what's wrong with Amy?" Edward demanded to know.

"What kind of a mother do you think I am? Of course I want to know about my daughter. Tell me what happened. Did she wreck that new car of hers? I suppose she was driving too fast. She never did care much about other people. I certainly hope she didn't hurt anyone else by her carelessness."

"Mom, she wasn't in a car wreck. Why would you even think that? Why didn't you bother to ask what was wrong with Amy instead of automatically assuming she had done something wrong?"

"She has a long history of doing the wrong thing, that's why. Besides, I've seen the way she drives that car of hers. Just the other night, I told myself she would end up killing some poor soul with her reckless driving, so I just naturally assumed that was what the problem was."

"Well, you assumed wrong, and besides, Amy is one of the safest drivers I know." Edward shook his head in disbelief as he sat down on the couch. "I just don't know where you get some of those ideas of yours."

"Well, if it wasn't an accident, why is she in the hospital?" Connie asked, frowning as she sat down next to him. "She looked perfectly fine the other night at her party. That is, until she drank too much and got sick. I told Ellen right then that Amy shouldn't be around her with the baby being due so soon. I hope it's nothing she could catch. How like Amy to think of herself before others. She should have stayed home, not run around exposing other people to her germs. I just don't know why that girl—"

"Mom, there are some questions I want to ask you, and I need for you to answer them as truthfully as possible."

"You sound so serious," Connie replied, patting Edward's leg as though he were a child needing comfort.

"I am serious. All this involves why Amy is in the hospital." As soon as he mentioned his sister's name, he saw a blank look come over his mother's face. She seemed to be automatically disassociating herself from anything to do with Amy. He didn't know how much truthful information he would be able to obtain from her.

"So, ask your questions."

"I need to know if Dad ever physically abused Amy."

"Where in the world would you get an idea like that?" Connie pursed her lips together so tightly it looked like she didn't even have any. Then she started ranting about Amy again. "Is that sister of yours telling lies about Randy? I can't believe she would accuse her own father of hurting her or doing those other terrible things. She lies all the time, you know. Why, a man would have to be sick even to think of behaving that way. Your father wasn't that kind of man."

As she raved on and on, Edward sat looking suspiciously at her. Finally he broke in on Connie's verbal tirade. "What kind of man, Mom? What are we talking about? Why did you automatically assume Amy had accused Dad of doing terrible things to her?"

"I'm not dumb, you know," Connie angrily replied. "What else was that question supposed to imply?" Connie started to rise from the couch, but Edward grabbed her arm, stopping her. Reluctantly, she remained seated.

"I seem to recall Amy having a lot of falls…bruises…black eyes. Why was that?"

"Just because your sister was an extraordinarily clumsy girl, always falling down the stairs and tripping over her own feet, doesn't mean she was abused. Especially by your father. He was a good man; he only did what he had to do for this family."

"What about all the broken bones she had? I don't remember any of my friends' sisters having that many accidents. And now that I'm finally thinking about it, it really does seem strange that she always had some kind of injury."

"If there had been any question about your sister being abused don't you think Dr. Jennings would have said something? It's the law that abuse has to be reported."

"Amy's injuries happened a long time ago, and I'm not sure there was even a law like that back then. Besides, family doctors seem to have a history of ignoring signs of abuse. Especially, if the people involved are influential, and we both know Dad carried a lot of influence in this town."

"Your sister is filling your mind with poison about Randy, and I won't stand for it!" Connie's eyes flashed with anger. "How would it look if it got around town that your father had done what you are suggesting?"

"Tell me Mom, what am I suggesting?"

"Don't get cute with me. Your sister would say anything to get back at Randy. She always hated him, but that didn't stop him from trying to be a good father. He just had to be a little more forceful with her than with you, that's all. She was always so strong-headed. He wanted her to grow up righteous, not like a little tramp. It would break his heart if he knew the way she turned out."

No longer worried how his mother would take the news about what Amy had said, Edward snapped at her. "You keep referring to Amy as *my sister*. Well she is also *your daughter*, and right now she needs your help. Your daughter swears Dad physically abused her for years...and there's more!"

"What do you mean there's more?" Connie turned ashen as blood drain from her face. "Isn't what she's saying bad enough? She's defiling Randy's good name, saying he beat her, and you're just letting her do it. I even think you believe her lies. You should be ashamed of yourself. What kind of son are you?"

"I was a good son. I worshipped Dad, and you know it. But that has nothing to do with what is going on in this family right now."

Edward had started to feel a little guilty for questioning his father's honor and almost didn't ask the main question that was preying on his mind the most. But he couldn't get the vision of

Amy's tear-stained face to disappear from his mind, so with a deep-seated fear settling in his heart, he forced the words from his mouth. "I need to know if you had any idea at all that Dad was sexually molesting Amy?"

"Lies...that's what she is telling you!" Connie shouted, springing up from the couch. She glared at Edward with that touch of madness showing in her eyes again. "Your father might have been a little strict, but he never abused anyone. And he sure wouldn't have molested your sister. He was a god-fearing man. He went to church every Sunday, and everyone in town trusted and depended on him to do the right things."

Edward stood up without breaking the eye contact between them. "Just because he went to church, doesn't mean he couldn't have molested Amy. A man can hold a bible in one hand and pull his pants down with the other one."

"How dare you even say such a thing about your father!" Connie's hand shot out connecting with Edward's face in a resounding blow.

Rubbing his reddened check, Edward's anger at his mother faded. "Mom, I just need to know if it was at all possible that Dad could have been hurting Amy. You of all people would know. I do remember a couple of times he got really mad at me and took a belt to my backside so hard it left bruises, and he got a lot madder at Amy than he ever did me."

"Your father never did anything wrong. He just had to be very strict with Amy, that's all. We didn't want her to grow up and get

442

into trouble like a lot of the other girls in town did. Sure he was a little more demanding with Amy than with you, but boys don't have to worry about the same things that girls do. Boys can't get pregnant and ruin their lives. Anyway, Randy never did anything different than my own father did, and I turned out just fine."

"What does that mean? Exactly what did your father do?"

Connie froze, not even drawing in a breath for the longest time. Then when she did breathe her eyes darted around the room as if she were expecting something to come at her from out of a darkened corner. From the look on her face, Edward halfway expected her to run from the room shaking with fear.

"Mom! What did your father do to you?"

Connie closed her eyes, almost pinching them shut. When she opened them and looked at him, Edward saw an emotion hovering in them that he didn't recognize. Shocked by her reaction, he remained silent and waited for her to continue.

For a few moments, Connie said nothing more, but then she began to defensively defend her own father. "Dad didn't believe in holding back the belt. I can still remember a few times when he tore into my brother and me with a vengeance for not following his orders, but that's just the way it was back then. The father was in control of the family, his word was law, and you had to respect him. If it was still like that nowadays, there wouldn't be so many snot-nosed kids running around telling their parents what do. If I had talked back to my father the way some kids do today, he would have beaten me until my legs bled."

"And you see this as a good thing? My God, Mom, no one deserves to be abused. No matter what the reason. There are other ways to discipline children besides beating them half to death."

"There is a big difference between discipline and abuse." Connie glared at him. "Abuse only happens to families that are so poor or so stupid they can't function properly. This family isn't like that. We're upstanding citizens in this town, and to even suggest such a thing could have happened in this house is blasphemous."

"Mom," Edward looked at his mother with distress as an awful thought occurred to him. "If you say Dad didn't do anything to Amy that your father didn't do to you...does that mean your father also molested you?"

Horror crossed Connie's face, and she stumbled back a couple of steps, almost falling over a chair. Catching herself with one hand, she held the other one out in front of her as if trying to ward off someone. "No! Don't you even dare think such disgusting thoughts. I wouldn't have ever let my father touch me. You know that's a sin. God would send me to hell for doing that. How could you even think such awful things?"

"But you just said Grandfather ruled over all of you like a tyrant. How could you have stopped him?"

"I don't want to talk about this anymore." Connie turned paler under Edward's deep penetrating stare.

"But this is something we need to talk about. It's important to both you and Amy." Edward thought his mother looked as though she might faint, and he grabbed her arm and eased her down in a chair.

"I think what you need to do is to go," Connie retorted angrily. "I told you I don't want to talk about any of this. Your sister is lying, and that's all I'm going to say. Now get out of here. This is my house, and I want you to leave, and if you don't, I'm going to call the police and have them throw you out."

Frustrated beyond belief, Edward turned away from his mother and headed for the door. He really had no choice but to leave. He would get no further answers from her tonight. His mother was beyond reasoning at that moment, and he desperately needed to go home. More than anything in the world he wanted to see Ellen right now and feel her arms around him. Maybe she would be able to make some sense from this craziness…because he sure couldn't.

Toni Auberry

Chapter 46

Connie forcefully slammed the front door behind Edward as he left. Her hands shakily bolted all three locks, and as the final lock slid into place, she leaned exhausted up against the door. Her wobbly legs failed her, and she allowed herself to slide effortlessly down to the floor. She remained there, sitting on the floor, hugging her knees tightly against her chest like a hurt little child, while tears flooded her eyes. Sobbing hysterically, almost to the point that she was gasping for breath, she couldn't stop the misery that was pouring out from within her heart.

Long ago, she had buried certain memories deep in her mind and had prayed that she would never have to dig them out. But her son's questions were making her think of those unthinkable things, even though she desperately didn't want to.

Good men didn't do wicked, immoral acts such as sexually molesting innocent children, at least not unless some evil presence had control of them. And both my father and my husband were good men.   How could anyone have known they had terrible, wicked demons controlling their souls?

Connie knew that a man couldn't fight a demon. Its powers were too strong, and no matter what a man did the demon would always win.

She knew that for a fact because her father had repeatedly told her so.

Crying uncontrollably, Connie also knew that she could never admit to anyone what had happen to her and then to her daughter under the roof of their own house. She had loved her husband and her father too much to ever tell a single soul about their demons. It hadn't been their fault that the evil creatures had somehow gained control of them and had made them do those sinful acts.

God would understand and would surely forgive them, but she wasn't so sure anyone else would.

"You have to understand what's happening to me, Connie," her father had said more than once, his voice pleading yet doubled-edged with another emotion that she hadn't been able to decipher. "The demons are in my head. They are trying to destroy me. They want to consume my soul and take me down to hell with them."

"No, that's not true," she had cried out, her fears for him filling her heart. "God wouldn't let them do that to you. I just know he wouldn't."

"They can do whatever they want to do," he had quickly replied, showing her a shocking picture from the newspaper. "See what they did to this poor man. He burst into flames right in front of his daughter's eyes. Look at what's left of him! Nothing but a couple of burnt bones sticking out of a pair of smoking boots. The fire marshal reported that the man simply burst into flames for no reason, but I know what the reason was. The demons were angry with him for telling their secrets."

"But surely that wouldn't happen to you!" she had sobbed in anguish, the horror of the gruesome picture making her stomach churn.

"Yes it could! At any moment I could burst into a ball of flames, just like that man, and I would be gone from you forever. Then who would there be to love you and take care of you?"

"But Papa—"

"Hush, Child," her father had said placing a finger upon her mouth. "You don't know what it's like having them in your head. With a single touch they can send my soul burning, blazing with pain."

"Can't you make them go away?" she had pleaded with him to try. "Can't you ask God to help you?"

"No. Only your sweet, pure touch keeps them from destroying me. You're my Little Angel, my only salvation. Without you I would surely die and be drawn down to hell with them."

"I don't want you to die!" she had cried out in misery from the ache he had placed in her heart.

"I know Sweetheart," he had said reaching for her. "That's why you have to help me keep them away. You calm them. Your touch is magic, easing this horrid pain pounding unmercifully in my head. Come here and let me hold you, let me feel the power of your innocence giving me the strength to fight them off."

And so she had gone to him letting him do what he had to do to survive because she had loved him with all of her heart and soul.

But she had hated every minute, every second, of it!

Yet she had no choice. She had to do everything she could to protect him. She had secretly watched from a crack in the door when the evil creatures had been in his mind tormenting him, sending him beyond reason. Once she saw him pounding his head against the wall until it had bled as he had tried to drive them away. The pain from their fevered touch must have been tremendous. She knew he had even thought about shooting himself. One time she had spied him sitting at his desk with a gun stuck in his mouth. She had watched in silent horror as his finger twitched at the trigger, but then he had thrown the gun against the wall in frustration and cursed the pain pounding in his head. Then he had called her name, and she had gone to him to ease his torment. It had to be that way, for there was no one else to help him. No one else knew about the demons. Their presence had been kept a secret from the rest of the world. If anyone else had found out about them, her father had said they would kill everyone in the family. And they could very easily do that. Her father had told her so, and he never lied.

+++++

Through tear-filled eyes Connie saw her father as she had seen him many, many years ago, moving restlessly in the library holding his head tightly between his hands, begging for his tormentors to leave him alone.

She curled into a tight huddle and backed up against the front door as far as she could go, as she tried to escape the scene that had started playing out in front of her eyes. It was a scene she remembered all too well, one she had never wanted to see again.

In the library she could see her father pacing back and forth like a caged animal. He was trying to find a way to escape the demons he knew were in the room with him. Through red, bloodshot eyes he was staring at the darkened shadows in the room. "Damn you," he yelled angrily, throwing an empty shot glass at whatever it was he had seen hiding in the darkness, "Damn you all to hell! Why can't you leave me alone?" He started pounding his head with tightly closed fists as though it would somehow drive the agonizing pain away. Then he collapsed into the high-backed chair at his desk and immediately grabbed the half-full whisky bottle that had been in front of him. He quickly gulped it down as though he was dying of thirst and the bottle was full of fresh spring water.

After several long swigs of the burning liquid flowed down his throat, he set the empty bottle down. His eyes darted around the room until he noticed her peeking at him through a tiny opening in the library door.

The moment his eyes locked onto hers, she wanted to run. Shocked by the wildness on his face, she felt fear surge through her tiny body. The frenzied look shining from his eyes only meant one thing.

The demons had to be there in the room with him!

There was no doubt in her mind what would happen next.

"Connie!" her father roared through a drunken slur. "Get in here. Right now!"

"But, Papa," she looked at him pleadingly, "I need to go upstairs. Mama wanted me to be sure to lock up all the windows tonight since she wasn't going to be home to do it."

"Damn the windows, Child. I said come here, and I meant it." The rage in his voice scared her so badly she couldn't make her legs move.

Seeing the fear on her face, he lowered his voice. "Now, Connie, come on over here. You know this really doesn't hurt. We both know you really like it, and I really do need you now. Your poor old father needs you to chase the demons away." Gesturing for her to come forward, he smiled slyly at her.

But she knew the smile didn't mean a thing. What he wanted to do did hurt. It hurt for days afterwards. But she couldn't refuse him. If she did, the demons might kill him, and she loved him too much to let that happen. So she reluctantly shuffled over and let him lift her up on his lap.

"Good girl, I knew you wouldn't let me down. Only you can make those demons in my head disappear." He pulled her up tightly against his chest as he nuzzled against her neck. Then he let his huge hands go down the back of her dress as he slowly released each tiny button. Pulling the dress down over her shoulders, he hungrily placed horrid, wet kisses all over her tiny, undeveloped breasts.

Connie shivered. His lips felt like slimy snails crawling over her.

He felt her starting to pull away, so he pulled her in closer, tightening his hold. "Calm down girl, you don't want to make the demons angry. They'll burn me for sure if you do. And you don't want that to happen do you? Just be a good girl, and it will soon be all over with. I promise not to hurt you."

But her father lied about it not hurting. It did hurt, and she wanted to die every time it happened. Why didn't those awful creatures just leave them alone?

Her tiny heart pounded fiercely in her chest. Doing things like this was sinful. She had heard her mother talking with the other women from church about it. You weren't supposed to let a man touch you in those private places unless you were married and had to.

Why didn't God stop it? Why wasn't he strong enough to stop the demons so her father didn't have to do those awful things to her?

More than once she had begged and pleaded with her father to let her tell her mother about the demons, but he had warned her that they would destroy anyone who found out about them. And she knew it was true. They had killed her little kitten, Charley, just to let her know that they could. She had found him dead one morning out by the back door, a charred, blackened pile of burnt fur with a red ribbon the color of fire wrapped around his neck. The odor from his singed fur had sickened her so much that she hadn't been able to eat for days. It had been her punishment from the demons because she had wanted to tell someone.

Her father had taken Charley, placed him in an old cardboard box, and then had buried him out in the back yard without letting anyone else see her beloved pet. She had learned the hard way that their secret had to be kept secret.

And Papa had said what they did together was a secret no one else must ever find out about it.

But it was so disgusting! She hated having his hands on her body, and hated it even more when he made her put her hands on him. But the worst was when he would put his man-thing inside of her, or made her use her mouth.

But she didn't want him to die. She loved him. When the demons weren't controlling him, he was a good man. He took her places, played hide-and-seek with her, and bought her wonderful presents. Presents he didn't get for her two older brothers. They were always so jealous, but they didn't know about the other things that her father did when they were gone.

Some days she worried about her own soul. Would she go to hell for doing what she was made to do? She knew God didn't like such things. It was sinful unless you were trying to make babies.

Once she had heard her mother screaming at her father as she had pushed him out of their bedroom, slamming and locking the door behind him. She had been shouting that he was inviting the devil into their home by asking her to do such wicked things.

Her mother didn't know the devil had already found its way there.

+++++

As she had grown older, Connie hadn't wanted the demons to find their way into her soul as they had her father's, so she had been very careful never to let herself enjoy anything at all involving sex. She knew the evilness that could spring from the touch of a man.

When her father had died of a stroke when she was fifteen, Connie had been sure those devil's servants had died with him. But how wrong she had been. The creatures had quietly laid waiting until her beloved husband had been weak enough to fall within their clutches. She had tried to tell Randy about how the demons could get to him if he kept submitting to the evils of sex, but he never listened. He had only laughed and had just kept on demanding she take care of those vile needs of his. Finally after ten years of marriage his demands had stopped, and she had been grateful. That is until she discovered the reason he had stopped seeking her out was because the demons had found their way into his body...just as she told him they would.

One night when she had awaken and found Randy wasn't lying beside her, she had crawled out of bed and sleepily went searching for him. For several days he hadn't been feeling very good, so she was worried. And as it turned out, she had been right to be concerned.

Her bare feet had carried her silently out into the hall. It had been very dark that night, and from out of that darkness, Amy's voice had reached her ears. The sounds of her daughter's muffled crying slowed her steps. She cautiously opened the door to Amy's bedroom, and to her horror, she had discovered that her father's demons were back.

She had quietly closed Amy's door so as not to be heard and had hurried noiselessly back to her own bed. There she had pulled her covers over her head, and she had prayed for God to destroy the evil things. But in her heart she had known her prayers wouldn't help, because if they would have, she would have been saved years ago.

She never told her husband that she knew what had happened to him. She had been positive the demons would kill her and the rest of the family if they ever found out she had discovered that they were back. So she had to tuck the secret far back in her mind where she couldn't even think about it.

After that night, she had been afraid to even talk to her daughter. Every time she looked upon Amy's face, she saw her father. Knowing what a good man Randy had been, she just couldn't imagine what terrible deed he had done to bring the demons back alive. Finally she had realized it must have been something Amy had done that had brought the evil spirits back into their home. After that, she could never look at her daughter without wondering what awful transgression Amy had committed.

She had tried to help Amy make up for whatever that terrible wickedness had been and had given her plenty of opportunities to repent. She had made Amy go to church every Sunday and any other time it was possible to get her there. She had made her pray every night before going to bed, sometimes for an hour, in hopes that the vile night creatures haunting their home could be stayed from their course. She had even let Randy punish her very forcefully, and maybe in a way it had been abusive, but the punishment needed to fit the crime if the girl's soul were ever to be saved.

Surely now, after all her hard work she wouldn't get blamed for Amy's sins. If Amy started telling everyone in the world about the private affairs of this family, the demons would get very angry. They might come back for her just like they promised her father they would if the silence were ever to be broken.

+++++

After Edward had left her home, Connie sat on the floor wrapped up in a daze for hours. Finally, her legs became so stiff and cold that she could hardly move. As she stood up, she wiped her tearstained face with the hem of her nightgown. Her mouth felt dry, and when she licked her lips, the taste of salt made her realize she had bitten her lip. She reached up and ran her fingers through her hair and found it damp with sweat.

She started back up the stairs to her bedroom, but the sound of movement just on the other side of the front door made her jump. And she began to worry. *What if one of the doors or windows weren't locked? The demons could still get in!*

After hurriedly checking all of the locks in the house, she peered out the front window. The neighbor's two dogs were over by the bushes next to the sidewalk leading to the door. She saw the male climb up on the haunches of the female. Her hand went to her mouth and she gasped. There could be no escaping the demons; they were watching her house. They were so bold as to present themselves right there for her to see. They were mocking her, letting her know that there could be no escape from them.

When Edward had left her house he had suggested that she needed to go to the hospital in the morning to see Amy, but there was no way she was going to do that. It wouldn't be safe to be around Amy at all. It was much safer to remain locked up behind the doors of her home then to go anywhere near her daughter.

She thought about Edward and wondered if he would be safe from the demons. Just in case he wouldn't be, she began praying feverishly that her first grandchild would be a boy. If it was a girl, the demons might seek out Edward to punish the family for telling the secrets that should never have been told. It would break her heart if her loving son were to fall prey to the hell-beasts that seemed to be following the family and destroying its god-fearing men.

Chapter 47

Right after Edward left Amy's hospital room, James' beeper went off. Glancing at the beeper's flashing message, he immediately recognized Windsong's phone number. A feeling of deep-seated dread instantly touched him. Somehow, he knew exactly what news the message would bring. It was times like this that his gift was more like a curse. He had discovered earlier in his life that there were some things he was better off not knowing until he had to actually face them.

"Is something wrong?" Amy asked as she watched James slowly replacing his beeper back into its tote on his belt. She was immediately aware of the transformation in his facial expression. Even wrapped up in her own anguish, she couldn't help but notice the change that had instantly came over him.

"I'm not sure," he replied in a voice that told Amy something different. "I need to go make a quick phone call, but I still want to talk with you a little more before I leave the hospital." Just before he left the room he looked over his shoulder at Amy. "I promise I'll be back in just a couple of minutes."

Amy watched James as he walked with reluctant steps toward the nurse's station, and she felt sorry for him. She could tell he knew the phone message would be bad news.

James picked up the phone receiver in one hand and stood for a second with the other hand paused over the phone's push buttons. Finally, he reluctantly punched in Windsong's phone number.

While James was waiting for someone at Windsong to answer, he turned toward Amy. She saw such sorrow surrounding him that for a moment she couldn't think of her own pain. Like a mother looking at a grieving child, she impulsively wanted to throw her arms around him to offer some measure of comfort. Through concern-filled eyes she continued to watch as he spoke a few words to the person on the other end of the line, then she saw him slowly place the receiver back in its cradle.

Amy found she was unable to remain in bed thinking only of herself. Rising, she walked over to the door and waited for James to come back into the room. When he returned, she reached out without saying a word and engulfed him in the circle of her arms for a brief hug. Then backing away, she looked deep into his eyes, feeling his anguish, knowing he was hurting. "The phone call was bad news, wasn't it?"

"It was about my grandmother." With a little catch in his voice, he told Amy the sad news he had just received. "She passed away over an hour ago. They think it was a heart attack." James sat dejectedly down in the chair next to Amy's bed. "I wish I could have been there with her. I have always promised her that she wouldn't have to die alone, but it happened so suddenly there wasn't any time for them to contact me."

With a look of astonishment, Amy stared at James for a moment. Then in a hushed voice she softly said, "Your grandmother wasn't alone. I was with her."

"What do you mean you were with her?" James' eyes locked with Amy's. "What in the world are you talking about?"

"I was with her when she died. Or at least immediately afterwards." A tiny, sad smile touched Amy's lips.

"That's not possible. There's no way you were with her. You were on the way to the hospital when she died." *Was Amy delusional now?* he wondered.

"My body was in the ambulance, but the rest of me wasn't. I was in the Gray world and your Grandmother was there with me. She kept me from going into the light. She sent me back here, but she went on ahead." Amy looked straight into James' eyes. She wanted him to see that she was telling the truth. "She wanted me to tell you that she was sorry she couldn't say good-bye, but not to worry because everything would be all right and that some day you'd see each other again."

"The Gray world? The light? I don't understand what you're saying."

"The Gray world was a place I went to when I was a small child to escape from my father. I didn't remember a thing about it

461

until I went back there again this afternoon. I really don't understand how I could've forgotten. It was the only safe place I could go to hide from my father, although this was the first time I ever saw the light there. The light was something different."

"What do you mean by different?" James asked, his interest growing stronger with each word spoken.

Pausing for a moment, Amy tried to think how to explain her world, her refuge, to someone who had never been there, someone who had never had the need to seek sanctuary within themselves. "My Gray world was a place completely surrounded by a very dense gray mist. When I would send myself there, I would spend all my time floating along on gently flowing air currents…feeling nothing…being nothing. Like an angel in the clouds I was free…and safe. It was peaceful, quiet, a place where no one could hurt me. But I wasn't stupid. Even though I was just a kid, I knew it was only my mind that was there and that my body was still back with my father. But it didn't matter. I realized as long as I could pull my mind away from him, I had a chance to survive."

"Tell me about this light you mentioned."

"Like I said, this time it was different. A brilliant light was glowing off in the distance. It seemed to be pulling me toward it, and all I wanted to do was to go to it."

"You said my grandmother kept you from doing that. How?"

"I was heading toward the light. I could feel its pull way down deep inside my soul. There was no fear, no dread, about what waited ahead. The glow from the light was warm, washing over me, making me feel clean inside instead of dirty like I feel right now. Then suddenly your grandmother appeared next to me and took my hand in hers. She told me it wasn't time for me to go yet, that I needed to come back here. I didn't want to, but she insisted. Without her, I would have gone on into the light. Just like she did."

Fascinated with Amy's story, James wanted to hear more...not only because she was talking about his grandmother but also because of the medical implications of her words. She was openly discussing one of the techniques she used to survive her childhood abuse. Somehow she had managed to disassociate herself from the physical abuse and mentally transport herself to a safe place. Intent on learning more about Amy's self-made world, he didn't immediately make any connection between Amy, his grandmother, and the light, but after a couple of minutes it hit him like a whack in the stomach with a baseball bat.

He had heard stories about people seeing such a light in near death experiences, but he wasn't exactly sure how that could be related to Amy's case. His grandmother, yes...but Amy hadn't been dying. Had she?

Thoughtfully, he considered how to approach the subject. "Tell me what you were thinking just before you went into this Gray world of yours."

"Plain and simple. I was desperately trying to will myself to die, and honestly part of me still wants to. I'm not sure why I came back here; I should have gone on. I should have died. I may never get another chance like that one. The world that was waiting for me might not be there again, and besides I'm so tired of this pain that is stealing my hopes and my dreams. I would have found peace up there. I know it. And now I will probably never know what it means to be happy. How can I be happy when I will have to face everyone when they find out the truth about me?"

"Find out the truth about you? What do you mean?"

"That I let my father touch me and use me like his whore. I shouldn't have allowed that to happen. I shouldn't have let him do it."

"You didn't *let* your father do anything. You were only a child. You had no choice. Your father forced you. Saying that you let him touch you would be the same thing as saying you let a rampaging grizzly bear rip you apart with his claws. It was no more possible for you to stop your father than it would have been to stop a grizzly bear."

"I won't be able to stop the talk either. I'm going to have to fight those awful battles over and over again now that those memories have found their place in my mind. There won't be any peace for me, not now, not ever. People will keep talking and they will keep asking questions, and I just can't handle that." Amy drew in a deep breath and then cried out with heartfelt pain, "Your grandmother should have let me go on!"

"Do you know what was waiting beyond the light?"

"Yes. Peace…wondrous peace and happiness."

"How could you possibly know that?" James asked.

"I could feel it," Amy replied, "deep down in my soul."

"Then why did you turn around and come back?"

"I told you...your grandmother sent me back. She said it wasn't my time to go yet. She said that there was someone here whose heart would break if I left. Then when I thought of Ted I suddenly started falling down a dark tunnel and the light was gone."

"Ted? Who's Ted?"

Amy didn't answer. Instead she turned her face away and stared down at the floor.

James felt Amy distancing herself from him again. He didn't want her to go back into the state she had been in earlier. He might not be able to bring her back. She obviously didn't want to talk about Ted. So he changed the subject.

"What did my grandmother do after she talked with you?"

"She went on ahead into the light without me. There was someone else who appeared out of nowhere in front of us. I couldn't see who it was, but I did hear your grandmother call him Steve. When she said his name her voice spoke with such joy, I think it must have been someone she was really happy to see. They joined up together and then walked into the light. So you see, she wasn't really alone after all. I was with her, and then Steve was with her, so don't feel so sad about not being there. Everything went just fine for her. She was really happy; I could tell."

"My grandfather's name was Steve," James spoke more to himself then to Amy. Looking intently at Amy's face, he wondered if what she had just told him had really happened or if it had all been a delusional fantasy. He hoped with all of his heart that it had been

465

real, but no one would actually ever know. At least not in his lifetime here on earth. Afterwards…maybe. But not now.

James suddenly felt exhausted and decided it was time for him to head home. "I think we've both had enough for tonight. The nurse will bring you some medicine to help you rest. I'll be back first thing in the morning to talk with you. Try not to think too much tonight about all of this. There will be plenty of time tomorrow to worry about what the future will bring. Just remember you have some good friends that will help you get though this."

Amy didn't reply. She just turned her back on James and headed for her bed.

James stayed with Amy until she was situated for the night. Then he took his leave and headed home.

+++++

Lying in bed with the blanket pulled securely up to her neck, Amy curled around her pillow, hugging it for comfort, just as she used to do as a little girl. James had mentioned she had some good friends who would help her, but he really didn't know how few friends she actually had. She thought of Edward and his wife Ellen. Then there was Susan and a couple of other women from work. And of course, now there was Raphael. Just like Thomas, she knew he would be there for her. Then last of all there was Ted, but she wasn't very sure she could count him on her list of friends. This morning, yes, she probably could have. But now, with all that has happened, how could he possibly still want to remain her friend? She'd be lucky if he would even speak to her once he finds out the horrible, awful truth about her. Why would he want to be with a woman whose father had used her like a prostitute to fulfill his own shameful needs?

Toni Auberry

Chapter 48

Three blocks from Charity Hospital Ted passed a small flower shop that still had its lights on and had an open sign placed in its window. He immediately decided that a bouquet of flowers might make Amy feel better, so he quickly turned at the end of the block and circled around until he found a parking place near the flower shop. Unfortunately, just as he climbed out of the car, the owner of the store was standing at the door with a set of keys in her hand locking up for the night. His eyes went to the closed sign that was now hanging lopsided in the dark window. He was too late.

"Please wait," Ted begged, "I really need a bouquet of flowers for a friend of mine who's in the hospital."

"I'm sorry, but I've closed for the night. I'll be open at nine tomorrow morning if you want to come back then."

"It's really important that I have them right now," Ted pleaded. "I promise that I won't take but a second of your time. I'll even pay you extra."

"No, I told you I'm closed," the woman replied. "Now, please go."

Ted saw her eyes were darting around as though she was looking for someone to help her. She was probably scared, he decided. After all, it was the middle of the night and no one else was on the street.

"Wait...look at these," he said, taking his billfold from his back pocket and pulling out his driver's license, a business card, and three credit cards. "See, here's my name, this is where I work, and here are my credit cards. Honestly, all I want is some flowers."

"Well, I don't know," she said, taking his business card and slowly looking it over.

"Please," Ted said as he suddenly kneeled down on one knee in front of her. Bowing his head in a majestic manner he begged, "Won't you help this poor knight perform a great deed? His queen is in great distress. The wicked sorcerer has cast an evil spell upon her and only a bouquet of the most beautiful flowers in the world will break his spell."

"I wouldn't say I have the most beautiful flowers in the world," she replied, smiling at his actions.

"Oh, but you do. The king's messenger told me so. He said that your flowers were beyond compare. The word all over the kingdom is that a single rose from—" Ted paused looking up at the sign on her door, "Crystal's, holds much power and could heal a sick heart. And I have much need for this power right now."

"Oh all right, if it's that important," she laughed. "I wouldn't want to keep you from completing your knightly mission."

"Thanks, you have no idea how much this means to me," Ted said, rising and following her into the shop.

"I don't have much of a selection right now. I'll be getting fresh flowers in the morning. Are you sure you don't want to wait?"

"Just pick out the best of whatever you have."

A grin suddenly brightened the florist's face. "You are a lucky one. I just remembered something. A man ordered a dozen red roses this morning, and he never did pick them up. You can have them. If the guy comes by in the morning, it will just be his bad luck. He should have called to let me know what his plans were. I'll go get them; they're in the back room."

Pleased by his luck, Ted completely forgot that Amy had mentioned at her birthday party that she had a severe allergy to roses. When the florist brought the flowers out, Ted was impressed with their beauty. They were a dark velvety red, and the softness of the petals reminded him of Amy's moist, inviting lips.

"They're absolutely perfect," he said, watching the florist wrap the flowers in pink tissue and then place them in a white flower box tied with a big red ribbon.

"These roses must be for someone very special for you to go to all this trouble," she said, flashing him a big knowing smile.

Ted picked up the boxed flowers and smiled back. "Yes, she is most certainly a very special person." *So special*, he thought, *that I want to spend the rest of my life with her.*

"Would you like a card to go with them? Here's a nice one. It has little hearts intertwined among a beautiful flower border. A lot of men choose this one for their wives."

Looking at the card's design, Ted instantly decided that it was perfect. He quickly added a short message, signed his name, and then tucked the card under the ribbon on the box. "Thanks, I really appreciate you going to all this trouble for me."

As Ted left the shop, the florist smiled. She had looked at the card as he was writing his message, and she had seen the note he had hurried scribbled on it...*I think I love you.* As she locked the shop and headed home to her husband, she felt so good inside. One of the benefits of working in the flower shop was watching the little dramas that sometimes played out right before her eyes. She knew somewhere tonight some woman was going to feel very special, and she had played one tiny part in that woman's happiness.

+++++

When Ted arrived at the hospital he stopped at the front desk to inquire which room Amy was in. The receptionist told him the room number, but then after a quick glance at the clock on the wall, she frowned. "I'm not so sure the nurses will let you on that unit this late in the evening unless you are a close relative. Unfortunately, the regular visiting hours for the mental health ward are already over with for the day."

Without blinking an eye, he smiled at the receptionist with what he hoped was a very convincing smile. "It's all right. I am a close relative. The patient is my sister. I just got back in town from a long business trip, or I would have been up here sooner. I promise not to stay very long. I just want her to know I'm back."

His smile charmed the lady, and she embarrassingly felt a rare flush color her cheeks as his beautiful blue eyes stared into hers. Flustered over her response to the tall handsome man with the sky-blue eyes that was standing in front of her, she quickly picked up the phone. "I'll call and find out if it is all right for you to go up."

Ted waited patiently, smiling at the receptionist while she placed her call to the nurse's desk on Amy's floor.

"Only people whose names are on the visitor's list can go up on that unit," she finally said. "The nurse needs to know your name so she can check to see if it's on the list."

Continuing to smile, Ted outright lied. "Edward Tedrow."

After the receptionist gave the name that Ted had claimed as his own, she was happy to learn it was on the visitor's list. She didn't want to disappoint the man. He seemed so worried about his sister. "You can go right up," she said pleasantly. "Only report in at the nurse's station before you go to the room."

"Thank you, you were very helpful," he replied as he turned and headed toward the elevator. Once he was in the elevator he punched the button for the fourth floor and waited impatiently for it to start moving. On the ride up, he wondered why Amy was on the mental health unit. After being with her yesterday evening when she had gotten hysterical and then had developed that migraine, he guessed that something must have happened today to trigger an even stronger reaction. Otherwise why would she be here in the hospital on that particular floor?

He immediately felt a little relieved at the thought that her problem might only be something like the post traumatic stress syndrome they had talked about last night, and he managed to relax a little. That was a problem he could help her deal with. If it had been a serious physical medical problem, who knows what her outcome would have been? He didn't want to have to face losing her, not now when he had just found her.

On the fourth floor he stopped at the nurse's station as he had been instructed to, and he again gave Edward's name as his. Then with the box of red roses under his arm, he turned toward Amy's room and headed toward the woman he now knew he loved.

+++++

Amy was lying in bed trying to read a magazine when she saw Ted stop at the nurse's station directly across from her room. She quickly burrowed down under the covers so only her face showed and pretended to be asleep. The last thing she wanted to do right now was to face Ted. She didn't want to have to try to explain to him why she was there. Closing her eyes, she lay as quietly as possible. But even though her body was perfectly still, her heart was racing, pounding so furiously that she was afraid it would make the covers move. Trying to control her breathing, she counted silently through each breath. *One...two...three...four...inhale, one...two...three...four...exhale.*

She heard Ted enter the room and place something on the bedside table. Pretending to be asleep, she continued to lie as motionless as possible. She didn't want him to find out that she was really awake, which she almost failed to do when he gently brushed a lock of hair away from the side of her face. As his presence loomed over the bed, she believed she could actually feel the heat coming off his body as he bent over her. Then when he started speaking, whispering so quietly in her ear that she had to strain to hear his words…she almost gasped in surprise.

"Hello, Angel. Am I glad to see you," Ted said tenderly, lovingly.

Thinking that he wouldn't be glad to see her if he knew what kind of person she really was, Amy fought back the tears that were threatening to pour forth.

"Do you have any idea what you mean to me already?" he whispered. "Somehow you have gotten under my skin with an itch that will not let up."

Amy struggled to remain quiet. If he only knew what kind of filth she had come from, he would think she was more than an itch. He would think she was poison ivy.

"I think I love you." He whispered, placing a gentle kiss upon her forehead.

"No!" Amy cried out, springing up in the bed, bumping her head against his in the process. "No…No…No. You can't love me. You don't know what I am."

"Yes I do," Ted said, rubbing the red area on his forehead where Amy's head had hit his. "You are a kind wonderful person. I only wish your brother had been able to convince me to meet you

475

long before now. When I think of all the time that was wasted because of my stupidity, it makes me sick." Reaching out, he tried to take Amy's hand in his, but she jerked it back before he had the chance.

"How can you say you love someone you don't even know?" Amy continued to struggle to hold back her tears. She still didn't want to cry. If she started crying, she wouldn't be able to stop.

"If that's what's bothering you, give me the chance to get to know you and you to know me. I will prove to you that I really do love you."

In desperation Amy scrambled out of bed, placing Ted on one side of the bed and herself on the other. She didn't want him to get close enough to touch her. If he were to put his arms around her, she might not be able to tell him what had to be told. "Would you love me if you knew my father forced me to have sex with him when I was a child? Would you love me knowing his filthy hands had touched my body? Would you love me knowing that it went on for years? Of course not!" Stopping only long enough to draw in a sharp intake of air, Amy almost screamed out her words. **"You can't love me, I am not worth loving."**

Surprised, but not truly shocked by her words, Ted didn't waste one second. Coming around the bed so they were standing face to face, he held out his arms to her. "Yes I can. Your love is worth more than I deserve."

Amy didn't reply. She had been shocked into silence by Ted's words. Tears starting to flow in a stream down her face. She looked at Ted through that river of tears as he stood in front of her holding out his arms, and she still couldn't make herself go to him. "You really think you can love me even knowing what awful things I did?"

"What awful things you did! I didn't hear you tell me anything about what you did. It seems to me the awful things came from your father...not from you. Let me show you that not all men are like that. I can love you with a love so strong, so powerful, you will think the weight of it would crush the world." Taking a step closer to Amy, Ted kept holding his arms out to her.

Finally, Amy took a hesitant step forward. Then Ted went the rest of the way, engulfing her within his massive arms. They stood together not saying a word, simply holding tightly to each other. Amy felt the soft puffs of air he breathed on her hair as he clung to her. He felt the small tremors flowing through her body.

Ted picked Amy up in his arms and then carried her back to the bed and carefully laid her down. Pulling a tissue from a box on the table, he gently wiped the tears from her face. When a tiny smile touched the corners of her mouth, he felt as if the whole world were smiling.

Amy looked upon Ted's face for a moment, then taking another tissue, she wiped his tears away.

Ted was surprised the tears were there. He hadn't even realized that he had been crying, but there was a difference between his tears and Amy's. He knew his were tears of joy.

A few moments later Amy's nurse started to enter the room. However, when she saw Ted sitting on the bed holding Amy's hand, staring into her eyes with a moonstruck look on his face, she quietly closed the door without saying a word. She knew instantly that the man sitting on the bed wasn't Amy's brother. No brother would be looking at his sister with love that strong shining in his eyes.

Chapter 49

Amy didn't like lying in the bed with Ted looming over her while he was talking. For some reason, she had started to feel confined and somehow trapped by his presence. The longer he remained near her, the more uncomfortable she became, and even though she wanted him to be in the room with her, he was just too close for comfort.

Ted noticed that Amy had started to avoid eye contact and seemed to be pulling away from him. He quickly guessed the reason why, and since the last thing he wanted to do was make her feel more uncomfortable than she already was, he stood up and crossed the room to look out the window. "The sky is exceptionally beautiful tonight," he said softly. "See how the stars are all shining so brightly, and if you look real close it seems like the man-in-the-moon is winking at you."

After a few moments, Amy joined Ted by the window, although she didn't stand next to him. "When I was a little girl I used to gaze out my bedroom window wishing that I could fly away up into the stars. It always seemed so peaceful and quiet up there."

"What else did you wish for?" Ted asked, his blue eyes focusing on Amy with such intensity that she felt as though he was looking right into her soul.

"I wished with all my heart that my mother loved me," Amy replied sadly, "At the park I would watch mothers walking with their daughters, holding hands, laughing, acting like they didn't have a care in the world. I could tell they loved each other very much, and I often wondered why mine hated me so much."

"I don't know why that had to happen to you," Ted said. "I only know I plan to spend the rest of my life trying to make up for all the love you missed when you were a little girl."

"The rest of your life? That's a very long commitment to make to someone you only met a few short days ago."

"Do you want to know what I used to wish for when I was a kid?" Ted asked Amy. "More than anything I wanted to grow up and marry a woman like my mother. I wanted to have the kind of relationship my parents had before my father died. There was a bond between them that was never broken, not even after my father's death. From the moment I saw you I felt that kind of bond. I can't explain it. I simply know it's there, and I'm going to try my best to convince you how strong these feelings are."

Amy felt a strange tightness binding her chest and tears forming in her eyes. "Sometimes when I watch Edward and Ellen together, I get so jealous because they have that kind of relationship.

I don't think there is anything in the world that could come between them. Even my brother's bossy attitude doesn't seem to dim Ellen's love for him."

"It can be that way between us, if you will only let it happen." Ted gazed lovingly into Amy's eyes and held out his hand, hoping with all his heart she would reach out and take it.

Drawn by Ted's hopeful gesture, Amy cautiously reached over and placed her hand in his. They stood together looking out at the stars, each dreaming a quiet dream and each feeling the power of love binding their hearts together.

After several minutes, Amy felt the compelling need to pull away. Doubts had started crossing her mind again, and she couldn't handle the confusion washing over her. She turned away from Ted and walked over to the bedside table. For the first time she noticed the box with the red ribbon that Ted had brought with him when he arrived. "Hey, what's this?"

Ted laughed at the glimmer that had suddenly sparked in her eyes. "Oh, that's just a little present I picked up for you on the way over to the hospital."

Amy took the card out from under the ribbon and opened it. She felt her heart flutter when she read the words Ted had written...*I think I love you.* For the first time she actually started to believe maybe there would be a chance for her to know what love was truly like. Maybe Ted would still be able to love her. If it were the other way around, she would still love him, so if her love could be strong enough not to let his past keep them apart, maybe his would be strong enough not to let hers.

She eagerly pulled the ribbon off the gift like a schoolgirl unwrapping a birthday present. Then she opened the box, and to her horror inside lay a dozen blood-red roses. Amy's grip on the box loosened, and it fell unhindered to the floor, spilling the beautiful roses out at her feet. Ashamed by her reaction, she began to apologize profusely as she quickly bent down and started picking up the flowers. In the process she accidentally pricked one of her fingers on a single missed thorn. As a tiny drop of blood formed on the tip of her finger, she stared at it through eyes wide with apprehension and fear.

When the roses fell to the floor, Ted immediately bent down to help pick them up, and he never saw the look of alarm that was crossing Amy's face as she watched that single drop of blood get bigger and bigger. Nor did he see her frantically wiping her hands on her gown as if she were trying to remove something hideous from them. In fact, he didn't notice anything strange was happening at all until Amy jumped up holding her hands out in front of her body as if those hands were covered with something very frightening and very terrifying.

In a frantic, hysterical, little girl's voice she began screaming, "Get it off! Get it off!" Wiping her hands on the bed covers and then on the curtains, she spun in a circle looking for anything that could be used to clean the imaginary mess from her hands. "Oh, the blood...the blood," she cried out in overwhelming panic. Then stopping suddenly, she looked down at her gown and began trying to rip it off. "Ooooooooh. It's all over me! Get it off! Please, please get it off." When Ted advanced toward her trying to grab her hands to keep her from tearing the gown, she shrieked, "NO...NO...NO. Keep away. Don't touch me." Beating at him with tiny, clutched fists, like a frightened little child, she pushed him away and ran taking refuge in the bathroom.

In her desperation to escape Ted, Amy managed to back into the bathroom until she had wedged herself between the wall and the commode in a kneeling position. She scrunched into an impossibly small space as though she were attempting to disappear into the wall.

Ted could only stare in disbelief. He had no idea at all how to respond to Amy's strange reaction and her unexpected flight from the room.

+++++

Amy's mind screamed out in silent terror as she watched the tiny drop of blood on her finger grow bigger and bigger. The hospital room quickly faded, wiped away by a wash of bright red. Suddenly, she was no longer standing next to Ted; instead she was standing beside her father in the rose garden that used to be in the back yard of her old home.

Her father, dressed in an old T-shirt and jeans, stood five feet away shoveling dirt out of a hole he was digging for the three new rose bushes he said he had bought for her eleventh birthday. A few minutes earlier when he had awakened her from a sound sleep, he had told her he was making a special rose garden just for her. But as she

483

watched him dig, she wondered why he was making the hole so deep. Looking around, she also wondered why he had chosen the middle of the night to do his digging.

Shivering from the chilly night air, she sat on the side of the pit watching him work. The oil lamp threw scary shadowy figures all around the yard. It was all so strange, but she knew better than to ask questions. Her father only seemed to want her there to watch him dig. He had been in such a hurry for her to join him that he wouldn't even let her change out of her nightgown. She didn't understand any of it, but then, she was only eleven years old (or at least tomorrow she would be), and she had learned a long time ago never to ever argue with her father.

Finally he finished. The hole was so deep he had trouble getting out of it. Standing on the edge, he ordered her to stand beside him. With a hostile glint in his eyes, he asked, "Remember what I said would happen if you ever told anyone what went on between us?"

She started to back away from him, but he grabbed her arm and held on so tightly that she thought it would break. She knew there would be bruises all over that arm by morning. That is…if she were alive in the morning. Maybe the hole was for her.

In a small, scared voice she answered. "You said you would kill anyone I told. But, Daddy, I haven't told anyone. I promise you, I haven't told anyone."

Thomas heard the terror in Amy's voice and came up to stand right behind her. A growl arose from deep in his throat. His lips curled showing the sharp points of his teeth. Thomas had made it known before that he didn't care much for Randy. The dog seemed to have a deep instinctive awareness there was something wrong with the man.

Amy saw the anger flaring in her father's eyes, and she became very frightened for Thomas. Her father released her arm, and she called out, "Hush, Thomas. It's all right. Be quiet now."

Thomas' growl faded, but he still stood with his eyes focused on Randy. Then he walked up and positioned himself between Amy and her father.

Randy looked down hatefully at Thomas. "You have been telling him! I've heard what you have been whispering to that stupid dog. Did you think I wouldn't find out? Haven't you realized yet that there isn't anything that goes on in this house that I don't know about? So now he's going to have to pay for your mistake."

Before she even had a chance to say anything in her own defense, her father picked up the large butcher knife that had been lying on the ground next to his feet, and then he deliberately, purposefully slit Thomas' throat. Thomas' blood sprayed all over her face and splattered her nightgown. At first she was too horrified to even scream out. She just stood frozen in time by the shock of seeing the great pool of blood pouring out from Thomas' throat. She watched in horror as it started to soak into the freshly turned dirt by her feet. She felt something sticky running into her eyes, and she reached up to wipe it away.

That's when she saw the blood on her hands and screamed.

Randy picked up Thomas as though the dog were weightless and tossed him into the grave he had just dug. He stared at the dead animal for a moment and then threw in the bloodied knife he had just used so ruthlessly. He smiled when it landed right next to Thomas' vacant, staring eyes. Picking up his shovel, he methodically started to fill in the grave. He paid absolutely no attention to his young daughter who was trying desperately to clean Thomas' blood off her hands.

"Get it off! Get it off!" she began yelling. "Ooooooooh. It's all over me! Get it off! Please, please get it off." She ran over to the patch of old brown grass by the porch and tried to wipe the blood away, but it wouldn't come off. She tugged and pulled at her nightgown trying to remove it, but she was so frantic and distraught she just couldn't do it.

"NO...NO...NO! Keep away. Don't touch me," she screamed as she saw her father move toward her with the shovel in his hand. She thought he was going to hit her with it and throw her body in with Thomas'. Running hysterically, she escaped into the house. She could hear him laughing in the background as she hid in the bathroom. Squeezing between the tub and the commode, she tried to make herself as small as possible. Maybe he wouldn't be able to find her if he couldn't see her.

She began praying with all her heart for someone to come and save her. Surely God wouldn't turn his back on her now...not after what had just happened. God couldn't let Thomas die in such a horrid way and not do something about it. Maybe her father would be struck down with lightning while he was out there in the yard. Maybe her mother and Edward would come home early and discover him out in the yard burying Thomas' body. Praying harder than she had ever done in her life, she begged God to help her. **"Please God, please let Mom get home right now. If she saw what Dad just did, I know she would help me."**

The bathroom light suddenly came on. She couldn't believe it. There in the door was her mother calling out her name. "Amy...Amy...I'm here now. It's safe to come out. There's nothing here to hurt you."

Rushing into her mother's arms, she started crying. "Mom, you did come! You do still love me, don't you?"

+++++

Amy's nurse had been down the hall working with another patient when she heard the commotion going on in Amy's room. Rushing into the room, she found Amy in the bathroom acting like she was trying to push herself straight through the walls in an attempt to escape whatever it was she thought she was seeing.

The nurse pulled Ted to the other side of the room and said, "Having you over there seems to be frightening her. I need for you to wait here where she can't see you. Let me try to talk to her." The nurse stood in the bathroom doorway and call out, "Amy...Amy...I'm here now. It's safe to come out. There's nothing here to hurt you."

Ted saw Amy look at the nurse with astonishment. Then he watched in surprise as Amy jumped up and rushed into the nurse's arms crying out, "Mom, you did come! You do still love me, don't you?"

+++++

Amy threw her arms around the nurse and held the woman in a tight, emotional embrace. This was her mother, who still loved her, and she felt overjoyed to finally be accepted back into her loving arms. Her mother would protect her from the man that had just destroyed her life. Her mother would not let him touch her again. God had heard her prayers!

The nurse held on tightly to Amy letting her cry upon her shoulder like a small child. She reached up and patted Amy's back saying, "There…there…it's going to be all right. Just try to settle down now."

Ted stood in the background not saying a word. His eyes never left Amy's face.

Amy looked up and saw Ted standing there watching her. The moment her eyes met Ted's she knew where she was and that the memory of Thomas' death was just that…a memory. But this time she realized something very important, something she hadn't been able to comprehend before now.

Nothing that had happened had been her fault.

The sins that had been committed were her father's and his alone. With the knowledge of how her beloved Thomas had died came the understanding that her father had been an evil man, a thief of childhood innocence, a murderer of what was good and joyful about life. And this realization gave her back the strength, the courage, to go forth and fight.

Stepping from the nurse's caring arms, Amy took the first step toward her new life. Reaching out to Ted, she felt the burning of a new flame deep within her soul. As Ted's loving embrace wrapped itself around her, the whole world took on a different hue. No longer was her future bleak and empty. The fire burning between her and Ted colored her world in a new brightness, promising the full colors of the rainbow to her weakened spirit.

Toni Auberry

Chapter 50

September 28, 1998
6 months later

Amy knew the meeting that James had scheduled today with her family would prove to be a landmark in her recovery from years of childhood abuse. Yet she was afraid. She could feel her heart rapidly beating, like the heartbeat of a scared baby bird. When she walked into James' office, she felt a disturbing heaviness settle upon her shoulders. "Is everyone here?" she asked nervously.

"Everyone but your mother," James replied, rising from behind his desk and walking over to the door to greet her.

"I knew she wouldn't come," Amy sighed unhappily. "She hasn't talked to me since I went into the hospital. She won't even open the door if she knows it's me on the other side."

"I'm sorry you haven't been able to convince her to meet with you. I know her attitude is making things more difficult for you."

"One of the hardest things I've had to accept is the fact Mom might never acknowledge that the abuse even happened."

"At least your brother has been very supportive, even though it's been very hard on him. I know part of him still doesn't believe your father abused you as badly as he did, but at least he's been trying to keep an open mind about it."

"I had to finally stop telling Edward everything I was remembering. I could tell he didn't always believe me, and the questioning look that is always in his eyes hurts so badly. But even so, I think it's time he heard the whole story." Amy took in a deep breath as she tried to force herself to relax. "I think it's going to be harder to tell Edward than Ted."

"That's because Edward will take it personally. After all, the man was his father, too, and he really did worship him. Plus he's going to feel guilty about not realizing what you were going through."

"Ellen has been very understanding. I was afraid she wouldn't want me to be around the baby."

"Why would you even think that?" James asked.

"Because I feel so tainted, as though there is something wrong with me, something I could pass on to my niece," Amy replied.

"Your sister-in-law is smart enough to realize what kind of person you are. Your father's destructive behavior wasn't your behavior, and she knows that. You're the one who thinks you've been contaminated, not Ellen, or Edward, or Ted."

"But my mother thinks that way," Amy said sadly.

"Right now you can't worry about what your mother thinks. You have to concentrate on healing yourself. Nothing else is more important."

Amy walked past James and went over to the window. Not quite ready to go into the conference room, she stood staring out at the blue sky. "In the beginning, I thought I was going crazy...seeing ghosts, hearing people's voices, dreaming about terrible beasts. What persons wouldn't have thought they were losing their minds?"

"A lot of people would have," James said, joining her. "But not too many people would have been strong enough to face their past like you did. Too often the victims of severe childhood abuse aren't able to pick up the pieces of their shattered lives and move on. Sometimes they get stuck in the nightmare and can't escape. A lot of them carry it on into their adult lives, reliving their abuse by subjecting their children to the same treatment they received...like a living legacy handed down from generation to generation."

"Well, it's stopping in this family with me. My children won't have to live the way I did. Neither will Edward's. I'll see to that."

"I know you will," James said with confidence. "And you're starting today by telling Edward everything. That will help him understand and keep him from making the same mistakes your father did."

"It's strange having lived for so many years with all those terrible secrets locked up inside of me. I still don't understand how I could have forgotten them. How could someone possibly forget a life of hell?"

"You really didn't forget them. You only repressed them...pushed them back into the furthest corner of your mind. That's how you survived. The trouble with repressed memories is that they don't like to stay hidden forever. They keep trying to surface, fighting their way from the unconscious mind into the conscious any way they can. Like smoke in a locked room slipping out through a key hole, the memories will try to slip around all the barriers you use to hold them back."

Amy reached over and placed her hand on James' arm. "I really wonder if Edward hadn't gotten me that painting for my birthday whether or not I would have finally remembered."

"Oh, I think so. The painting was only a catalyst. If it hadn't been the painting, it would have been something else. Raphael and Gary are proof of that. You were ready to face your nightmares, even though you really don't believe that." James smiled encouragingly. "Come on. It's time. They're all waiting for you."

+++++

Edward, Ellen, and Ted were seated in big comfortable leather chairs in James' conference room. Amy and James walked in and sat down in the two remaining chairs. Amy looked over at her family, and when her eyes sought Edward's, he looked down at the table as if he were ashamed to face her. Ellen saw what was happening and placed a comforting hand on her husband's arm.

Amy knew her brother still didn't totally believe her. He was holding on to some deep hope that their father hadn't been a monster. In a way, Amy understood. If she had loved her parents as much as

Edward had, it would be very hard to believe the story she was about to tell. But the parents she knew weren't the same ones Edward knew, and the truth needed to be told. Not only for her sanity, but also for her brother's.

"This is very hard for me to do," Amy said, laying a large notepad down on the desk in front of her. "As part of my therapy I wrote down everything I have been able to remember, and now I'm going to read to you what I've written. To make it easier for me, I wrote the story as if it had happened to another little girl...a girl named Amy."

Opening the note pad, she began. "This is *Amy's Tale—*"

Toni Auberry

Chapter 51

Amy's Tale

Amy's nightmare started late one stormy night…just like some nightmares do. Lightning flashed everywhere, and its fiery tentacles illuminated the sky like a multitude of brilliant neon lights. Thunder boomed, echoing down, shaking the whole house. A forceful wind threatened to blow the trees right up out of the ground. Through it all, Amy, a little seven-year-old girl lay curled under her covers, shivering in fright. She knew the house would be blown away if the wind got any stronger because she had seen it happen last night on the news.

Lying in bed with her new puppy, Thomas, she cringed with each loud explosion of thunder. She hugged Thomas so tightly that he yelped, and she felt so alone and frightened. If her brother had been home, she would have run into his room and curled up in bed with him. He would have thrown a cover over their heads so they could pretend they were deep in a cave far away from the storm.

Except Edward wasn't home. He and their mother were out of town visiting relatives all weekend, and that left her in their big gloomy house with only her father and Thomas for company.

Over the noise of the storm, she suddenly heard her father's heavy footsteps coming down the hall. She tried hard to keep Thomas quiet because he wasn't supposed to be upstairs in bed with her. But she couldn't still his yapping as he struggled to escape her tight hold.

The door flew open, and her father's big frame filled the doorway. "You know that mutt isn't allowed up here. If you can't obey the rules, I'll have to send him to the pound. And you know what happens at that place. They kill dogs, especially dogs that don't behave."

"I'll take him back downstairs right now," Amy promised. "He got scared by the thunder, so I brought him up here to keep him from crying. He's better now. It's not his fault. Don't take him to the pound. Please."

"Well, I'll overlook your disobedience this one time. Go ahead and take him down where he belongs, but he'd better be quiet. I can't stand hearing a dog yelping all the time." Her pleading voice had let him know he had gotten his point across. He hated it when his orders weren't obeyed.

Amy didn't give her father a chance to change his mind. Grabbing Thomas, she practically ran down the stairs. She put him in his bed in the utility room and then gave him a little kiss on the head.

"Now you have to be very quiet down here. You don't want to make Dad mad. He might send you to the dog pound, and I don't want that to happen. I love you too much for that." She closed the door to keep him safely where he was supposed to be and hurried back upstairs.

When she got back to her room, she found her father sitting on the side of the bed waiting for her return.

"I just wanted to be sure you didn't try to sneak that dirty little mutt back up here," he said, looking at her with watchful eyes as though he expected her to do something wrong. "Come on now, climb into bed, and I'll tuck you in. It's been a long time since I've done that."

Hungry for the least bit of affection from her father, she flashed him a big smile and ran to the bed. Practically jumping, she climbed up and sat next to him. Happy just to have her father being nice, she reached over and threw her arms around him. "Thanks, Daddy." Hugging him as tightly as she could with her tiny, thin arms, she turned her face up and kissed him on the cheek. "I love you," she whispered.

It felt so good not being scolded that she held on to him with all her might. For one second, she was her daddy's little girl...loved and cherished. Then her whole world began changing, and there was nothing she could do to stop it.

Surprised at the intensity of Amy's hug, Randy held back; he wasn't the hugging type. The presence of her arms around him made him instantly tense up. But then, as the warmth of her small body flowed into his, he felt a driving need to hold her. This was his little girl, his daughter, and he did love her. Slowly he brought his huge arms up and engulfed her small frame. He felt his love for her building from deep within. She was flesh of his flesh, blood of his blood.

He loved her. He needed her.

A desire stirred by the devil flared up in his soul. The intensity of it heated his blood and clouded his mind. There was no thinking of what was right or wrong. There was only the presence of an intense need to possess that which he needed and wanted—his daughter. She was his and would always be his.

With Amy still wrapped up in his arms, he lay down with her upon the bed, and his desires became her nightmare, a nightmare that would haunt her the rest of her life. When she cried out for him to stop, he couldn't hear her voice over the roar of the blood pounding through his head. Madness clouded his eyes; he couldn't see the look of terror on her face as he forced her legs open and ripped apart her body and soul. Her screams were lost in the storm outside. No one heard. No one came to save her. She could do nothing except to lie there under his heavy weight and hurt.

When the flames burning in his soul cooled and the hysterical sobbing of his daughter finally sounded in his ears, he threw himself off the bed in horror. What had she done to him? He would be condemned to hell for her actions. Angered by the wickedness she had displayed by seducing him, he struck out, and his hand found its mark on the side of her face.

The impact knocked Amy from the bed. She fell on the floor in a jumbled heap of broken spirits and injured limbs. The product of her father's love began seeping down her legs onto the floor.

He backed away from her in horror. "You are from the devil. Look what you have done to me." Turning, he staggered to the door. The weight of his deed lay heavy upon his shoulders. He stopped with his hand on the doorknob, and without even looking back he spoke to her with disgust. "Go clean yourself. Your filth is soiling this room." Then he left.

Amy heard the slam of his bedroom door echo through the whole house. Unable to stand up and walk to the bathroom, she crawled on her hands and knees across the wooden floor. In the bathroom she managed to pull up to the sink and clean herself off.

Downstairs she could hear Thomas barking excitedly. Afraid her father would carry through with his threats, she attempted to negotiate the steps down to Thomas. Each step sent sharp pains across her groin. Halfway down, she felt blood seeping down her legs, but that didn't stop her. Thomas was barking louder and louder, and her fear for him helped carry her the rest of the way.

Taking Thomas into her arms, she sank down in his bed hugging him tightly. Whispering quietly, so as not to disturb her father, she told Thomas the story he would hear time and time again over the next four years, a story that would ultimately be the cause of his death.

The next morning her father found her curled up with Thomas in the utility room. He grabbed her arm and pulled her up. Then he made sure no one would ever find out about what had happened during that terrible, awful night.

"What you did last night was an act by the devil himself. I don't understand how a daughter of mine could have been so wicked. If you ever tell anyone about what you did, I will have to cast you out of this house, just like God cast the devil out of heaven for his wickedness. No one would take you into their home once they learned about you, so you better never tell anyone at all." Then looking over at Thomas, he spoke again. "If you ever say one word, I promise you I will kill Thomas. I will slit his throat and let him bleed to death."

Amy looked up at him with eyes open wide in terror. "I won't tell anyone...ever. I promise."

From the look on her face, he knew she understood, but just to be sure, he jerked Thomas out of her arms and held his hand over the puppy's mouth and nose.

"No!" she screamed. "Don't do that. He can't breathe." She grabbed her father's arm and tugged, trying to pull his hand away from Thomas' face. She watched in horror as Thomas struggled and then went limp.

Her father finally released his death grip on Thomas and brushed Amy's hand away. Then he wiped his own hand on his shirt, as if he were cleaning it after touching something soiled. "You had better keep that promise...or else," he threatened, handing over a limp, but alive Thomas. Satisfied with the look of fear on his daughter's face he turned and walked away, leaving Amy shivering from fright.

When she finally heard the front door close and her father's car pull out of the drive, she quit shaking. Feeling contaminated by her father's touch, she went upstairs and ran the bathtub full of the hottest water she could stand, and she scrubbed at her skin till it felt like it was going to rub off, but the feeling of filth just wouldn't go away.

+++++

Before the first time that Amy's father crawled into her bed, he had never actually hurt her. He had acted like she was a great nuisance to have around, but he had never really hit her, at least not hard enough to leave any bruises. But after he had raped her, beatings became a routine part of Amy's life, as did the trips he made to her bedroom in the dark of the night. At least two or three times a month, he would seek her out for the use of her body. And after each nighttime trek, the physical abuse intensified. The guilt from his sins would eat at his soul, and the only way to relieve himself of the pain within his own heart was to inflict a greater pain upon his daughter. The greater his guilt...the great Amy's pain had to be. In fact his guilt turned out to be so immense that he carried the physical abuse out years beyond when the sexual abuse finally ended sometime after Amy's twelfth birthday.

When Amy was a teenager, she figured out that a lot of the beatings seemed to be directed at the parts of her body that were somehow connected with sex. The bruises would show up the worst

503

around her breasts, near her pelvic area, and on her buttocks. It was as if her father had tried to eradicate those parts of her that had anything to do at all with sexual maturation. Today, she wonders if she will ever be able to have children because she is sure there must have been a lot of damage to her womb with all the trauma inflicted upon that area of her body. Maybe one day when she is feeling very brave she will see a doctor to try to find out how intensive the damage might be. But not right now. She still doesn't trust doctors...except of course for Dr. Perry.

+++++

Not one doctor had sense enough to figure out that the great Randy Tedrow's daughter was being sexual and physically abused. If they did, they never did anything about it. The closest any doctor came to recognizing the truth occurred when she was fourteen. She remembers sitting in the emergency room and hurting so badly she thought she was dying. She had two broken ribs from where her father had knocked her into a wall after she spilled a coke on the new carpet in the living room.

The pain had been so great she thought she would pass out. She could hardly breathe and had collapsed on the kitchen floor. Finally, her mother had made Randy carry her out to the car so they could take her to the emergency room.

"Don't say a word," he threatened when the car arrived at the emergency room doors. "You know what will happen if you say one single thing," he whispered as he carried her in and laid her on the bed in the ER.

Randy insisted he be allowed to remain in the room while the examination was being performed. Every time the emergency room doctor asked Amy a question, her father would answer it. After the doctor looked her over and ordered x-rays, he finally asked her father to leave the room. The doctor explained he wanted to talk to Amy alone.

Indignant at the request, Randy demanded he be allowed to remain, but the doctor refused. Her father ranted and raved like a mad bull, all the while continuing to insist that no one had a right to talk to his daughter alone without his permission. Finally though, he had no choice but to leave, and he stormed from the room in a huff.

After her father was gone and Amy was alone with the doctor, he looked at her with compassion in his eyes. "Do you want to tell me what really happened?" he spoke in a quiet voice. "There isn't anyone in here that will hurt you. If you can tell me how you got injured, I just might be able to help you. I really don't think you fell down the stairs like your father is saying."

Speechless, Amy stared at him. She wanted to tell him. His eyes were so kind, but the words simply would not come. Sometimes, she wonders how different the next few years of her life might have been if she could have only said something.

"Did someone hurt you?" he asked, his voice calm and full of sympathy. "Is that what happened? It's safe to tell me. I'm a doctor, and it's my job to help kids like you."

For the first time, Amy almost told someone the truth. The doctor seemed so sincere. Maybe he could have helped her, except before she had the chance to speak, her father returned followed by the hospital's administrator and her family physician. The emergency room doctor was severely reprimanded for his actions right there in front of the rest of the staff and then instructed to leave.

As the kindhearted doctor left the room, Amy realized her chance to finally speak had disappeared just as quickly as it had appeared. Dr. Stevenson treated her fractures without asking Amy one single question; instead he spent the entire time discussing political matters with her father.

Amy never saw the kind doctor again. She heard her father bragging a couple of days later about how he had managed to get the man transferred out of town to another hospital. After that, no one ever questioned any of her injuries. Everyone in town, including all the doctors, accepted Randy's word as truth.

+++++

Poor Amy. She had no one to talk to except her dog, Thomas. He was the only one she could tell her terrible secrets to, but even when she was talking to him, she had to be very secretive so no one else could hear. As the abuse had intensified, so had the threats her father used to keep her silent. Knowing how much she loved her brother, her father eventually directed the threats toward him.

She can still recall the hiss of her father's voice as he whispered in her ear. "If you tell anyone about what you do, the shame would be too great for this family. I would have to kill everyone, including Edward. I couldn't let him live with the terrible disgrace you have placed upon this family. It would be so wrong, so you'd better keep it a secret if you love your brother."

Sometimes she had wanted so badly to tell Edward what was happening, but she could never be sure if the threats against him would really be carried out. From the way her father treated Edward, she didn't think he would really kill him, but what if she was wrong? So to protect her brother, she kept the silence. She had to…Edward's life was worth ten times more than hers, and she couldn't let anything happen to him.

+++++

When the beatings first started, Amy tried to turn to her mother for protection and comfort, but her mother had turned away, offering nothing to ease Amy's awful burden. If her mother was in the room when the beatings were happening, she simply got up and left. She even helped hide the evidence of the abuse. She was the one who had insisted Amy wear the long-sleeved shirts to hide the bruises, the one who took Amy to the doctor and lied about the injuries, and the one who very carefully applied makeup around all the black eyes so they wouldn't show.

Amy never really knew for sure if her mother realized that her beloved husband had started crawling into his daughter's bed at night, but how could she not have known? Her father had to leave the bed he shared with her mother to come to hers. Wouldn't her mother have guessed what was happening?

But when she was growing up, Amy didn't want to admit that her mother actually knew because to admit such a thing would have meant she wasn't loved at all. Through all those terrible years, it had been very important to Amy to hang on to the belief that deep down inside her mother's heart there had to be some love left for her.

For years Amy dreamed of living in a happy home where her mother wanted to be with her. One of her most favorite daydreams was the one where they would be out on a picnic together laughing and talking just like all the other families she had watched at the park, but that dream never did come true. Her mother never did laugh and talk with Amy after the night that her father raped her. Instead, she acted as though she actually blamed Amy for what was happening in their home.

+++++

To protect herself from the awful feelings that would materialize when her father would come for her in the middle of the night, Amy learned how to send herself far away. Of course, when she did that, she had to leave her body behind, and since it was the only way she could survive without losing her mind, that's what she did.

When she would send herself away, her memory would disappear, like someone had used scissors and snipped off bits and pieces of her life, and then had pasted them back together leaving some of the parts out. One minute she would be in her bed looking into her father's stone-cold, gray eyes glaring down at her, and the next minute she would find herself somewhere else. Maybe it would be at school, or at church, or eating breakfast, and it might be the next day, or the next month, or even the next year. It was really scary waking up as if from a long, dreamless sleep and finding herself someplace she had absolutely no memory of how she got there.

Blank spots are what she called the memory lapses because there existed only emptiness where there should have been memories. And even today, her mind is still full of those blank spots. Hours, days, months are missing. In fact, her entire eleventh year is lost as though it had never happened. From the day she turned eleven until the night before she walked out in front of a car when she was twelve, there exists a huge, gaping, black hole in her memories. And no matter how hard she tries, most of what happened to her during that time period seems to be irretrievably lost.

+++++

Despite that huge blank spot after her eleventh birthday, she now remembers in very clear detail what happened the night before. That was the day her dear childhood friend, Thomas, was murdered. Right before her eyes, her father slit his throat. Now when she closes her eyes, she can sometimes see the blood as it sprayed out covering her face and hands and soaking her nightgown until it clung to her skin.

She remembers her father throwing Thomas' blood-soaked body and the knife he had used to kill Thomas into the grave he had dug in the flower garden out in their back yard. Then he had planted three red rosebushes over the grave to mark it. After that, every year on her birthday, he gave her a present of a dozen blood-red roses. The roses were to be a reminder so she wouldn't forget what would happen if she broke the code of silence.

The funny thing was, her father didn't really have to go to all that trouble every year, because by the time she was thirteen, Amy had already suppressed all her memories about the sexual abuse. All she could remember was that she hated red roses and her birthday.

+++++

The sexual abuse, which had started at age seven, finally stopped when Amy turned twelve. The last time her father raped her was the night before she walked out in front of a car in an attempt to kill herself. She remembers that particular night very clearly now. Just a few hours before her father came to her room, she started menstruating for the first time. When her father discovered she now had "the curse" he refused to look upon her face. After seeing the blood all over his groin, he treated her like a filthy whore who had given him some deadly disease. He cursed and called her horrible names, and then he took his belt to her like an obsessed demon. The pain had been terrible, and she had prayed for death long before the final swing of the belt slapped against her skin.

Sometimes late at night when darkness settles around her, she can still hear the sound of that belt as it whooshed through the air before it struck her again and again.

At that time Amy had no idea what "the curse" was. No one had ever told her about that part of being a female. Her mother hadn't mentioned one word to her about it. When she saw the blood on her underpants, she thought that she was dying, and in a way she had actually felt happy about it. She thought God had finally decided to grant her what she had been praying for…*death*. However, when her father started ranting and raving about her sinfulness, Amy finally realized she couldn't handle living any more. She decided at that moment not to wait for God to take her away. The next morning she went outside and walked down the driveway and then deliberately marched out to the street directly into the path of an oncoming car.

Their neighbor had been right when she reported Amy had purposely walked right out in front of the car. It wasn't an accident like her parents told everyone. She didn't trip and fall, but until the repressed memories surfaced, Amy didn't remember any of that. All she could recall was one day she was almost eleven years old and the next she was twelve and in the hospital with a cast on both of her legs and pain exploding through her entire body.

+++++

When she was thirteen, Amy stole her father's new camera, the one that could be used for self-portraits. Then she started taking pictures of every bruise, cut, and scrape her father gave her. She took great risks in getting those pictures. She had to be very careful where she bought the film, traveling clear to the other side of town where people didn't know her in order to buy it without getting caught. If her father had ever found out what she was doing the punishment would have been severe. But she knew she had to have the pictures. From the beginning her father had said no one would ever believe a word she said. So, she had to collect proof. Unfortunately, she never found someone she could show the proof to. She couldn't even get the pictures developed. She somehow knew that the information would have gotten back to her father.

Somewhere up in the attic of her mother's house is a cardboard box wrapped and tied with old twine that contains a camera and seven rolls of undeveloped film. After her father's death, there had been no reason for her to even look in that box again. As far as she knows, it's still lying right where she had last placed it, hidden back in a corner where no one could accidentally find it.

Even though those rolls of film were never developed, the pictures upon them were in essence what finally saved her from her father. The knowledge of their existence became the primary cause of his death. When she was eighteen she had threatened to post the pictures all over town if he ever touched her again. It made him so angry that his heart exploded, which hadn't bothered her one bit. She was glad when he died. Maybe that was wrong for her to feel that way, but she was very glad. When she had first heard the news, her heart had rejoiced, and her soul had lifted itself upward and soared with its newly found freedom…a freedom from the fear and pain she would never have to face again.

Chapter 52

October 4, 1998

The staircase leading to the attic was dark and gloomy, just like Edward's mood. Years ago the attic had been his favorite hideaway. With its gross accumulation of family castoffs, it had been a young explorer's dream. Unfortunately, he wasn't making the reluctant trek up the stairs simply to relive childhood fantasies.

Supposedly, somewhere buried among the attic's trash and treasures lay one of the keys he needed to unlock the mystery of Amy. According to his sister, she had hidden a box in one of the dark, remote corners of the room, far beyond the casual glance of the eye. It was a box that presumably contained proof of his father's guilt.

The climb up the stairs was slow and deliberate. His legs felt heavy, as if they were made of lead instead of flesh and bone. The journey was one he didn't want to be taking. He wasn't sure he really wanted proof of Amy's abuse. Without proof he could at least hold onto a shred of the feelings of love that he had for his father. With proof, he had nothing. How could he feel any type of love for a man who had systematically destroyed his own daughter?

Fatigue overwhelmed him, and he had to stop for a moment. He leaned his weight against the banister and sighed. *Maybe I wouldn't be feeling quite so bad if I didn't have to do this alone,* he thought wearily. *But Mom wouldn't let anyone else come into the house, especially Amy. With each passing day she's getting more and more unreasonable, and I just don't know what to do.*

He listened to her shouting angrily at him from the first floor. The hysteria in her voice made him wonder what would happen if she got any worse.

"You're a traitor to this family," Connie shrieked at him like a banshee. "I can understand your sister turning against us, but not you. How could you even think of believing those lies Amy is telling everyone? You know what the truth is."

"That's exactly the reason why I'm here," Edward shouted back at her. "I want to find out what the truth really is."

"I want you to stop right now and come downstairs. I won't help in despoiling the family name, and I refuse to allow you to do it either."

"Mom, I'm going up to the attic to look for those rolls of film, whether or not you want me to."

"Your sister is crazy; you know that, don't you? Your father didn't abuse her. Discipline isn't abuse. Amy was just too wild, and someone had to keep her under control."

"How? By beating her so severely she couldn't walk? By breaking her arms so she couldn't fight back?"

"You don't know how unmanageable she was. Your father only did what he had to do to save her soul."

"Save her soul! Amy's soul wasn't in need of saving. She was just a normal little kid."

"You can't talk about something you know absolutely nothing about. Amy wasn't a normal little girl. She—"

"Mom, that's enough. I've got things to do." Forcing himself to start moving again, Edward resumed his journey up the stairs. As his feet slowly worked their way upward, his ears tried to tune out his mother's voice. At the top of the stairs Edward paused before opening the door to the attic. Downstairs he could hear his mother shouting scriptures at him about honoring his mother and father.

How he wished that Amy was with him. She could have simply walked in, found the box, and then they could have left. But that just wasn't possible because she wasn't even allowed to enter the house anymore. So there wasn't anyone else to do the job. It was all up to him, and he needed to find the film before their mother decided to look for it. Somehow he knew if she found it first it would disappear forever.

He slowly opened the door, walked in, and then headed to the center of the room. Reaching overhead, he found the string to the only light fixture in the room. With a swift tug the single hundred-watt light bulb instantly flickered on, casting its cheerless glow across the cluttered attic.

His eyes quickly scanned the dusty, cobwebby room. No one had been up there for years. He could see where his footprints were the only ones crossing the dusty floor. *Amy's box with its hidden film should still be here somewhere. That is, if it really does exist,* he thought warily, allowing his doubts to besiege him again.

+++++

After an hour of rummaging through dusty shelves and haphazardly piled boxes, crates, and old furniture, Edward was becoming increasingly frustrated. There was no sign of Amy's box anywhere in the room. *Could Amy's story have been a lie or a hallucination,* he wondered for the hundredth time. *Maybe Amy really is sick. Maybe she did imagine it after all.*

He slammed his fist down on an old, dust-covered table and cursed. *Damn it, who am I supposed to believe? If I can't find the film, I'll never really know which one is telling the truth...Amy or Mom.*

In his frustration he turned too quickly and tripped over a pile of discarded magazines. When a box full of old picture frames came crashing down on his head, he let out a whole string of obscenities.

He could hear his mother downstairs yelling for him to give up his foolishness and come down and have tea with her. He had just about decided to join her when out of the corner of his eye he saw a piece of twine sticking out from behind a pile of old books. Moving aside a stack of outdated encyclopedias, he discovered a small cardboard box hidden deep in the shadows. It had been wrapped several times with twine and then had been tied very securely.

All of a sudden the air around him felt heavy, making it hard to breathe. His chest tightened, and his heart began pounding so hard he could hear the sound of his own blood pulsating through his ears.

Was this Amy's hidden proof?

With shaky hands he slowly picked up the box. Written in childlike handwriting were the words *AMY'S PRIVATE PROPERTY. KEEP OUT.* Moving over to the small, grimy, attic window for more light, he very carefully undid the box's bindings. As the twine fell to the floor, he felt lightheaded and dizzy. He did not want to lift the lid. He was too afraid of what he would find hidden inside.

But there was no stopping the hands of fate; he knew what had to be done. Blowing the dust off the top of the box, he stared at it for a few seconds more. Then he lifted the lid. Securely placed between rumpled pieces of old newspaper were several rolls of undeveloped film and his father's lost camera. Picking up each roll, he started counting; one…two…three…all the way up to seven. It was exactly as Amy had told him it would be.

He put the film back into its box and then headed down the stairs. He found his mother waiting for him at the last step. Her eyes went directly to the box he carried in his hands.

"No! There can't be any pictures," she screeched at him. Grabbing for the box, she actually clawed his arm in her attempt to take it from him. "Give that to me. I have to destroy it right now before it can destroy this family."

Edward held the box over his head far away from her reaching hands as he headed toward the front door. "Mom, this family has already been destroyed. Dad did it a long time ago. We just didn't know it until now."

"It wasn't Randy's fault. He was a good man." Connie's voice took on a hysterical tone. "My father's demons did it all. First they destroyed my father and then they came back for Randy. There's no way anyone can fight them. Don't you know that?"

Bewildered Edward turned toward his mother. "Demons! What in the world are you talking about? There never were any demons in this house, except maybe my father." Then he looked at his mother's frantic face and sadly said, "And maybe your father."

Connie's hand flew to her mouth. She shouldn't have told her son about the demons. They might come for her. Like a crazed wild woman, she turned and ran up the stairs. Locking herself in the bedroom, she got down on her knees and started praying. She tightly clutched the silver cross hanging around her neck as she pleaded with God to save them all.

+++++

Without a word of goodbye, Edward left the house with the film still in his possession. In the car, he placed Amy's box right next to him on the seat. He didn't want to lose sight of it for even a second.

As he drove down the road, he was able to relax a little for the first time in months. He carefully drew in several deep breaths and felt the tightness in his chest finally abate. In a way the worst was over. He knew exactly what the pictures would show. It wouldn't matter if the film couldn't be processed. Amy had been telling the truth. His sister wasn't crazy after all.

+++++

Edward turned on to Interstate 57 and headed out of town. There wasn't any place nearby that he could safely take the film to be developed. The pictures weren't exactly the type a person would want to take over to the neighborhood drug store for processing. Fortunately, Justin, a friend of his over in the next county, had agreed to help.

At Justin's, Edward very cautiously handed over the box of film. "Here are those pictures I need for you to develop. The rolls are several years old and have been stored in an old attic. They might not be any good. Just do the best that you can."

"From the way you are handling it, one would think there's a bomb inside," Justin said, taking Amy's box from Edward's shaking hands.

"In a way, that could be true. These pictures are going to cause an explosion that will be heard all across the county, and my whole family will be at the very center of the blast."

Justin didn't know exactly how to reply, so he simply kept quiet.

"Give me a call as soon as you get finished," Edward said, turning to go. "You're going to want to talk to me anyway. According to Amy, there is some pretty shocking stuff on this film. So don't freak out. I'll explain it all later. And as a favor, please keep all of this between you and me."

"Sure thing, at least as long as it's nothing illegal," Justin jokingly replied.

+++++

Edward climbed back in his car and headed home. All of a sudden he had an overwhelming need to hold his new daughter, Christi. Lately it seemed like the only time he felt good about himself was when he held her tiny body in his arms. Christi was proof there were still some good things about life.

As he drove home, he made a promise to his daughter that he would never do to her what had been done to Amy. One important fact he had learned from James was that childhood abuse often became a familial pattern of living, being passed down from generation through generation. Just as children learn how to read or write as they are growing up, they also learn behavioral patterns. If they are repetitively exposed to abusive situations, as they grow older they unconsciously model their behavior to follow that same destructive pattern.

It was a vicious cycle, one that must be broken, and it was going to start right there in his own home. It hadn't been until this nightmare with Amy had started that he had realized how controlling and manipulative he was. While he had thought his marriage had been perfect, he was now finding out it had only been an illusion. Ellen had been overwhelmed by his need to always be in control. He had very seldom allowed her to make any of the decisions in their marriage. He had been acting just like his father and his grandfather…like he was the king and his wife was his servant.

But he was lucky. Ellen still loved him, and he still loved her. They were now going to counseling together and learning a whole new way of communicating. People used to say he and Ellen had the perfect marriage. Well, it had been that way for him, but not for her. However, that was going to change. He was going to do his best to make it as perfect as he could for both Ellen and Christi. The legacy of violence handed down within his family would end with him and his sister. He and Amy were going to start a new family tradition, one that was centered around love...not hate. It would take some help from people who knew how to go about making changes, but the cycle of abuse would be broken.

Toni Auberry

Chapter 53

Justin worked all night on Edward's project, and his shock and disgust increased with each picture developed. He had grown up with Edward. They were best friends all through high school and had spent hours, sometimes days, at each other's homes. Yet not once had he ever suspected what had been going on at Edward's house.

Who could have done such terrible things to Amy? he wondered in amazement.

Whoever it had been, he had kept it up for years. The pictures showed Amy battered and bruised through several years. In the earliest photos she was in her very early teens with small budding young breasts. Later pictures showed that the abuse had been carried out until Amy must have been old enough to graduate from high school.

Justin understood now why Edward hadn't wanted the film developed anywhere else. The photos definitely would cause an explosion…an explosion of repugnance and loathing toward anyone who could have committed such shameful acts.

As he stood looking at the battered images of Amy, he also realized why Amy had seemed so strange when she had been younger.

All through high school, Justin had wondered why Amy didn't date. He had thought she was beautiful, and if she had shown the least bit of interest in him, he would have asked her out in a heartbeat. She'd had the most kissable lips of any girl in the whole school. There had even been a couple of times he had caught himself daydreaming about what might happen if they ever got the opportunity to be alone together, but that chance never came. Amy avoided being around people. He had thought it was because she was stuck on herself, like other people weren't good enough for her, but he had been wrong on that one! If he had been through the hell she had, he wouldn't have wanted to be around other people either.

As he carefully studied each picture, he became even more appalled. It seemed as if whoever had hurt Amy had zeroed in on her breasts and pelvic area. In a couple of the later photos in which Amy had fully developed breasts, the breasts were nothing but one big mass of bruises. It was if someone had tried to rip them off of her chest. No wonder she never dated! After experiencing something like that, who would want some guy pawing at your body?

It dawned on Justin that there was the possibility Edward might have had something to do with Amy's injuries. Before his friend had left yesterday, he had asked that the contents of the box be kept a secret between the two of them, but Justin wasn't sure he could do that. Lying in front of him was proof of a very horrendous crime. He couldn't let it go unattended. Edward was a good friend, but the cost of remaining silent would be too great for his own conscience. Whoever had hurt Amy and then had the audacity to actually take photographs should be hung without a trial.

Disturbed by the pictures, he knew he had to talk to Edward. He picked up the phone and wasted no time in placing that call. Justin didn't even bother to be cordial. As soon as he heard his friend's voice on the phone line, he started talking. "You had better have a good explanation why you have those pictures of Amy. Otherwise, as soon as I hang up the phone, I'm calling the police."

There was a short pause on the line before Edward spoke. "I guess there's no doubt Amy has been telling me the truth."

"The truth about what? That someone beat the hell out of her and then took pictures of it!"

"I was hoping the pictures wouldn't be that bad," Edward said, feeling more downhearted than he had ever felt in his life.

"Well, they are more than just bad. They are horrendous! And those pictures aren't leaving this house with anyone but the police unless you can explain to my satisfaction why you have them in your possession."

"It's a long story," Edward said, knowing his friend well enough to realize Justin wasn't bluffing. So for the first time outside of the family and Amy's small circle of friends, Amy's tale was told, except with the pictures as proof, it was no longer a tale—it was a reality, a reality he would have to live with for the rest of his life.

Justin listened silently, shocked speechless by what Edward was revealing about his father. The whole story was almost too fantastic to believe. Randy Tedrow had been someone he had wanted to be like. The man had possessed power, money, success, and a good standing in the community. How could he have been the one that had abused Amy? How could he have molested his own daughter? The man had been a key church member, one of the influential leaders in the town's youth groups, and an icon in their hometown.

"Are you sure that's what happened?" he asked Edward, the sound of disbelief strong in his voice. "I knew your Dad, and I can't even begin to imagine him doing to Amy what I saw in those photos."

"When Amy first told me, I didn't believe it either. I thought she was hallucinating, or had gone crazy, but you saw the pictures. Does it look like it was all lies to you?"

"Are you sure it was your father? Could it have been someone else?"

"I've racked my brain trying to find someone else to blame, but denying my father's involvement doesn't make the story any less true."

"So what are you going to do now?" Justin couldn't begin to imagine how bad Edward had to be feeling right now. To learn such dreadful things about your father would have to be devastating.

"I don't know. I guess I need to talk with Amy again now that I have the pictures."

"Speaking of these pictures…what do you want me to do with them?" Justin asked. "I just can't pretend they don't exist."

"I'll swing by your place later on today and pick them up. This whole matter is not getting washed under the bridge. I promise you that. Amy is already in therapy, and so am I. It's been very hard on both of us, but I think we're going to make it. The pictures are the end point of all that has been going on since early this year. I guess I just needed some kind of proof to validate what Amy has been telling me. I didn't want to accept it, but now I really don't have a choice."

"Once you see these pictures, there won't be any doubts left in your mind. I sure don't have any. I was ready to turn you over to the cops. Your sister must have a very strong spirit to have survived. I'm not so sure I could have."

"In a way, she gave up her whole childhood just to protect me. I would say she is one of the strongest, spirited women I have ever met. I can only hope some of that spirit dwells in me. Once all this reaches the public ears, the Tedrow name isn't going to be worth much. At least not until I can prove I'm not my father's son."

"All of my life I have wished I was in your shoes. You seemed to have everything. Now for the first time, I'm very glad that I'm not."

"This is one time I really wish I wasn't in my shoes either," Edward replied, his voice trembling from the sorrow in his heart.

+++++

After talking with Justin, Edward felt emotionally drained. Collapsing exhausted on the couch, he didn't even have the energy to hang up the phone. It was taking every bit of his strength to deal with the fact that he no longer had the memories of a loving father to hold on to. Instead, all he could see in his head were the images of his father looming over his sister in her bed like a beast in the night. And worst of all was the guilt he felt weighing down his soul. Why hadn't he recognized what was happening to his sister right under his own nose? How could he have been so self-centered and so wrapped up in his own little world that he had missed all the signs of Amy's abuse?

Edward started crying as a cataclysm of guilt consumed his senses. If he had just once taken the time to see beyond his own little world, maybe there wouldn't have been the need for Amy to take those pictures.

Overwhelmed with shame, he wanted to curl up into a ball and stay on the couch forever. His father had used Amy's love for him to keep her quiet, and he certainly didn't deserve a love like that. He hadn't paid enough attention to his little sister to even notice the hell she had been living through. How could she possibly still care for him now that she remembers everything? He wouldn't be that generous. He would probably leave town and never get in touch with any of his family again.

Damn It, Dad! Edward cursed bitterly. *Why did you do it? Did you think your actions weren't affecting anyone but you? Did you even bother to consider what you were doing to the entire family...Amy, me, Mom?*

Edward knew there were no answers to his questions, and it infuriated him to think his father would never have to face the consequences of his reprehensible conduct.

It would be the rest of the family that would pay for his father's sins, not his father, and there was no justice in that at all.

Toni Auberry

Chapter 54

As he pulled into his mother's driveway, Edward began preparing himself for the battle that would soon be happening. Armed with the stack of pictures he had just picked up from Justin, he was going to confront his mother with the proof of his father's guilt. After seeing the pictures, she would finally have to admit that Amy hadn't lied. The evidence was right there in his hands in full living color. Every bruise on his sister's body screamed out the truth.

After banging on the front door for ten minutes and getting no response, Edward moved to the back entrance and tried again. But he had no luck there either. His mother still didn't respond. Finally he broke out one of the windows on the back door. Then he reached in and quickly undid the locks. All the while, he had the feeling that something just wasn't right.

"Hey, Mom, don't be scared, it's only me," he shouted. "I let myself in the back door because I need to talk with you." When he didn't hear a reply from his mother his alarm rose sharply. He was afraid something might have happened to her.

"Mom! Where are you?" he shouted.

Only a strange empty silence echoed though the house.

Edward quickly checked all the rooms downstairs and found nothing. Everything was exactly as it should be, except his mother wasn't anywhere to be found. He was seriously considering calling the police when he heard a noise coming from the direction of his mother's bedroom. Cautiously he started upstairs.

"What's going on?" Edward anxiously asked. "Why aren't you answering me?"

Silence remained the only reply.

When Edward reached the top of the stairs he paused for a moment. All the doors in the foyer were closed tight making the hall look very dark and foreboding. He halfway expected an ax-swinging maniac to burst from one of the rooms.

He forced himself to remain calm and tentatively knocked on his mother's bedroom door.

"Mom, are you all right?" he asked. When he didn't get a reply his anxiety intensified. *Maybe she was hurt and couldn't get to the door. Yesterday she had seemed very unsteady on her feet. She might have fallen and broken a hip, or something worse could have happened. What if she'd had a heart attack like Dad?*

But just as he was considering the idea of trying to bash in the bedroom door, he heard the sound of a sliding door chain came from inside her room, and he felt his fears immediately ease.

"Is that really you, Edward?" Connie asked, opening the bedroom door only far enough for her to see her son's face.

"Yes, it's really me. Who else would it be?" Edward replied shocked by the crazed look in the eyes that were staring at him through the opening in the door.

After a long pause, Connie slowly opened the door and then stepped out in the hall.

Edward was stunned by her slovenly appearance. Her uncombed hair fell down across her face, and she was wearing the same clothes she had on yesterday. When she moved closer, he noticed that a stale, sweaty odor seemed to be oozing from her skin. She smelled as though she hadn't bathed for several days.

"What is happening to you?" he demanded to know as his eyes focused on the deepening flush that was coloring her cheeks bright red. When he received no response, he shifted his gaze from her face and saw that she had the silver crucifix he had given her on Mother's Day clutched tightly in her hand.

"Here, put this on...right now," Connie insisted, pressing the crucifix into Edward's hand. "I don't want the demons to get to you. This cross has been blessed by the priest, so you should be safe if you wear it."

Edward didn't want to upset her any further so he allowed her to hang the crucifix around his neck. "Mom, I think you need to see the doctor," he said with concern. "Why don't we do that right now while I'm here to help you?"

"Absolutely not. I'm not going to go see any doctor. No doctor can help us. No one can. We have to find a way to fight them ourselves."

"Fight who?" Edward asked.

"I can't say it out loud," Connie said. Lowering her voice she whispered. "They might hear me."

"I'm not worrying about anyone hearing us," Edward replied. "Right now the only thing I'm worrying about is you. You don't look well at all. Have you even eaten anything today?"

"I'm not hungry! I have more important things to worry about than food."

"Let me fix you a bowl of soup or a sandwich?" Edward begged. "You can't go without eating."

"How can I eat when they're watching every move I make?" Connie said, her voice edged with hysteria.

"Mom, I'll make sure *they* don't bother you while you eat," Edward promised. He took his mother's arm and helped her navigate down the stairs. He was surprised at how unsteady she had become. She almost fell twice on the way to the kitchen. He didn't know what to do, but if she refused help, there wasn't a thing he really could do…at least for now.

In the kitchen, she didn't offer any objections while he fixed a bowl of hot soup. As she sat at the table eating, she looked over at him. "I know why you're really here. You want to apologize for believing all those awful rumors your sister has been spreading about your father. I told you nothing would show up on those photographs.

Those stories of hers were nothing but hateful lies. Amy has always been such a wicked child. That's why the demons were able to use her to get at your father."

Edward rose from his chair and without saying a word he walked out to his car. When he returned he brought back the box of Amy's pictures that Justin had developed. Silently he spread them out on the table in front of his mother. With Amy's proof right in front of her face, he believed that she couldn't deny his father's guilt any longer.

"See…Amy hasn't been lying!' he said. "It really did happen. Mom, I want you to take a good look at these pictures and tell me you didn't know about this. Tell me you didn't allow Dad to rape and beat your daughter."

Connie quickly scanned the pictures that Edward had spread across the table, and she didn't even blink an eye when she saw the battered images of a broken child staring at her. Then with an angry sweep of her hand, she knocked the photos off the table onto the floor. "Trash, it's all trash. Somehow your sister has managed to fix those up to make it look like she had been hurt. She's a tricky one. See how she has managed to trick you in to believing her. Those pictures aren't proof of anything."

Anger colored Edward's vision. He wanted to shake his mother until she admitted Amy's story wasn't a lie. How could she not see the truth when it was right there in front of her eyes captured on film? He couldn't understand how she could turn her back on Amy. It just didn't make any sense at all.

He felt the need to put some distance between him and his mother, so he walked over to the back door. Through the broken windowpane he could see the flower garden his father had built so lovingly in the back yard. All at once, he had a vision of his father standing out in the middle of the garden slitting Thomas' throat while Amy stood watching, her eyes open wide in horror.

"You want positive proof of Dad's guilt. I'll give you positive proof." Edward marched from the house, letting the door slam noisily behind him. He practically ran to the small garden shed next to the garage and grabbed a shovel from the tool rack.

"What do you think you're doing?" Connie demanded, coming up behind him.

"I'm giving you more proof, that's what!" Edward said, walking to the part of the garden where Amy's three rose bushes used to be. He shoved the shovel into the ground with a vengeance and started digging.

"Stop that right now!" Connie shouted. "You're going to ruin my garden."

"I really don't give a damn about your garden. What I care about is Amy. If I have to dig all the way to China, I'm going to prove to you she isn't lying."

+++++

After an hour of digging, Edward finally saw something other than dirt. In the ground, at the tip of his shovel, lay a small rib bone. Digging more carefully now, he slowly started uncovering the rest of the skeleton.

"Looks like a dog, doesn't it Mom? I'd even go as far as saying it would have been the same size as Thomas. Don't you agree?"

Connie refused to look into the pit that her son was digging. She remained on the porch swing with a dazed expression in her eyes. "Edward, I don't understand what you're trying to prove. So what if there's a dog buried in the backyard? Big deal. There are probably animal bones all over the place. A house has been on this property for over a hundred years. I'm sure more than one dog has been laid to rest here."

"Do you remember the part of Amy's story about how Dad slit Thomas' throat and then buried him out here in the garden and how he then planted those rose bushes over the grave? Well, whose bones do you think these are—Mrs. Grime's dead cat?"

"That story about Thomas is just another one of the fairy tales she's dreamed up in her head."

"Isn't this exactly where Dad planted those rose bushes he gave Amy for her eleventh birthday?"

"Yes. So, what's your point?" Connie said irritably, frustrated her son was acting so crazy. *Couldn't Edward see that Amy was nothing but a liar and couldn't be trusted to tell the truth?*

"If Amy's story is only make-believe, why is there a dog's skeleton buried out here just as she said it would be?"

"You don't know those are Thomas' bones. You just think they are because she told you they were. Can't you see what she's trying to do? She's trying to make you angry with me so you won't

537

come over here anymore. She's evil. It was her fault that the demons got to Randy. If she hadn't been such a bad child, they wouldn't have been able to come back into this house. Everything that happened to her was her own fault, not Randy's. Can't you see that?"

"The only thing I want to see right now is the butcher knife that should be here next to Thomas' bones. If Amy's story is true, then somewhere buried nearby is the knife Dad used to kill Thomas. Remember what Amy said? After Dad slit Thomas' throat and tossed him into the pit, he threw the knife in before he covered the dog up. If it's buried here, then you will have to believe her."

"No! No! No! I don't have to believe anything," she shrieked. Connie covered her ears with her hands so she couldn't hear Edward anymore and ran back into the house.

Edward kneeled down and started shifting through the dirt with his bare hands. *The knife has to be here somewhere*, he thought. Unexpectedly, he felt a sharp prick on one of his fingers. When he pulled his hand out of the dirt, he saw a thin line of blood appear on his little finger. He started scooping dirt from the site where he had received the cut, and within minutes he uncovered the knife that his father had so unmercifully used upon Thomas.

Edward pulled a handkerchief from his pocket. Then he carefully wrapped it around the knife. He crawled from the opened grave and headed toward the back door carefully carrying the knife in his hands. As soon as he opened the door, he smelled smoke. At the kitchen sink, Connie was frantically trying to burn the photographs of

Amy that he had brought into the house to prove his sister's innocence.

"Don't!" Edward shouted, as he watched his mother lighting another match. He pushed her aside and grabbing a dishtowel, he started beating at the flames that were licking eagerly at the edges of the photographs. "Why did you do that?" he yelled as he carefully gathered up the singed photos.

"Those pictures were put here by the devil to deceive me, but I know the demons' tricks, and they can't fool me. And you'd better beware, or they'll get you just like they did your father...and your grandfather. They'll use your own daughter, Christi, against you. You don't know what they can make you do."

"What is all this talk about demons? There are no demons here. Who put such foolishness in your mind?"

"I know what I'm talking about. I've seen how the evil creatures work. They took over my father's soul and then my husband's. I don't want to see them do the same thing to my son. Please, you have to understand. Your sister is part of them now, and if you keep seeing Amy, you are putting yourself and your daughter in danger."

"Putting my daughter in danger of what? What does Christi have to do with any of this? All of it happened long before my daughter was ever born."

"The demons can get to you through her. They can make you do terrible things to Christi, things you know are wrong." Connie reached forward trying to snatch the wrapped knife from Edward's hand.

"What kind of terrible things, Mom? Tell me. What happened to you? What did your father do to you?"

"Not my father! The demons! My father wouldn't have ever hurt me. Now give me that knife," Connie cried out, hysterically grabbing for it again. "I know what they can make you do. I've seen it. Once they get into your mind, you can't escape them. It's too late to save your sister, but not too late for you. Do you want to end up hurting Christi?"

Edward dropped the knife and the pictures and grabbed his mother's shoulders. He forced her to look deep into his eyes. "What will the demons make a man do?" he demanded to know. "Will they make him go to his daughter's bedroom and seek her out? Is that what they made your father do? Is that what they made my father do?"

Connie struggled to escape Edward's clutching hands. She pushed him with her frail hands, but she wasn't strong enough to break away. "I can't tell you," she cried out with fear underscoring each word. "They'll come after me. You have to stop asking questions. I don't want to talk about it."

"Mom, you have to talk about it. It has been a secret for too long now. Can't you see? It's eating you up inside!"

"I told you I can't talk about it. Now get out of here. Right now." She finally managed to shove Edward away. She ran to the door and flung it open. "Go on, get out of here, get out of my house.

I don't want to ever see you again," she shouted as tears streamed from her blood-shot eyes.

Edward picked up Amy's pictures and the knife his father had used to kill Thomas and reluctantly walked out the door. Just outside on the steps he turned back toward his mother. "Please won't you let me take you to see a doctor?"

Without replying, his mother slammed the door in his face.

Edward walked away with a heavy heart. How quickly his whole world had changed with all of the truths in his life turning into lies. Where would it all end, and would he still have a small part of his heart left intact when it did?

Toni Auberry

Chapter 55

October 26, 1998

Amy sat on the front steps of the town library enjoying watching Raphael chase a butterfly across the library's beautifully landscaped lawn. She felt comfortable and safe because Ted was standing protectively beside her. James, Edward, Ellen, and Christi were also nearby. Her friends and family were there to give her moral support.

Located in the library's front courtyard was the memorial the town had erected in honor of Amy and Edward's father, Randy Tedrow, for his commitment to the community. The memorial was a miniature flower garden that took up a quarter of the front lawn space. A walkway allowed people to casually stroll through the small garden and enjoy the beauty of the artistically spaced flowers and shrubbery. It was a peaceful place, quiet and pleasing to the eye. The shade from two ancient oaks offered comfort from the sun's burning rays, and a person could sit with a book on one of the four stone benches and simply relax. The garden also had a limestone wall that ran along the backside of the garden. At the end of the wall was a bronze plaque dedicated to Randy Tedrow.

Amy reached over and took Ted's hand and then stood up. "This is a beautiful place. The only thing I hate about it is that plaque they put up honoring Dad. He might have done a lot of good for this community, but he never did one decent thing for me."

Ted's eyes went to the bronze plaque located at the far end of the garden. *This garden is dedicated to a great man...a man who gave of himself to help this town grow and prosper. We will forever be grateful for the help and support Randy Tedrow provided to many individuals here. As you pass this spot, please take the time to pause for a moment and offer up a prayer of thanks to him for all he did during his lifetime to make this town a better place for all of us to live.*

"I guess the town council decided it wasn't a good idea having a memorial dedicated to a child molester," Amy said, watching the city workers as they started removing her father's bronze plaque from its place of honor on the stone wall.

"I don't think too many people will be praying for him now," Ted said, holding Amy's hand tightly. "Most of them are going to be too busy praying for their own souls. They all have a long list of sins to repent for. They shouldn't have ignored what was happening to you."

"Just like me," Edward spoke up quickly, his voice full of guilt. "I was too wrapped up in my own life to see what yours was like. I will have to pray for forgiveness for that stupid mistake for the rest of my life."

"There's nothing to forgive," Amy said, reaching over and hugging Edward. "I would do it the same way again if it meant you would be all right. I never wanted Dad to hurt you. You're the one who gave me the strength to go on. Without you I would have given up."

Ellen shifted Christi's weight in her arms. "We're all going to be all right now. It's over with, and none of us are going to make the same mistakes your father did. Our children won't have to live with such terrible secrecy and lies."

Edward sighed, "I just wish it was over for Mom. I hated committing her to that mental health hospital, but I really didn't have a choice."

"The new therapist, Ms. Tolson, is really good," James said. "At least your mother is starting to talk to her. That's more than she would do with anyone else. Maybe Ms. Tolson will be able to get through to her."

"I hope so for her sake," Amy replied. "At least now that I know what happened to her I can understand her a little better."

"I guess our grandfather must have really laid some trip on her with that demon routine," Edward said looking at Amy. "I know it's not going to be easy for you to forget what Mom did by letting the abuse continue, but maybe someday you will be able to forgive her enough to have some kind of relationship with her."

"Maybe," Amy replied doubtfully.

"I'm glad there's not at lot of people hanging around here today," Edward said, watching his father's bronze plaque being pried from the stone wall. "I halfway expected a crowd to be here watching so they could have more to gossip about in town. Especially since the news about Dad has been the main topic for weeks around here. As soon as I walk into a place it instantly gets quiet, so I know they're talking about us."

"I'm glad, too," Amy said, looking over at Ellen and Christi. "I was afraid everyone would be here gawking and staring at us like it was a freak sideshow. I'm not sure I could have handled that, and it wouldn't have been good for the baby to see."

"Well," James said, "it looks like the people around here have wised up a little. They did have the decency to leave you alone today. After all, this really is only a private family matter."

"Maybe now," Ellen said, "but when Amy was going through all that abuse, it should have been the concern of every citizen in this town. Teachers, doctors, neighbors, the other kids at school...all of them should have gotten involved. Even if your dad had been the president, that wouldn't have automatically given him the right to step beyond the boundaries of human decency like he did. Someone should have stopped him."

"I pray the next time one of them suspects a child is being abused it will get reported instead of ignored," Amy said. "I hope and pray I never have to read in a newspaper again about the victimization of a child, but I know that's an impossible dream."

"Yes, but a dream worth dreaming," James said, his eyes taking in his group of new friends. In the beginning he had been so sure fate had brought them all together so he could help them rebuild their lives. Now as he stood among them feeling the friendship and caring they gave so freely to each other and to him, he wasn't so sure that was the case. This time fate played a much different hand than what he had expected. His grandmother, Elizabeth, had been the last member of his family. Without her he would have been totally alone. But now here he was with four people who had taken him into their hearts with the promise of a friendship that was truly real and honest. Life had taken from him someone very dear to his heart, but had replaced the loss with friends who would help him recover from his pain. Amy had given him more peace of mind than she could ever have imagined. By telling him of his grandmother's journey into the light, she had given him the hope that someday he would be able to see his family again. Maybe when it came his turn to walk into the light, Grammy would be waiting for him, just as his grandfather had been there waiting for her.

+++++

When the bronze plaque was finally lifted into the back of an old, rusty, pickup truck, there was a feeling of finalization among all of them, as if this act were the end of some long journey, which in a way it was for Amy.

"There's one thing that I can promise you," Amy said, watching the truck drive away. "I will never keep silent again. Not only for myself, but also for the children out in the world who are facing the same nightmares I went through. I haven't told any of you yet, but I just got accepted into law school and—"

"Law school!" the others exclaimed in unison.

"Yes, law school. I know it's going to be hard, but I can do it. I want to help end the secrecy of sorrow so many children live under. By becoming a lawyer, I can be a voice for those who can't speak for themselves and have to cry in silence."

Ted didn't say a word, but his eyes told her all she needed to know. He would support her and help in any way possible.

Edward and Ellen also kept quiet, for what else was there to say.

Amy called to Raphael. "Come on boy, it's time to head home." Gathering her purse, she turned to head toward the car. After taking a few steps away from the others, she realized no one else was following. Turning, she looked at them, and she saw Ted smiling at her mischievously.

"Hey, isn't anyone else going home?" Amy asked suspiciously.

"You don't want to leave just yet. There's something else you need to see," Edward said, beckoning for her to rejoin them.

"All right you guys...I can tell you're up to no good. I've seen that look on my brother's face before, and it usually means he's getting ready to spring a surprise on me."

Taking Amy's hand, Ellen began pulling her back to join the group. "Come on. We do have a surprise for you."

Raphael followed behind the two women with his tail wagging as he pranced around in a little dance. He ran circles around Amy and the others while they all stood watching two city workers that were just starting to remove a blue tarp from something on the ground near the stone wall where Randy's plaque had been.

Raphael wanted to play, and Amy and Ted weren't paying the least bit of attention to him. So he decided to try his luck with someone else. Racing over to where the workers were, he clamped his teeth down on the blue tarp and started pulling. With one big tug, the tarp fell away exposing what lay underneath.

Worried that Raphael was bothering the workers, Amy immediately dashed over and grabbed the dog by his collar. Apologizing for Raphael's behavior, she started to pull him back out of the way. That was when her glance fell upon the new bronze plaque Raphael had just uncovered. Astonished, she read and then reread the words written upon the plaque.

Amy's Garden.

This garden is dedicated to a woman who showed great strength and courage when faced with insurmountable odds. We hope and pray that those who pass through this garden who are in need of comfort will be able to find a peace and joy that will help give them the strength and courage to face a new day. As you pass this spot,

Toni Auberry

please take the time to pause for a moment to offer up a prayer for this town that those who live here may never again turn their backs on someone in need.

About the Author

Toni Auberry, a registered nurse and occupational therapist, is a survivor of domestic violence. She extensively studied the dynamics of family violence as a means of gaining back control of her own life. In her studies, she learned that survival is directly related to making the right choices instead of consistently repeating the wrong ones. *Whispered Secrets* was written to hopefully help abuse victims realize they do have the power to change their lives by making choices that will lead them down a different path...one toward freedom from fear...if they can only find the courage to take that first step. Though it isn't easy, the choice to live free from abuse can be a reality instead of only a dream.

Printed in the United States
17920LVS00003B/106-153